I0138077

Written Scots
in Scotland and Ulster

CORPUS TEXTUUM SCOTICORUM
Volume 2

Scale:
0 10 20 30 40 50 60 miles
0 10 20 40 60 80 100 km

Shetland

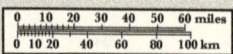

Insular Scots

Orkney

Thurso
Wick

North Northern Scots

Dingwall
Elgin
Fraserburgh
Inverness
Peterhead

Mid Northern Scots

Aberdeen

Stonehaven

South Northern Scots

Forfar
Dundee
Arbroath
Perth
St Andrews

North East Central Scots

Stirling
Kirkcaldy
Dumbarton
Greenock
Glasgow
Edinburgh
Paisley

South East Central Scots

Berwick-upon-Tweed

West Central Scots

Lanark
Galashiels
Kelso
Selkirk
Ayr
Cumnock
Hawick

South West Central Scots

Moffat
Langholm

Southern Scots

Coleraine
Lochmaben
Dumfries

Derry
Ballymena
Larne
Stranraer

Ulster Scots

Belfast
Newtownards

CORPUS TEXTUUM SCOTICORUM
Volume 2

Written Scots in Scotland and Ulster

*A review of traditional spelling practice
and recent recommendations
for a normative orthography*

By
Andy Eagle

Edited and with a foreword and afterword by
Michael Everson

evertype

2022

Published by Evertype, 19A Corso Street, Dundee, DD2 1DR, Scotland. *www.evertype.com*.

© 2022 Andy Eagle.

Editor: Michael Everson.

First edition 2022. First published in PDF format in 2006 (with subsequent updates to 2016) under the title *Aw Ae Wey: Written Scots in Scotland and Ulster*. Reprinted with corrections May 2022.

All rights reserved. No part of this publication may be reproduced, stored in a retrieval system, or transmitted, in any form or by any means, electronic, mechanical, photocopying, recording, or otherwise, without the prior permission in writing of the Publisher, or as expressly permitted by law, or under terms agreed with the appropriate reprographics rights organization.

A catalogue record for this book is available from the British Library.

ISBN-10 1-78201-263-X
ISBN-13 978-1-78201-263-4

Typeset in Baskerville by Michael Everson.

Map on page ii: Michael Everson, based on the map on p. xxxvii of the 2017 edition of the *Concise Scots Dictionary* (ISBN 978-1-4744-3231-3). Alterations made by permission to "Scotland vector Map, 5m scale", © 2021 RH Publications, www.atlasdigitalmaps.com. All rights reserved.

Illustration on page 192: John Tenniel, 1865.

Cover design by Michael Everson. The photo shows lines 20–26 of Cowie MS 50/1, the original letter written by Robert Burns to William Nicol (used as a sample text in § 9 below). Photo © CSG CIC Glasgow Museums and Libraries Collection: The Mitchell Library, Special Collections.

TABLE OF CONTENTS

FOREWORD

Nobody likes spelling reform.

I have long been involved in questions of orthography and spelling for the world's languages. I have worked to encode modern and historic characters and alphabets in the Universal Character Set[1] for languages worldwide, including many letters used in Old English, Old Norse, Middle English, Middle Scots, Middle Welsh, Middle Cornish, Primitive Irish, and Modern Irish (to name languages of likely interest to readers of this book). I have worked with the inventors of newly-invented writing systems (like Adlam and Wancho) to help them avoid structural defects that might lead to problems in spelling, and I have worked extensively with other experts to help improve practical orthographies of languages like Revived Cornish.

In 2003 I published Nicholas Williams' Irish translation of *Alice's Adventures in Wonderland*; this led to the publication of his Cornish translation in 2009, and since then I have published *Alice* in more than 80 languages, including (as of this writing) nine dialects of Scots.

Nine dialects of Scots. With two more on the way.

Now, *Alice* is notoriously difficult to translate—which, of course, is the fun. Certainly, many puns in a translation from Standard English to a language closely related to it—whether Scots, or Scouse, Cornu-English, Low Saxon, Viennese German, Elfdalian, Icelandic, or even Old English— are easier to devise than they are for languages belonging to the Bantu, Polynesian, or Turkic language families. Still, puns are not all there is in *Alice*—much of the nonsense doesn't require wordplay—and in Evertype's Scots *Alices*, there is a very great deal of rather joyous linguistic creativity expressed.

But...

Alas, there's always a *but*. And here the *but* derives from some assumptions made by some linguists and lexicographers in the mid-1980s—which is that (for tacit and unexplained reasons) Scots doesn't *need* any sort of regular spelling system, because (without parallel elsewhere in the world) it is somehow "better" to focus on the differences between the dialects than to provide speakers of the language with a robust, inclusive orthography, and the tools that can make use of a normative orthography in order to help them to write their native language in normal, day-to-day use.

---

1   The International Standard ISO/IEC 10646 and its better-known industrial implementation, Unicode.

Many Scots who know about this situation have a view about it. Some favour the dialect-centric approach, thinking that a phonetically accurate representation of the sounds of a particular dialect is the most important thing. Some disfavour that, realizing that a divided linguistic community is less healthy than a united one. One of the things that makes the situation particularly problematic, however, is that a rather large number of Scots who might not have been in the position of being writers of their native language in the 1980s and 1990s are now quite frequently in the position to write it—on social media venues like Facebook and Twitter, for instance. And what makes this problem an acute one is that the paradigm that prevailed from the mid-1980s has created a situation where many speakers of Scots pretty much make it up as they go along, guided by a few graphs that they learn are "Scots" rather than "English". Moreover, many of them, mistakenly believe that (at least some) Scots words which are historically identical to English ones benefit somehow by spelling them differently where there are no grounds to do so.

There isn't much to be gained by blaming anybody for this.[2] In the mid-1980s and after, scholars interested in Scots seem to have tended to focus on the differences between the dialects. They did not seem to be concerned about Scots being used as a day-to-day language. Rather, they seemed to prefer to treat it in the same way that Swiss German is treated in Switzerland—as something suitable for historical texts, and for modern writing of folk songs, poetry, and the occasional joke—but not a vehicle for serious (or even ordinary) writing. Spoken Swiss German is very strong—everybody speaks it[3]—but most speakers do not write it or rarely try to do so. They write Standard German. Scots is in a similar situation. Pavel Iosad, a senior lecturer in the department of Linguistics and English Language at the University of Edinburgh, has said:

> Most pro-Scots policy is run in arts and education, where it is essentially a vehicle of personal identity and creativity. This means we don't get any serious policy for language planning and no unified front: when most people publicly performing Scots are creative types, who often put a premium on how it's something malleable that belongs to no-one and everyone, the hard work of policy is just a boring downer.[4]

---

2   In fairness, John M. Tait has written rather extensively and acerbically on this topic, and with a great deal of rather satisfying wit.

3   No, not necessarily those speakers of French, Italian, or Romansch. All of the Swiss Germans speak it, though.

4   Quoted by Andrew Learmonth "Calls for a Scots language act as attacks on speakers increase" https://web.archive.org/web/20210124063808/https://www.thenational

A look at Facebook groups or Twitter threads shows that this is not the case in Scotland. Scots *want* to write their language. But most of them haven't been trained to do so, and although even as recently as the middle of the 20th century[5] a certain familiarity with Scots literature—literary or popular—was more widespread than it is today, there hasn't been much in the way of a concerted effort to encourage a convergence on a written standard. In fact, though one often finds some people advocating for such convergence, one also finds others making claims about what they assume is the importance of being able to write exactly as they speak. Such a view isn't based on sound linguistic analysis or forward-thinking sociolinguistic policy, but it's reinforced by text in every modern dictionary in which the editors throw up their hands and say that Scots spelling is not fixed.[6]

Well, as a publisher of Scots texts, I can tell you that this second attitude has forced me to face a particular problem over and over again.

I *cannot* help my translators spell-check. Tools for spell-checking Scots could be (and should be) devised, but not if there isn't a target to hit. Websterian reforms were largely cosmetic, and even what's now called "British" vs "American" English isn't as straightforward a thing as many think (Oxford recommends *colour* and *civilize*, other British authorities recommend *colour* and *civilise*, and American authorities recommend *color* and *civilize*)—but nevertheless robust and useful tools exist to help English-speaking writers avoid spelling errors.

We can't do that in Scots. In (written) Scots we have arrived at a dialect-based free-for-all, and even within any given dialect we find variation which is more or less random, depending on a set of graphs that the writer likes, or is used to, or thinks are the "right" ones.

For example, in the 1985 edition of the *Concise Scots Dictionary* the only spelling for the negative form of *can* was the traditional literary form *canna*.

.scot/news/19034578.calls-scots-language-act-attacks-speakers-increase/ accessed 2021-10-30.

5   Examples of such school text books are *Paterson's Scotch Readings, Recitations & Sketches* (1925–1948) by T. W. Paterson (Edinburgh & Glasgow: John Menzies & Co.), and A. MacMillan's *The New Scots Reader* (Edinburgh: Oliver & Boyd, 1972. ISBN 0-05-002565-1); both probably inspired by Alexander Mackie's *Readings in Modern Scots* (London & Edinburgh: W. & R. Chambers, 1913).

6   See § 4.1.7 below for examples of this current practice. Yes, it's "descriptive", not "prescriptive". There are proper venues for such descriptive linguistics, too. But such an approach does not help children to learn to write their language, and no modern language in Europe eschews normative orthography as a matter of principle. An authoritative reference work like the *Oxford English Dictionary* is descriptive in terms of language use (recording incorrect usage of "literally" for instance); it's carefully inclusive, but not preposterously so, in offering different orthographic forms in the headwords, (chiefly European v. American forms). One can follow such a dictionary for guidance in spelling. *It's gey fickle tae dae that wi maist o the Scots dictionars aboot the nou.*

FOREWORD

The 1996 edition of *The Essential Scots Dictionary* includes *canna* and *cannae*,[7] the 2017 edition of the *Concise Scots Dictionary* includes *canna*, *cannae*, and *canny*. In addition to these, I've seen *canni* and *cannie* on Facebook and Twitter myself.

Yes, this one extremely common word does have several pronunciations in different parts of Scotland: ['kanə], ['kanɛ], ['kanɪ], and ['kane] are all found. But is it normal for any language to write one common word in three or four different ways? Honestly, we must ask ourselves: Whom does plurality in spelling this one word serve?

In English there was once a sort of orthographic chaos, but by and large things were settled by Samuel Johnson (1755) in Britain and by Noah Webster's subsequent reforms (1806) in the United States. As Andy Eagle will show in this book, the situation for Scots was a bit more complex. Middle Scots had a number of relatively stable conventions, which were, after 1600 or so, retained with some alterations based on the influence of the emerging Standard English orthography. The graph *quh-* was lost to *wh-*[8] and some other English spellings came to be adopted, though it is clear (from rhymes for instance) that even where those graphs had a different pronunciation in Standard English, the Scots pronunciation was not impeded and Scots writers were unconcerned by the spelling. It is important to note that many conventions used in Middle Scots (and later) are much the same as those used in modern Standard English, and as such are seldom perceived as Scots conventions—even where they were used in Scots before the introduction of Standard English orthography to Scotland!

An example of this is *house*, which was and is pronounced [hus]. Nowadays (because of the strength of Standard English, naturally enough) many Scots speakers prefer the spelling *hoose*—which is fine, even though it is a shift from the more-or-less "standard" Scots orthography which writers like Burns used. A new normalization for Scots might well take the influence of some very common English graphs on board and choose some which differ from those where confusion could occur.

Another interesting example is the word *ane* 'one'. This word has three quite distinct pronunciations in Scots dialects ([en], [jɪn], [in]), but we can again tell from the rhymes that Burns wrote *ane* but was saying [jɪn] ("yin"). Note that Old English *án* [aːn] ended up as Modern English *one* [wʌn]

---

7   In the introduction to the *The Essential Scots Dictionary* it states: "In this little dictionary there has of course been no space for more than a few different spellings"—indicating that more variation, not less, is the objective!

8   Along with a shift from /xʍ/ to /ʍ/? Grant and Dixon 1921 §121 remark that in some dialects "the back action of the tongue is very marked so that the result might be represented almost by **xʍ** or **x**ʍ" (§ 121).

"wun".[9] Everybody writes ⟨one⟩ though, which ought to rhyme with *stone*, right? But it's an orthographic *convention*. And everyone who speaks Standard English uses that spelling, and nobody thinks about it, any more than Robert Burns did think twice about *ane* though he pronounced it "yin".

The Scots language is not a dialect of the English language. Linguistic history supports this quite well: English is based on dialects of Southern Middle English, and Scots is based on dialects of Northern Middle English, which had (amongst other things) a rather greater influence from Norse than English in the south, and a very different relationship to borrowings from French. There is a continuum of dialects within English, from Cornwall to Middlesborough, but the isoglosses that separate Scots from northern dialects of English are a very serious border indeed.

The study of Scots was blessed by the work of a number of extremely gifted linguists. I'm a linguist myself, so it is easy for me to recognize and appreciate the genius of analysis that A. J. Aitken (1921–1998) made in describing the vowel system of Scots. It is that system which unifies Scots and speakers of Scots, and which distinguishes it from the various systems which make up English and its dialects.

Scots speakers understand one another fairly readily, though of course in some places there are different words for things. That's not unusual. "Pants" means 'underwear' in British English but 'trousers' in American English. Within American English, small freshwater crustaceans are known as *crayfish*, *crawdads*, and *crawfish*, with lesser-used names like *freshwater lobsters*, *mountain lobsters*, *mudbugs*, and *yabbies*. Evidently the number of names for seagulls is legion in Scots.[10] That's a matter of lexicon—the words people

---

9   As few people know much about this, it would be useful to cite here the Oxford English Dictionary etymological note on *one*: "The expected Middle English form in the south and midlands would have open *ō* (< Old English *ā*: see *O n.1*), a shortening of the reflex of which is reflected in the modern English regional pronunciation /wɒn/. The vowel in the usual modern pronunciation arises from shortening of /uː/, the reflex of Middle English close *ō*, in a variant showing the result of raising of the vowel from open *ō* to close *ō*. The usual modern pronunciation also reflects the development of a back glide before Middle English open *ō* and, more rarely, close *ō*, although this has been only rarely reflected in the spelling; compare OAT *n.*, OAK *n.* The widespread nonstandard enclitic *'un* (evidenced in rhyme at least as early as the late 17th cent: compare quot. 1675 at sense C. 13b) represents the survival of a form without the back glide. English regional (northern) and Scots forms in *y-* reflect the development of a front glide before *e*; compare OAT *n.* and see further A. J. Aitken & C. Macafee *Older Sc. Vowels* (2002) §22.2.1. On the pronunciation history see discussion in E. J. Dobson *Eng. Pronunc. 1500–1700* (ed. 2, 1968) II. §§ 36, 37, 150, 429, 431."

10   **gou** 'gull'; **seagou** 'seagull'; **skaitie-gou** 'Arctic skua, *Stercorarius parasiticus*'; **willie-gou** 'herring gull, *Larus argentatus*'; **maw**, **blue maw** 'common gull, *Larus canus* or other similar gull'; **foumaw** 'fulmar, *Fulmarus glacialis*'; **gormaw** 'cormorant, *Phalacrocorax*

use—and it is *not* an indicator of pronunciation or a definer of language. The essential thing is that there is a core set of vowel phonemes in Scots, and even though the audible "realization" of those differs from place to place, it is their cohesion as a set of sound relationships that makes it possible for Scots from one region to understand Scots from another. This is what we know as "accent".

We know that in English some speakers say *bath* as [bɑːθ] and some say [bæθ]. We know that *butter* is pronounced ['bʌtə] and ['bʌtəɹ] and ['bʌdə] and ['bʌdəɹ] and ['bʌɾə] and ['bʌɾəɹ] and ['bʌʔɐ] and ['bʌʔəɹ] and ['bʊtɐ] and ['bʊtəɹ] and ['bʊʔɐ] and ['bʊʔəɹ] and other ways in different parts of the world. *Three* and *brother* typically have /θ/ and /ð/, but in North London, Manchester,[11] and other places, now /f/ and /v/ are found much more widely, and in Ireland /t/ and /d/ are common.

Yet we don't (and don't want to) write anything but *bath*, *butter*, *three*, or *brother* in Standard English. Doesn't it make sense to have an inclusive, agreed way of spelling for Scots?

Scots dialects have many more similarities *between* them than dialects of English have one from another, though of course there are some similarities between Northern English and Scots. Despite diglossia—the ability of Scots speakers to switch to the Standard English that has been the foundation of literacy in their primary education for nearly three centuries—there are no compelling arguments that "prove" that the Scots language is a variety of the English language. Scots speakers are well-used to having naysayers claim that Scots is "just" a form or English, or that it is a substandard "slang". There aren't any good linguistic arguments for this, of course.

We must recognize the status and use of Scots has political ramifications. Scots is recognized as a regional language by the UK via the European Charter for Regional or Minority Languages. Concerted efforts have been made in Scotland's schools, by the Scottish government, and in the Scottish media. As respect for Scots is restored, its status as a genuine language suitable for use in all areas of public life must bring with it a number of

---

carbo'; **gou maw** 'great black-backed gull, *Larus marinus*'; **gowden maw** 'glaucous gull, *Larus hyperboreus*'; **herrin maw** 'lesser black-backed gull, *Larus fuscus*'; **huidie maw** 'black-headed gull'; **pickmaw, pickiemaw** 'black-headed gull, *Larus ridibundus*'; **pirr-maw** 'black-headed gull, *Larus ridibundus*'; **whitemaw** 'herring gull, *Larus argentatus*'; **willie maw** 'guillemot, *Uria aalge*'; **pewl, pewlie** 'herring gull, *Larus argentatus* or similar seagull'; **plee** 'the thin piping cry of a bird, usually a seagull, or the (young) seagull itself'; **scorrie** 'the young of any species of gull while still in its brown-speckled plumage; the cormorant *Phalacrocorax carbo* or shag *Phalacrocorax aristotelis*; **muckle scorrie** 'glaucous gull, *Larus hyperboreus*'.

11 See for instance Baranowski, M. & D Turton. 2015. "Manchester English", in R. Hickey (ed.), *Researching Northern Englishes* (pp. 293–316). Amsterdam and Philadelphia: John Benjamins.

ramifications. Educational policy *must* deal with the language question seriously. Education through Gaelic is already available in places outside the Gàidhealtachd. What shall be done about education through Scots? Is it possible to set a national curriculum in Scots where there is no standard by which students' work can be evaluated? Can the Scots language thrive in Scotland with a spell-as-you-speak approach? What if more than one "standard" were developed and promulgated? Broad Scots speakers from across the country can readily understand one another with or without a little acclimation. Should a little girl taught to spell in school in Glasgow have to learn a different spelling if her family move house to Aberdeen?

In Ireland, there are constitutional-level legal ramifications with regard to the official status of both Irish and English. A law drafted in English can easily be translated into Irish.[12] Since Scots is a language in its own right it must, in Scotland, actually be treated as one. Scots must be its frame of reference. Standard English is the right frame of reference for local dialects of English. Its use for Scots has the effect of weakening Scots. But the Irish example is worth considering. Is government information to be made available in writing to Scots speakers all across the country? In what spelling? What about legal instruments? Orthographic plurality could certainly be a recipe for inaccuracy and dispute. How can any law, for instance, be translated unambiguously into Scots if there is no normative orthography?

A word of warning: Some readers may find that they have issues with words like "regularization", "normalization", and "standardization". Everyone must understand that in terms of *orthography* or *spelling*, these are all the same. They must also understand that a standard orthography *never* forbids any dialect word (*gou, maw, pewl, scorrie*), and never prescribes one pronunciation as the only correct one. It just sets out that *guid* is the way to spell the word meaning 'good', whether it's pronounced [gød], [gyd], [gjød], [gɪd], [ged], [gwid], or [gid]. Scots is not made stronger or safer or better if it offers spellings like *gid* or *geed* or *gweed* alongside *guid*.

Andy Eagle has given us the best way forward to sorting this out. All right, you may say, what's "best" about it? It is pandialectal. It is inclusive. It is polyphonemic. It draws upon prestigious literary conventions common to Modern Scots.

This book explores ten modern suggestions to approach the problem of Scots spelling. Here Andy analyses each of those proposed reforms, all of which have tried to make alterations here and there where they considered

---

12   Unfortunately it is common that Irish laws are written in English and translated into Irish. Some of the ramifications of this with regard to the constitutional status of the language have been explored by Micheál Ó Cearúil in his *Bunreacht na hÉireann: a study of the Irish text* (Dublin: Office of Public Works ISBN 0-7076-6400-4).

it made sense. This study begins with the linguistic reality, analysing the phonemes of Scots and the various graphs traditionally used for them. It then examines the various proposals for refinement of Scots orthography which have been suggested since 1947 when the Scots Style Sheet was published. Comparing and contrasting traditional graphs with these proposals, Andy proposes a sound, natural-looking compromise, aiming toward an inclusive orthography that serves all dialects, and does not favour any one over any other.

We (I include myself with Andy here) recognize that the convergence aimed at here does not solve every problem (some phonemes unique to Shetland might merit special dialect-specific representation, for instance). But *marginal* dialect phonemic distinctions cannot be the focus of a normative orthography for Scotland. Remember your children—and their children, and theirs. Do you want them to have the choice of an education through Scots? Then you must realize and accept that they need a single unified spelling for Scots, regardless of whether they live in Ayr, or Caithness, or Aberdeen, or Dundee, or Glasgow, or Orkney, or Shetland, or even Ulster.[13] From my point of view, the translations of *Alice* I have published are all wonderfully unique and creative, each one a different take on the playfulness of the original—but reading them can be difficult. For each one, sometimes something as simple as the personal pronouns and the forms of the verbs *tae hae* and *tae be* have to be puzzled out. The dialect spellings *mask* the language—they don't enhance the reader's experience.

Nobody likes spelling reform.

But there's no alternative. We must agree a spelling for Scots. The right way to do that is to look at the linguistics, look at the options, and choose a coherent, robust, inclusive system, with a sound etymological basis, which will do justice to the Scots language. Nobody will be satisfied by everything. But Scots is a modern European language no different from English or German or French, and speakers of Scots deserve and require better support for their national tongue then the present chaos offers them.

It is time to grasp the thistle of spelling reform, for the good of Scotland. Andy Eagle's proposal is the best and most comprehensive one I have yet seen.

Michael Everson
Dundee 2022

---

13 For audio samples of various dialects written using the same spelling conventions see https://web.archive.org/web/20210506191505/https://www.scots-online.org/audio/index.php accessed 2021-10-30.

PREFACE

Under the European Charter for Regional or Minority Languages[14] the British Government committed itself to protecting and encouraging autochthonous regional or minority languages, one of them Scots. Among the objectives were:

> the facilitation and/or encouragement of the use of regional or minority languages, in speech and writing, in public and private life; (Part II Article 7, 1.d.)

Here, in particular, the facilitation of the use of written Scots in public life, especially in transactional texts intended to impart information to the general public, raises the issue of orthography. Historically Scots has never had a standard orthography in the sense that modern Standard English does. Recent written Scots, especially in the 20th century, encompasses some orthographic diversity reflecting historical, regional, circumstantial, and idiosyncratic practices. That would seem to reflect a somewhat anarchic situation, however, the literary record, especially in the 18th and 19th centuries, shows that not to be the case.

In this monograph the nature of Broad Scots orthography, in particular that of the 18th and 19th centuries, will be examined along with some of the more recent well-known or exhaustive suggestions for a normative orthography. The suitability of various traditional practices and the various suggestions made by others will be discussed as regards the establishing of a "standardized" pan-dialectal normative orthography—although I prefer "regularized". There is no intrinsic reason why a normative orthography should prescribe one spelling for each word if a variant pronunciation cannot be predicted from the graphemes used to represent the underlying phonemes.

The abbreviation *SND* refers to the *Scottish National Dictionary* (Grant, William *et al.*, eds. 1931–1975) and *DOST* to *A Dictionary of the Older Scottish Tongue* (Craigie, William *et al.*, eds. 1931–2002).

Andy Eagle
www.scots-online.org, 2022

---

14   Council of Europe. "European Charter for Regional or Minority Languages". Strasbourg, 1992-11-05 (European Treaty Series – No. 148) http://web.archive.org /web/20211030120419/https://rm.coe.int/1680695175 accessed 2021-10-30.

1
AN OVERVIEW OF SCOTS ORTHOGRAPHY

1.1 HISTORICAL CONTEXT

The earliest occurrence of Scots words in writing originating in Scotland was in texts written in Latin. These were usually Latinized forms of geographical names or titles.

The principle chronological periods in the history of Scots are usually defined as follows (Robinson 1985: xiii):

Old English:	to 1100
Older Scots:	to 1700
Pre-literary Scots:	to 1375
Early Scots:	to 1450
Middle Scots:	1450 to 1700
Early Middle Scots:	1450 to 1550
Late Middle Scots:	1550 to 1700
Modern Scots:	1700 onwards

The fragment of the *Dream of the Rood*, carved in runes on the Ruthwell Cross in Dumfriesshire (? *c*. 800), might have been carved, as far as linguistic propriety is concerned, at Edinburgh or at York. (Smith 1902: xii)

The thing which most basically and consistently separates Scots and English is pronunciation. Starting from the same base as Standard English, Scots has developed along a very different phonological path beginning with the separate development of Old Northumbrian in the Old English period. (Tulloch 1980: 182)

As Murray (1873) has pointed out, Scots developed out of the Northumbrian dialect of Old English, and one should presume that it inherited the written traditions of the north as well, language developments and writing traditions which have never been seriously studied. (Kniezsa 1997: 24)

By the second half of the 15th century all the characteristic features of Scots orthography had been developed. Those consisted of graphemes derived from forms carried over from Old English, general features introduced by scribes trained in the 11th- and 12th-century Norman French and Parisian traditions, forms shared with northern English and Scots innovations or archaic forms no longer used in northern English. (Kniezsa 1997)

The analysis in section 2.3 above has made it evident that all the spelling features which count as diagnostic in Scottish orthography were already found in Northern English texts, and earlier than the examples written in Scotland. [...] the Scottish scribes learned their writing tradition from the north, and it formed a spelling continuum in the first appearance of texts written in the vernacular. (Kniezsa 1997: 32)

That this is true, even as late as Late Middle English (1300–*c.* 1450), is shown by the comparison of the authenticated writings of John Barbour, Archdeacon of Aberdeen (? 1320–1395), and Richard Rolle, the hermit of Hampole near Doncaster, who wrote about 1340. (Smith 1902: xii)

The uniqueness of the orthography therefore lies, not so much in the invention of entirely new notational forms, but in being a special system which Scots scribes developed from shared features and the later developments of major variants out of earlier marginal ones. (Kniezsa 1997: 34)

Despite certain internal differences, which we shall see were less idiosyncracies than the sporadic effects of influences from without, the uniformity in the practice of Middle Scots is one of its most striking features. (Smith 1902: xii)

If variability was the rule in EmodE before conventions became stable around 1700, then the coexistence of two largely unsettled systems in late 16C Scotland allowed for even greater variation. (Görlach 2002: 69)

1.2 OLDER SCOTS ORTHOGRAPHY

Scots orthography had become relatively stable between 1450 and 1700, sharing some of its conventions with those of contemporary Standard English. There was scant evidence of dialect variation in contemporary written Scots, although Müller (1908: 143), commenting on "dialect spellings" in 16th-century Aberdeen documents, mentioned *fat* for *quhat* 'what', *quintray* for *countrie* 'country', and the occasional marking of the /i/ realization of Anglo-Saxon /oː/, Older Scots /ø/, which is still current today.

> Osc. seems to have had a more or less standardised orthography, in the sense that according to our present understanding, few texts give orthographic clues about the provenance of author or scribe; but did it have the first, lexicalized orthographic system, or the second grapheme-phoneme kind of system, or a system which was neither of these? The answer to this question is not immediately apparent. (Agutter 1987: 75)

> The Lothian dialect had been elevated to the status of the official language of local and national government, and was the basic medium for the brilliant literary tradition of 15th- and 16th-century Scotland. Local dialect features in Middle Scots writings (literary and non-literary) are not common, though some can be found; and if the spelling of Middle Scots was far from standardised, the language was in this respect no different from other national vernaculars of the period preceding and immediately following the advent of printing. (McClure 1995: 22)

> First, just as Tudor English is, Scots is in the process of developing a Standard by the beginning of the sixteenth century, based on the Mid-Scots dialects spoken in Edinburgh and other important Central Belt centres. Like sixteenth-century English, there is still a large amount of variation within it, especially in the orthography, and there are no Scots grammarians or dictionary-makers to codify what is 'proper' Scots. Indeed, it is not even certain that anyone had a notion of that would be, or even used this dialect in the spoken mode, although it certainly could have served as the sort of koiné that could be used among people of diverse origins who are thrown together, as might happen in the court, the chancery, the universities or religious houses [...] (Johnston 1997a: 50)

More important is the fact that speakers of Scots had developed a separate spelling system and prescriptive norms for the language (Meurmann-Solin 1993, 1997, Kniezsa 1997), associated in the main with a metropolitan variety used in the court at Edinburgh. Other 'dialects' of English also had distinctive spelling patterns; Scots managed to maintain and propagate its system well into the age of print, however. Indeed, the middle to late sixteenth century was when this separate system was most healthy. It was broadcast through the medium of print, and written both by considerable writers, and by some of the most prominent people in the country (Jack 1997). (Millar 2005: 90–91)

Among the particularly Scottish characteristics (Smith 1902; Aitken 1977; 2002, Görlach 2002) were the representation of long vowels by an added ⟨i⟩ or ⟨y⟩ in words such as *streik* 'stretch', *weil* 'well', *weit* 'wet', *foirseing* 'foreseeing', *opteynit* 'obtained', *weycht* 'wight', *meteyr* 'metre', *gairding* 'garden', *mair* 'more', *pairt* 'part', *waittir* 'water', *cloik* 'cloak', *coill* 'coal', *coird* 'cord', *bluid* 'blood', *buik* 'book', *fluid* 'flood' *fuill* 'fool', and *puir* 'poor'. Depending on adjacent consonants, ⟨y⟩and ⟨o⟩ were often used instead of ⟨i⟩ and ⟨u⟩ in order to aid legibility, as was a free variation between ⟨u, v⟩ and ⟨w⟩. Vocalized ⟨l⟩ usually became unsounded after ⟨ā⟩ and ⟨ō⟩, but the grapheme remained as a marker of vowel length and often occurred in words that historically had no ⟨l⟩, such as *walkinit* 'wakened', *chalmir* 'chamber' *waltir* 'water', *rolkis* 'rocks', *golkit* 'foolish', *als* 'as', and *poulder* 'powder'.

This is an outstanding characteristic of M.Sc. It is in reality an orthographical device to indicate a long vowel. (Smith 1902: xxiii)

When, by a sound change, the spelling *ai*, which had represented a separate diphthong in Middle English, can to have the same sound as the spelling *a* used for a long vowel, a new way of representing the length of the vowel came into being. In Middle Scots this convention was applied to *e, u* and *o* as well so that a following *i* or *y* became a standard indication of a long vowel. (Tulloch 1980: 200)

⟨oa⟩, which survives in a great many words in present-day English e.g. *board, boat, coat*, was introduced to distinguish the more open long vowel /ɔ:/ from /o:/, which was represented by ⟨oo⟩. (Scragg 1975: 77)

[…] with the possible exception of ⟨oa⟩ which is a late development in southern English and did not appear in Scots earlier than the sixteenth century (Müller 1908). (Kniezsa 1997: 34)

There is a mysterious grapheme which surfaces in the sixteenth century—at least, mention is made of it in connection with texts written in this period. It is the digraph ⟨ae⟩, an allograph of Scots ⟨a⟩—⟨a-e⟩—⟨ai/y⟩: *maer*, *sae* and so on. […] from the eighteenth century it gained ground and became an important part of the non-anglicised Scots orthography. (Kniezsa 1997: 42)

Among the particularly Scottish consonant graphemes were the longer retention of the characters Thorn ⟨þ⟩ and Yogh (Scots *Yoch*) ⟨ȝ⟩, often rendered ⟨z⟩, used initially for /j/ in, for example, *ȝour* or *zour* for *your*. Less well-known is the Middle Scots S ⟨ß⟩ (roman ⟨ß⟩, italic ⟨ß⟩), an elaborately formed ⟨ss⟩ deriving from ⟨fs⟩, similar to the German Sharp S ⟨ß⟩ (roman ⟨ß⟩, italic ⟨β⟩) which derived from ⟨fz⟩ (blackletter ⟨ſʒ⟩). Among the particularly Scottish consonant clusters were ⟨quh⟩/xw/, now ⟨wh⟩, ⟨sch⟩ /ʃ/, now ⟨sh⟩, and ⟨ch⟩ for /x/, etymological ⟨gh⟩ in Standard English. In written texts a number of abbreviations were commonly used, for example, *w*[t] for *with* and *E*[t] for *Edinburgh*.

Other common conventions were the use of ⟨k⟩ and ⟨ll⟩ in words such as *crak* 'crack', *cukis* 'cooks', *infekkit* 'infected', *paddok* 'frog', *sikkerlie* 'surely', *stamok* 'stomach', *angell* 'angel', *haill* 'whole', *littill* 'little', *maternall* 'maternal', and *sempill* 'simple'. Further conventions included consonant doubling in words such as *crappe* 'crept', *doubbis* 'puddles', *innemy* 'enemy', *lawchtter* 'laughter', *myshappis* 'mishaps', *proffect* 'profit', *tcheir* 'chair', and *wyffis* 'wives'. Common word ending conventions included ⟨-ir⟩ and ⟨-(i)oun⟩ in words such as *bettir* 'better', *bittir* 'bitter', *maneir* 'manner', *marineir* 'mariner', *wattir* 'water', *commoun* 'common', *delectatioun* 'delectation', *inclynatioun* 'inclination', and *occasioun* 'occasion'.

Plural nouns were generally formed by adding ⟨-is⟩ or ⟨-ys⟩, probably realized /ɪs/ and later /s/, /z/ as in Modern Scots, similarly as in *Scottis* 'Scottish' and *Inglis* 'English'.[1] The present participle and gerund were generally distinguished as ⟨-and⟩, ⟨-ant⟩ and ⟨-ing⟩, ⟨-yng⟩, ⟨-yn⟩, ⟨-ene⟩ or ⟨-en⟩ in words such as *scrapand* and *cummyng* 'coming'. The past participle of verbs was usually ⟨-it⟩ or ⟨-yt⟩ in words such as *perysit* 'perished' and *sirculit* 'encircled'. The negative particle was ⟨-na⟩ in, for example, *haue na* 'have not' and *mak na* 'make not'.

---

1   The recessive modern form, '*Ingles*' can still be found in surnames and place names as Ingles [ɪŋlz] and Ingleston etc.

Anglicization occurred rapidly during the 16th century, when in Scot-and, Scots and Standard English spellings became interchangeable, and by the end of the 17th century Scots was virtually absent in official writing.

> Among the conditions favouring this trend were the Scots' failure to produce a translation of the Bible in their own language and Protestant [...] reliance on Bibles in English, so that the Biblical language of Scotland was English. (Aitken 1992: 894)

> The history of the relationship between Scotland and England is one of constant political, linguistic and cultural influence of the south upon its northern neighbour. From the sixteenth century onwards, there were some developments in Scottish writing which led away from a distinctive Scottish orthography towards a general, all-English one by the end of the seventeenth century. (Kniezsa 1997: 43)

> In the late sixteenth and early seventeenth centuries, even those authors who are counted as considerably anglicised restrict the use of southern spellings to individual lexical items rather than mix the two systems [...] (Kniezsa 1997: 44)

Stylistically speaking, the appearance of anglicized spelling depends on the typology of writing; it is generally stated that the most anglicized texts were the religious treatises, while the most conservative Scottish were official papers, such as those of the Privy Council, local authorities and so on. The spelling in private papers seems to depend on the personal history of the authors, and whether and for how long they lived in England [...] and even there their early training wins considerable ground against later English influence. (Kniezsa 1997: 46)

1.3 MODERN SCOTS ORTHOGRAPHY

Scots of course remained the vernacular of the vast majority of the Scottish population but, from the sixteenth century on, written Scots generally survived only in vernacular literature, usually poetry and the centuries-old ballads. Although the spellings used often drew on Standard English many conventions from Older Scots were also employed. Some the same or similar to those of Standard English (see §10, p. 190). That continued to the end of the 18th century a revival of written Scots, based largely on contemporary colloquial Scots, occurred, and although the spellings used were often highly anglicized, some conventions based on sixteenth-century written Scots were also employed. That continued to the end of the nineteenth century, receiving a further boost through the repeal of the Stamp Act in 1855, which led to increased availability of newspapers and magazines, many of which had some Scots content.

> And the Scots tongue has an orthography of its own, lacking neither "authority nor author." (Stevenson 1905: 152)

> [...] Scots remains the one British dialect which may be represented today by a consistent (and traditional orthography). (Scragg 1975: 37)

> Instead most use the standard form of the language as developed by Ramsay, Fergusson and Burns in the poetry of the eighteenth century. This was a descendant of the old court Scots, which was basically the Scots of sixteenth-century Edinburgh and, although some of the more distinctive old Scots spellings like *quh* for *wh* and *sch* for *sh* had been dropped, this Standard Scots had in its spelling caught up with all recent changes in Edinburgh Scots. This is evident in poetry in the rhymes. (Tulloch 1980: 249)

> They wish to address themselves to all Scotsmen and accordingly follow the general literary convention, but every now and again they use a spelling that indicates a local pronunciation, or employ a word or an idiom that betrays their district origin. (SND I: xv)

> We can be quite sure that Scott's Scots is actually thicker than it looks. As one might expect, his spellings are irregular and inconsistent but, if they have any tendency at all, it is in the direction of making it more intelligible to an English reader [...] This indeed was in the tradition of the eighteenth-century Scots writer[s] from Ramsay onwards, but it has the unfortunate effect of obscuring the proper pronunciation and rhythm which enhances the author's effects in using this broken language to its maximum capacity. (Murison 1969: 220)

> The mixed spelling he adopted made an Englishman's task of understanding much easier. And, apart from intelligibility, there is probably another reason why Scott wanted to introduce English spellings. He was interested in presenting his Scots-speaking lower-

class characters as dignified human beings and not as ignorant, stupid and laughable fools. (Tulloch 1980: 303)

According to the prevailing view of Scottish culture, the nineteenth century after the death of Scott was a period of decline and failure in which Scottish writers, recoiling from the spectre of industrialisation, immersed themselves in rural fantasy following Sir James Barry, 'Ian Maclaren' (Dr John Watson) and other writers of the 'Kailyard School'. The present study seeks to modify this view, suggesting that Scottish culture was (and is) a popular culture, and that its major vehicle during the period was not the London-dominated booktrade, but the Scottish newspaper press, owned, written, and circulating within the country. It suggests that in the Scottish context fiction published in the press was much more extensive and important than might otherwise be concluded on the evidence of a book-culture produced for an all-UK literary market, and that during this period popular newspapers provided the environment for a vernacular prose revival of unprecedented proportions. (Donaldson: 1986 xii)

There were poems in the vernacular, novels with vernacular dialogue, editorial or near-editorial comment in the vernacular, vernacular advertisements, and quite enormous quantities of antiquarian, historical, folkloristic and musicological feature writing which dealt with every aspect of Scottish life and culture in which the vernacular also, and inevitably, figured largely. There was a growing awareness of the complexity of the language situation in Scotland which showed itself in a tendency to report Scots speakers verbatim without silently translating what they said into standard English. (Donaldson 1986: 60–61)

The book-trade had long been tied into the English market and obliged to conform to the cultural values which prevailed within it. Most of Walter Scott's readers would have been English—he could never have built that Gothic extravaganza at Abbotsford on returns from the Scottish book-trade alone—and he had to write about things they could understand in a way that they would tolerate. And that is true for most Scottish book-novelists during the nineteenth century. But the newspaper press was wholly free from this constraint. It could address a specific audience at national, regional or local level, and this had important consequences when we consider the cultural role it came to perform. [...] Above all, they used vernacular Scots to deal with an unprecedented range of topics [...] (Donaldson 1989: 2–4)

This book presents evidence [...] of a major vernacular revival during the second half of the nineteenth century. Revival. In a sense the word is ill-chosen. How could Scots be revived? It had never declined. Not, at least, its spoken forms which continued to be the language of the people [...] (Donaldson 1989: 1–2)

If the textbooks were right, this volume would contain nothing but empty pages; because the medium in which its authors wrote—i.e. discursive Scots prose—became extinct more than two hundred years before any of them were born. (Donaldson 1989: 10)

After the Union of the Crowns in 1603, and still more after the Union of the Parliaments in 1707, the intercourse between Scotland and England became much closer, with the natural result that the influence of English spelling, then gradually becoming standardized, upon the spelling of Scotch rapidly increased; more especially as Scotch writers found it to be to their interest to secure a wider audience by making their works, even when composed in Scotch dialect, more easily intelligible to English readers unfamiliar with Scotch pronunciations. (Wilson 1926: 194)

The key achievement of Ulster-Scots literature—those works on which its claim to our attention rests—lie in this field. It is possible to extend the cannon by including, for instance, the utilitarian prose of the plantation period or the Kailyard newspaper fiction of the mid-nineteenth century. (McIlvanney 2005: 214)

By the end of the eighteenth century, any written Scots was produced in a melange of orthographical styles which lent themselves to seeing it as a corrupt English. (Millar 2005: 191)

By analysing the orthographic practices of a number of 18th and 19th century revival writers from various parts of Scotland and Ulster it is possible to establish which orthographic tendencies prevailed in literary Scots and also to identify those which may be considered typical or traditional Scots forms. The analysis of the vowels is based on the numbering scheme devised by A. J. Aitken.

I shall not attempt to squeeze Scots phonology into the mould of Wells' (1982) keywords. This is an excellent tool for the description of Standard English and closely related varieties, but it cannot be matched up with Scots (or indeed English dialects north of the Humber) without serious distortion, because of differences of lexical incidence, going back in some cases to late OE. Here, we use instead the system of vowel numbers established for Scots by Aitken (1977), and revised by Aitken and Macafee (2002). (Macafee 2004: 63)

Vowel number	Vernacular Scots	Scots vowel
8a	**ay** 'always', **gey** 'very', **May, pay, way**	əi
10	**quoit, avoid, join, point, oil, choice, poison**	
1 short	**bite, bide, price, wife, tide**	
1 long	**five, size, fry, aye** 'yes', **kye** 'cows', **fire**	ɑ·e
2	**meet, need, queen, see, seven, devil, here**	i
11	**ee** 'eye', **dee** 'die', **dree** 'endure', **lee** 'untruth'	
3	**meat, breath, dead, head, steal, pear, mear** 'mare'	(Merges with 2, 4, or 8)
4	**ake** 'oak', **ate** 'oat', **bate** 'boat', **sape** 'soap', **baith** 'both', **hame** 'home', **stane** 'stone', **hale** 'whole', **tae** 'toe', **twae** 'two' (SE dialects); **late, pale, bathe, day, say, away, mare** 'more', **care**	e
8	**bait, braid, hail, pail, pair**	eː (in many Central Scots dialects merges with 2, 4, or 8)
5	**throat, coat, thole** 'endure', **rose, before**	oː (merges with 18 in some e.g. Central and South Scots)
18	**cot, God, on, loch, bocht** 'bought', **horse, Forth**	o
6	**about, bouk** 'bulk', **poupit** 'pulpit', **loud, powder, room, shouder** 'shoulder', **mouth, house, louse, cow, now, fou** 'full', **pou** 'pull', **plow** 'plough', **oo** 'wool', **hour, sour**	u
7	**boot, fruit, good, muin** 'moon', **use** (n.), **use** (v.), **love, do, moor, poor, sure**	Ø (North Mainland: merged with 2, Central and South Scots: merged or merging with 4 (SVLR long), 15 (SVLR short))
9	**Boyd, choice, noise, boy, joy**	oi
12	**faut** 'fault', **saut** 'salt', **fraud, mawn** 'mown', **auld** 'old', **cauld** 'cold', **hauch** 'meadow', **cause, law, snaw** 'snow', **aw** 'all', **faw** 'fall', **twaw** 'two' (except in the SE), **far, daur** 'dare', **waur** 'worse'	aː/ɔː (in some Northern dialects merged with 17)
13	**nowt** 'cattle', **cowt** 'colt', **gowf** 'golf', **sowder** 'solder', **louse** 'loose', **chow** 'chew', **grow, know** 'knoll', **four, owre** 'over', **row** 'roll'	ʌu
14	**duty, feud, rule, heuk** 'hook', **neuk, beuch** 'bough', **teuch** 'tough', **news, dew, few, blue, true, plewis** 'ploughs'	iu/ju
15	**bit, put, lid, hiss, give, gird** 'hoop', **his, next, whether, yird** 'earth', **fir**	ɪ
16	**met, bed, leather, meh** 'cry of sheep', **serve, Perth, Ker**	ɛ
17	**sat, lad, man, jazz, vase, warst, mar**	a (see vowel 12 above)
19	**butt, bud, bus, buff, buzz, word, fur**	ʌ

2
PHONOLOGY

A chart of the Scots vowel system (Aitken 1981b: 132–133, 1984: 95–98) appears on page 10.

2.1 WRITTEN SCOTS FROM CENTRAL SCOTLAND

Fergusson's Scots poems are not purely in the Edinburgh or in the Lothian dialect, any more than Burns's are purely 'in the Ayrshire dialect.' Dialect poetry—in the sense of a deliberate effort to record the speech mannerisms of a definite locality—is relatively rare in Scotland. [...] Scots is therefore composed in some sort of a standard language rather than in dialect; or if dialect we must call it, then it is a literary dialect created by men of the pen. This is certainly true of most of the Scots prose of Sir Walter Scott and Robert Louis Stevenson. It is also true of the Scots poetry of Ramsay, Fergusson and Burns [...] (Mackie 1952: 123–124)

These observations are mainly useful as evidence for my contention that the poet, like Scott and Stevenson later and Allan Ramsay before him, is trying to write in traditional Scots rather than record something accurate for the dialect student. (Mackie 1952: 128–129)

By his rhyming in most cases Fergusson makes it clear that while he uses English spelling he intends usually Scottish pronunciations of the words that the two tongues have in common, but that are differently sounded in the sister languages. (Mackie 1952: 131)

[...] as evidently most of the writers (including of Ayrshire, like Kennedy and Nisbet) aimed at writing, not in their own local dialect, but in the then accepted literary Scots. (Wilson 1926: 168)

[...] as we have seen, Scott uses Standard Scots [...] (Tulloch 1980: 182)

Scott's answer was characteristically an inconsistent use of both [English and Scots] conventions. This was also the way most of his eighteenth-century predecessors had settled the question. (Tulloch 1980: 198)

In fact the transcriber does not seem to have made a lot of changes to Scott's spelling and the author always had a chance to approve, or even amend, the results of the transcription. In the circumstances it seems reasonable to talk of the spelling as Scott's own. (Tulloch 1980: 193)

[...] and since Ramsay at times used the spelling of an English word to represent its Scots phonological cognate—a practice current among Scottish writers since the seventeenth or even, arguably, the late sixteenth century [...] (McClure 1987: 262)

[...] His [Allan Ramsay's] glossary is not large (about 750 words); there are perceptive observations on the Scots vowel system [...] but also because the spelling provided a model for Scots poets widely followed in the eighteenth century and far on into the nineteenth. The main object seems to have been to spell identically with or as near as possible to the English spelling, e.g. ⟨gh⟩ rather than ⟨ch⟩ in *bright*, *night*, ⟨-ed⟩ for ⟨-it⟩ in past participles, ⟨oo⟩ representing /øː/ as well as /uː/ as in *good*, *soon*, *poor*, ⟨ou⟩ and ⟨u⟩ for /uː/, while ⟨ow⟩ is sometimes the simple vowel /uː/ and sometimes the diphthong /ʌu/. The affects of this mixter-maxter of Scots and English in the minds of people accustomed to associate language with its printed form can be heard to this day in the unhappy attempts of performers to sing a Scots song or recite a Scots poem [...] (Murison 1987: 18)

Wilson's analysis[2] showed that Ramsay, Fergusson, Burns and Scott followed the following orthographic practices.

---

2   Wilson, James (1926) *The Dialects of Central Scotland*, London: Oxford University Press. pp. 194–221.

2.1.1 Use of *gh, ch, wh, th, sh*

All generally used ⟨**gh**⟩ for the older ⟨**ch**⟩ /x/ but occasionally used ⟨**ch**⟩, ⟨**wh**⟩ for the older ⟨**quh**⟩ in words such as *whase* 'whose' and *what*, ⟨**th**⟩ for dental fricatives /θ/ and /ð/, and ⟨**sh**⟩ /ʃ/ for the older ⟨**sch**⟩. Ramsay generally adopted ⟨**y**⟩ for the older yogh ⟨**ȝ**⟩ but occasionally used ⟨**z**⟩ (used by early printers to replace yogh, which was not extant in contemporary printing sets)[3] in words such as *cunzie* 'a coin' (now *cuinyie* [ˈkyn(j)i]) and *fenzie* 'feign' (now *feingie* [ˈfeŋ(j)i]).

> Burns [...] leaves it to be understood that the Scots pronunciation of the *gh* is the rough aspirate [...] (Wilson 1923: 37)

> Fergusson would, however, use the guttural [gh], and most of his contemporaries would, including judges and other dignitaries. (Mackie 1952:127)

> He [Fergusson] has a marked fondness for the old Scots 'z' which after 'n' or 'l' has the effect of the initial 'y' in 'yes,' making the 'l' into Spanish 'll' and the 'n' into French 'gn.' So we get 'cunzied,' 'fenzying,' [...] 'spulzie' (for spoil, dialect 'spile', 'tulzie,' 'brulzies,' 'ulzie' (oil, dialect 'ile'. (Mackie 1952: 138)

> Apart from an archaic passage in *Chronicles of the Canongate* [...] the only survival of *quh* in Scott is, as we might expect, in the legal term *umquhile* '(the) late' [...] and even this is often spelt *umwhile* [...] Scott like Ramsay, preferred the *gh* spelling. (Tulloch 1980: 198)

2.1.2 Use of the apostrophe

All generally used an apostrophe to represent perceived "missing letters" in the likes of *an'* 'and', *awa'* 'away', *mak'* 'make' *o'* 'of', *wi'* 'with' and for root-final ⟨**l**⟩ vocalization in words such as *a'* 'all', *ca'* 'call', *fa'* 'fall' and the suffix *-fu'* 'full' but in medial positions traditional graphemes were preferred in words such as *fause* 'false', *faut* 'fault', *gowd* 'gold', *gowff* 'golf' and *saut* 'salt'. In older Scots the ⟨**l**⟩ represented vowel length (Smith 1902: xxiii). Scott did much the same but often used the Standard English spelling or even

---

3   It should be noted that the shape of ⟨**ȝ**⟩ and ⟨**z**⟩ fall together in the manuscripts from a fairly early period throughout Britain—even in Cornwall, where ⟨**ᴣ**⟩ is used in the late 14th-century *Charter Fragment* for both ⟨**ȝ**⟩ /θ ð/ and ⟨**z**⟩, and where ⟨**ꝫ**⟩ is similarly used in the early 15th-century *Pascon agan Arluth*. (Williams, Everson, and Kent 2020). Printers in Scotland (or of Scots elsewhere) may well have simply used ⟨**z**⟩ because the distinction was not being kept up, at least by some writers. The letters ⟨**þ**⟩ and ⟨**y**⟩ also fell together during this period, though in some manuscripts the latter is written with a dot, ⟨**ẏ**⟩. [ME]

13

inserted ⟨**l**⟩ where it was no longer usual, perhaps as a deliberate archaism, for example *almery* for *aumry* 'cupboard', *calsay* for *causey* 'pavement', *halse* for *hause* 'throat', *maulkin* for *maukin* 'hare', and *nolt* for *nowt* 'cattle'.

> In our study of Fergusson's Scots […] is the Ramsay trick of spelling Scots as if it were English, with occasional apostrophes to show clearly the relationship of a Scots word with its English cognate. (Mackie 1952: 130)

> Scott spells relatively few words with apostrophes but his page is nevertheless dotted with them because these words include some very common ones, in particular *a'* 'all', *o'* 'of' and *wi'* 'with'. (in a few rare cases *a'* is replaced by *aw* […] (Tulloch 1980: 194)

2.1.3 Use of *-na*

All used *no* 'not' and generally used ⟨**-na**⟩ for the negative particle equivalent to ⟨**-n't**⟩ in words such as *canna, dinna* 'don't' and *maunna* 'mustn't'.

2.1.4 Deletion of terminal *-d*

Ramsay and Fergusson often rendered the elided terminal ⟨**d**⟩ in ⟨**nd**⟩ and ⟨**ld**⟩ as an apostrophe in words such as *an'* 'and', *en'* 'end', *han'* 'hand' and *stan'* 'stand'. Burns regularly used an apostrophe indicating the characteristic Ayrshire pronunciation. Scott tended to write the ⟨**d**⟩.

> Fergusson […] drops the 'd' when it suits him for rhyming purposes. (Mackie 1952: 136)

2.1.5 Use of *ae* and *ane*

Ramsay, Fergusson and Burns used *ae, ane* 'one',[4] although they probably pronounced them [je, jɪn]. Scott used both *ane* and *yin*.

> Curiously enough, although in A[yrshire]. 'one' *num.* is pronounced **yin**, 'once' **yins**, and 'one' *adj.* **yay**, Burns spells them 'ane', 'ance', and 'ae'. (Wilson 1923: 37)

2.1.6 Weak verb past tense endings in *-it*, *-ed*, and *-'d*

Ramsay often rendered past tense of weak verbs /ət/ ⟨**-it**⟩, but also used Standard English ⟨**-ed**⟩ and ⟨**-'d**⟩. Fergusson was much more consistent,

---

4   "*Ane* corresponds in its usage for the most part to St.Eng. *one*, but AE (*q.v.*) is the usual Sc. form for the adj. before a noun." (SND I: 58 s.v. "ANE")

preferring ⟨**-it**⟩. Scott mixed ⟨**-it**⟩ and ⟨**-ed**⟩, along with such forms as *sell'd* 'sold' and *tell'd* 'told'.

> As it happens Scott, while using the *-it* ending quite frequently, rarely uses it where it has been elided to *-t*, and this may explain the *-ed* forms here. (Tulloch 1980: 305)

2.1.7 Present participles in *-an*, *-in*, and *-ing*

Ramsay often rendered the present participle /ɪn/ ⟨**-an**⟩, or ⟨**-in'**⟩ but also ⟨**-ing**⟩. Fergusson was much more consistent preferring ⟨**-in**⟩. Burns used all three. Scott preferred ⟨**-ing**⟩.

> Throughout the M.Sc. period the distinction between the pres. Part. (verbal adj.) and the gerund (verbal noun) is generally kept, the former being in *-and* (or *-ant*), the latter in *-yng* or *-yn*, and *-een* or *-en*. (Smith 1902: xxxvi–xxxvii)

> Though he [Burns] often spells the present participle with the termination *an*, he as often spells it *in* or *ing*. In his later editions he drops the distinction, and spells both the present participle and the verbal noun as ending in *in*, or the English *ing* [...] (Wilson 1923: 37)

> Both are now pronounced *in* throughout Central Scotland. (Wilson 1926: 197)

> [...] Allan Ramsay, not always, represented the ending of the present participle as 'an' [and] again not in every case, gives the gerundive ending 'in.' [...] Fergusson uses 'ing' and 'in' indiscriminately for both participle and gerundive. (Mackie 1952: 132–134)

> Scott [...] almost invariably uses *ing* and only very rarely *in* or *in'*. (Tulloch 1980: 197)

2.1.8 Vowels 1, 8a, and 10 in *i*, *y*, *-ay*, and *-oi*

Vowels 1, 8a, and 10 were usually written ⟨**i**⟩ or ⟨**y**⟩, with a mute ⟨**e**⟩ after a following consonant in words such as *ay* 'yes', *aye* 'always', *byre* 'cowshed', *dyke* 'wall', *fire*, *kye* 'cattle', *side*, *syne* 'ago', *tine* 'lose', and *tyke* 'dog'. Burns held with Standard English spellings ending in ⟨**-ay**⟩ in words such as *hay*, *pay*, *way*, and *oil* . Scott used *gey* 'very' and *quey* 'heifer' but *pay* and *way*. All used

⟨**oi**⟩ (vowel 10) in most words with /ɔi/ realizations such as *boil, join, point* and *toil*.

2.1.9 Vowels 2 and 11 in *ee, ei,* and *ie*

Vowels 2 and 11 (root-final) were usually written ⟨**ee**⟩, but ⟨**ei**⟩ and ⟨**ie**⟩ also occasionally occur in words such as *brier* 'briar', *ee* 'eye', *flee* 'fly', *green, neibour* 'neighbour', *slee* 'sly', *steek* 'shut', and *wee* 'little'.

2.1.10 Vowel 3 in *ea, ai,* and *ei*

Vowel 3 was usually written ⟨**ea**⟩ in words such as *beast, clean, dead, east, head, meal* and *meat*, or ⟨**ai**⟩ as in *daith* 'death' but Scott also used ⟨**ei**⟩ in *heid* 'head'.

2.1.11 Vowels 4 and 8 in *ai, a-e,* and *ae*

Vowels 4 and 8 were variously written ⟨**ai**⟩, ⟨**a-e**⟩ or ⟨**ae**⟩, for example initial and medial *ain* '(one's) own', *braid* 'broad', *laid* 'load', *skail* 'spill', *taid* 'toad', *yaird* 'yard', *gane* 'gone', *hale* 'whole', *lave* 'rest' *nane* 'none', *wame* 'belly', *claes* 'clothes' and root-final *brae* 'hillside', *flae* 'flea', *frae* 'from', *gae* 'go', *sae* 'so', *strae* 'straw'.

2.1.12 Vowels 5 and 18 in *oa, o-e,* and *o*

Vowels 5 and 18 were usually written ⟨**oa**⟩, ⟨**o-e**⟩, and ⟨**o**⟩ as in Standard English cognates, in words such as *cod* 'pillow', *corn, flock, horse,* and *morn* 'morning'.

2.1.13 Vowel 6 in *ou, ow, oo,* and *u-e*

Vowel 6 was variously written ⟨**ou**⟩ or ⟨**ow**⟩, and occasionally ⟨**oo**⟩ or ⟨**u-e**⟩, in words such as *doun* 'doun', *fou* 'full', *jouk* (v.) 'duck', *oor* 'our', *oot* 'out', *pou* 'pull', *roust* 'rust', *south, sow, throw* 'through', and *toun* 'town'. Burns was particularly fond of the Standard English spellings. Scott often used ⟨**ow**⟩ but also ⟨**oo**⟩.

> He [Burns] generally also follows the E. spelling in the many words which in A[yrshire]. Are pronounced with the sound of *oo*, and in E. with the sound of *ou* or *ow*, and so spelt in E. (Wilson 1923: 43)

> Fergusson repeats Ramsay's inconsistency in the spelling of the 'ou' (oo) and 'ow' (diphthong) sounds. He will spell 'cow' for 'cou', 'dowr' for 'dour,' and yet he will use 'loup' for 'lowp.' In one rhyme sequence he gives us 'doup,' 'coup,' 'stoup' and 'sowp' (backside, upset, draught and sup). It is evident that he, like Ramsay before

him, relied on his Scottish readers knowing how the words were
expected to be pronounced, but a reader not of his day might be
excused for getting hopelessly bogged among these 'ou's' and
'ow's.' (Mackie 1952: 132)

The traditional Scots spelling of this sound is *ou* [...] as we shall
see in the discussion of Scott's spelling he rarely uses the English
alternative *oo*. (Tulloch 1980: 184)

2.1.14 Vowel 7 in *u-e*, *ui*, *oo*, and *eu*

Vowel 7 was variously written ⟨**u-e**⟩ or ⟨**ui**⟩, but also ⟨**oo**⟩ as in Standard
English cognates, in words such as *bluid* 'blood', *guid* 'good', *coof* 'fool', *loof*
'palm', and *clute* 'hoof'. Burns was particularly fond of using ⟨**oo**⟩. Scott
tended to use ⟨**ui**⟩, but also ⟨**oo**⟩.

[...] Burns generally follows the E. spelling or spells it with *oo*, but
sometimes with *ui* or with *u* followed by a mute *e* after a consonant
[...] (Wilson 1923: 42)

The 'ui' vowel of many Scots words, corresponding in sound to
the German modified 'o' in 'Goethe' or the French '*œu*' in '*hors d'*
œuvre,' has become quite unrounded in Edinburgh and the
Lothians, but the process had not gone so far in the poet's time.
[...] If the unrounding was not so far advanced in Fergusson's time
it would excuse his rhyming of such words as 'moon' and 'aboon'
(above) with such words as 'toun' and 'doun' [...] (Mackie 1952:
127–128)

The result of vowel 7 before /k/ and /x/ was often written ⟨**eu**⟩ in words
such as *beuk* 'book', *eneugh* 'enough', *neuk* 'nook', and *teugh* 'tough'.

Me. *eu*, *ęu* hat im Schott. genau dieselbe Entwicklung genommen
wie in der Schriftsprache: *ẹ̆u* > *iu* > *jū* [...] Jetzt können wir auch
die Schreibung *eu* für msch. *ọ̄* vor Guttural (§64) verstehen. Der
Laut ergab nämlich in dieser Stellung ein *jū*. Da nun auch *eu* in
seiner Entwicklung denselben Lautwert erreichte, vermischte man
beide und gebrauchte schließlich die historische Schreibung des
Entwicklungsprodukts von *eu* zur Bezeichnung für beide; und zwar
eu wohl deshalb, weil die Entsprechungen von msch. *eu* häufiger
waren und mehr gebraucht wurden, als solche von *ọ̄* + Guttural.
(Steiger 1913: 41–42)[5]

5   'Middle English *ęu*, *ęu* developed the same way in Scots as it did in the written language

[...] in Scott's own dialect but it is not apparent in his spelling which is Standard Scots *u-e* or *ui* inherited from Middle Scots. [...] Before a back consonant [...] the *eu* spelling is used [...] (Tulloch 1980: 184)

2.1.15 Vowel 9 in *oy* and *oi*

Vowel 9 was usually written ⟨**oy**⟩ or ⟨**oi**⟩, as in words such as *boy* and *noise*.

2.1.16 Vowel 12 in *au*, *aw*, and *a'*

Vowel 12 was usually written ⟨**au**⟩ medially and ⟨**aw**⟩ initially and finally, and ⟨**a'**⟩ usually for historic ⟨**l**⟩ vocalization (see above) in words such as *auld* 'old', *bauld* 'bold', *haud* 'hold', *hauf* 'half', *braw* 'fine', *craw* 'crow', and *snaw* 'snow'.

2.1.17 Vowel 13 in *ow* and *ou*

Vowel 13 was variously written ⟨**ow**⟩ or ⟨**ou**⟩ in words such as *gowd* 'gold', *gowk* 'fool', *howe* 'hollow', *howk* 'dig', *knowe* 'knoll', *rout* 'roar', and *stoup* 'pitcher'. Scott was particularly fond of ⟨**ou**⟩ in medial positions.

2.1.18 Vowel 14 in *ew* and *ue*

Vowel 14 was usually written ⟨**ew**⟩ in words such as *brew*, *dew*, *few*, *grew*, *spew*, and *new* but ⟨**ue**⟩ was also used in words such as *blue* and *true*.

2.1.19 Vowel 15 in *i* and *u*

Vowel 15 was usually written ⟨**i**⟩ in words such as *sic* 'such', *clim* 'climb', *fit* 'foot', *ingan* 'onion', *night*, *rigg* 'ridge', *rin* 'run', and *simmer* 'summer', but ⟨**u**⟩ was also often used for vowel 15 after /w/ and /ʍ/.

2.1.20 Vowel 16 in *e*

Vowel 16 was usually written ⟨**e**⟩ in words such as *het* 'hot', *snell* 'severe', and *yett* 'gate'.

2.1.21 Vowel 17 in *a*

Vowel 17 was usually written ⟨**a**⟩ in words such as *aff* 'off', *drap* 'drop' *saft* 'soft', *sang* 'song', and *wast* 'west'.

[Standard English]: *ę̆u* > *iu* > *jū* [...] We can now understand the spelling *eu* for Middle Scots *ǭ* before a guttural (§64). In this position the realization resulted in *jū*. Now that *eu* had developed the same realization, the two were merged and finally the historical spelling of the historical outcome of written *eu* came to represent both; particularly *eu* because the equivalents of Middle Scots *eu* occurred and were used more frequently than those from *ǭ* + guttural.' [AE]

2.1.22 Vowel 19 in *u*

Vowel 19 was usually written ⟨**u**⟩ in words such as *curn* 'a few', *lug* 'ear', *lum* 'chimney' *muckle* 'much', and *wud* 'mad'.

2.1.23 Other comments

Fergusson's spellings closely followed those of Ramsay. Burns was clearly influenced by both but used anglicized spellings much more often. Scott was influenced by all three but also regularly used anglicized spellings. Like Burns, Scott was inconsistent but often much more idiosyncratic, using for example, six different spellings for the cognate of dovecote—*doucot, doocot, dooket, dookot, dow-cote* and *dukit*.

2.2 WRITTEN SCOTS FROM NORTH-EAST SCOTLAND

A selection of writing by north-eastern writers taken from McClure[6] shows a similar pattern, though a few spellings representing the local pronunciation do occur.

> Charles Murray in *Wha draws a Blade* is addressing all Scotsmen, and on a dignified subject—therefore he uses the conventional literary dialect. In *Fae France* he puts the "braidest Buchan" into the mouth of the poacher who becomes a soldier. (SND I: xvi)

> In view of Murray's enduring local popularity and well-established reputation as the archetypal poet of the North-East, it is somewhat surprising to observe that the distinctive linguistic features of the "Doric" are much less conspicuous in his poetic language than that of Mary Simon, and often absent altogether. (McClure 2000: 44)

> Soon after the Vernacular Revival had been initiated in Edinburgh […] the North-East made the first of its many and distinctive contributions to Scotland's literary culture; and though local dialect features were less conspicuous in poets of the eighteenth century than in the more deliberately regional literature of later times, they were sufficiently in evidence to establish an unmistakable local identity. (McClure 2002: 79)
> All these writers draw on existing literary models […] (McClure 2002: 80)

---

6   McClure, J. Derrick (2002). *Doric: The Dialect of North–East Scotland*. Amsterdam: Benjamins. pp. 21-152.

2.2.1 Use of *gh* and *ch*

All generally used either ⟨**gh**⟩ or ⟨**ch**⟩ for /x/ but Ross used both. Murray used ⟨**ch**⟩, except in *mith* 'might', which indicates the dialect realization.

2.2.2 Use of *wh*

All generally used ⟨**wh**⟩. The graph ⟨**quh**⟩ never occurred but occasional forms showing the local pronunciation /f/ did occur as ⟨**f**⟩, for example, Ross's *fump'ring* 'whimpering' and *fustle* 'whistle', Burness's *fan* 'when', Symon's interrogative *fa* 'who', *faur* 'where', *fulp* 'whelp' and *futtled* 'whittled', and Caie's *fan* 'when' and *fat's* 'what's'. Skinner also used *fow* 'how'.

2.2.3 Use of *th* and *sh*

All used ⟨**th**⟩ for /θ/ and /ð/ (except in dialect forms with /d/ such as ⟨**d(d)**⟩ *swidder* 'dither') and ⟨**sh**⟩ for the fricative /ʃ/.

2.2.4 Use of *ȝ* and *z*

The older yogh ⟨**ȝ**⟩ occasionally occurred as ⟨**z**⟩ in words such as *broolzied* 'brawled' and *gaburlunzie* 'beggar'.

2.2.5 Use of the apostrophe

All generally used an apostrophe to represent perceived "missing letters" in words such as *an'* 'and', *awa'* 'away', *mak'* 'make' *o'* 'of', *wi'* 'with' and for root-final ⟨**l**⟩ vocalization in words such as *a'* 'all', *ca'* 'call', *fa'* 'fall', and the suffix *-fu'* 'full' but in medial positions traditional graphemes were preferred in words such as *hauf* 'half' and *saut* 'salt'.

2.2.6 Use of *nae* for *no*

The negative *nae* for 'not', instead of *no*, occurred as is usual in the north-east.

2.2.7 Use of *-na*

The negative particle was always ⟨**-na**⟩ in words such as *canna* 'can't', *didna* 'didn't', *haena* 'haven't', *wadna* 'wouldn't, and *winna* 'won't'.

2.2.8 Deletion of terminal *-d*

Simplification of ⟨**nd**⟩ to ⟨**n**⟩ generally did not occur except in *norlans* 'northlands', though examples of ⟨**ld**⟩ simplification to ⟨**l**⟩ did occur, as is typical in the north-east in words such as *aul'* 'old' and *caul'* 'cold'.

2.2.9 Use of *ane*

All used *ane* 'one', although they probably pronounced it /in/.

2.2.10 Weak verb past tense endings in *-it*, *-ed*, and *-'d*

The past tense of regular verbs /ət/ ⟨**-it**⟩, was usually written ⟨**-ed**⟩ and ⟨**-'d**⟩ but Murray did use *chappit* 'knocked' and *happit* 'covered'.

2.2.11 Present participles in *-in'*, *-in*, and *-ing*

The realization /ɪn/ for the gerund was usually written ⟨**-in'**⟩ '-ing', though ⟨**-in**⟩ and ⟨**-ing**⟩ did occur.

2.2.12 Vowels 1, 8a, and 10 in *i(-e)*, *y(-e)*, *-ay*, and *-oi*

Vowels 1, 8a, and 10 were usually written ⟨**i**⟩ or ⟨**y**⟩ with a mute ⟨**e**⟩ after a following consonant in words such as *bide* 'stay', *blythe* 'cheerful', *by*, *cry*, *fire*, *hynd* 'farm labourer', and *tyne* 'loose' but ⟨**ay**⟩ and ⟨**oi**⟩ (vowel 10) were used in words such as *may*, *pay*, *stays* 'steps' *way*, and *doited* 'foolish'.

2.2.13 Vowels 2 and 11 in *ee*, *ei*, and *ie*

Vowel 2 and 11 (root-final) were usually written ⟨**ee**⟩, but ⟨**ei**⟩ and ⟨**ie**⟩ also occasionally occur in words such as *chiel* 'fellow', *dreep* 'drip', *green*, *feet*, *free*, *leefu'* 'sorrowful', *neiper* 'neighbour', *see*, *speel* 'climb', *speer* 'enquire', and *weel* adj. 'well'.

2.2.14 Vowel 3 in *ea* and *ei*

Vowel 3 was usually written ⟨**ea**⟩ in words such as *beast*, *clean*, *dead*, *east*, *head*, *meal*, *meat* but Mary Symon also used *deid* 'dead'.

2.2.15 Vowels 4 and 8 in *ai*, *a-e*, and *ae*

Vowels 4 and 8 were variously written ⟨**ai**, **a-e**⟩ or ⟨**ae**⟩, for example, initially and medially *ain* 'own', *aith* 'oath', *bairn* 'child', *braid* 'broad', *care*, *claith* 'cloth', *faith*, *graith* 'equipment', *hame* 'home', and root-finally *fae* 'foe', *frae* 'from'. Murray used *fae*, *hae* 'have', *sae* 'so', and *strae* 'straw'. Note the cluster ⟨**ane**⟩, usually /i/ in this dialect. All used *ane* 'one', *ance* 'once', *bane* 'bone', *gane* 'gone', *lane* 'lone', *nane* 'none', and *stane* 'stone' but Symon used *aince* 'once'.

2.2.16 Vowels 5 and 18 in *oa*, *o-e*, and *o*

Vowels 5 and 18 were usually written ⟨**oa**⟩, ⟨**o-e**⟩, and ⟨**o**⟩ as in Standard English cognates, in words such as *bonny* 'beautiful', *cogue* 'bowl', *cost*, *mony* 'many', *on*, *road*, and *roast*.

2.2.17 Vowel 6 in *ou, ow, oo,* and *u-e*

Vowel 6 /u/ was often written ⟨**ou**⟩ and ⟨**ow**⟩ as in Standard English cognates but also ⟨**oo**⟩ or ⟨**u-e**⟩ in words such as *about, broo* 'brow', *down, drouked* 'soaked', *drouth,* 'thirst', *drown, gown, now/noo, power, shoud* and *sude* 'should', *shower, south, stout,* and *town/toon.*

2.2.18 Vowel 7 in *oo, o, u-e, ui,* and *eu*

Vowel 7, in this dialect, usually /i/ and after /g/ and /k/ rendered /wi/, was often spelled ⟨**oo**⟩, ⟨**o**⟩, or ⟨**u-e**⟩ as in Standard English cognates *aboon* 'above', *do, good, soon, mools* 'mould' *smoor'd* 'smothered', and *sure.* Among the Scots forms used were ⟨**ui**⟩ as in *fuish* 'fetched', *guid* 'good', *muir* 'moor', *puir* 'poor', and *shuitit* 'shot' but forms indicating the local pronunciation also occurred such as ⟨**ee**⟩ in *beets* 'boots', *bleed* 'blood', *eese* (v.) 'use', *fleer* 'floor', *gweed* 'good', *leems* 'looms', *queet* (*cuit* = 'ankle'), *reets* 'roots', *sheen* 'shoes', *squeel* 'school', and *teem* 'empty'.

Before /k/ and /x/ vowel 7 was often written ⟨**eu**⟩ in words such as *aneugh/eneuch* 'enough', *beuk* 'book', *cook, feugh* 'puff', *leugh* 'laugh' *nook,* and *pleugh* 'plough'.

2.2.19 Vowel 9 in *oy* and *oi*

Vowel 9 usually written ⟨**oy**⟩ or ⟨**oi**⟩ was only found in *coy,* James Beattie's *capernoited* 'crazy' and *doited* 'crazed' may represent vowel 10.

2.2.20 Vowel 12 in *au, aw,* and *a'*

Vowel 12 was usually written ⟨**au**⟩ medially and ⟨**aw**⟩ initially and finally, and ⟨**a'**⟩ usually for historic ⟨**l**⟩ vocalization (see above) in words such as *aumry* 'pantry' *auld* 'old', *aw* 'all', *cauld* 'cold', *chaumer* 'chamber', *claught* 'seize', *fauld* 'fold', *faw* 'fall', *flaucht* 'a flash', *hauf* 'half', *haul, hauld* (n.) 'hold' *lauchin* 'laughing', *maun* 'must' *snaw* 'snow' *taunty,* and *vaunty.* Burness also used *tald* 'told'.

2.2.21 Vowel 13 in *ow* and *ou*

Vowel 13 was variously written ⟨**ow**⟩ or ⟨**ou**⟩ in words such as *couped* 'overturned', *fouk* 'folk', *hows* (hollows), *knows* 'knolls', *ower* 'over', *rows* 'rolls', and *trow* 'believe'.

2.2.22 Vowel 14 in *ew*

Vowel 14 was usually written ⟨**ew**⟩ in words such as *new, spew,* and *clammyhowat* 'a heavy blow'.[7]

---

7   McClure's note "[...] The more usual spelling is *clamihewit*: Skinner's ⟨ow⟩ suggests the NE [jʌu] corresponding to [ju] in other dialects."

2.2.23 Vowel 15 in *i*

Vowel 15 was usually written ⟨**i**⟩ in words such as *anither, ilka* 'every', *him, lingle* 'cord', *mids* 'middle', *night, sic* 'such', *stirk* 'bullock', *swidder* 'dither', *will,* and *wind* (n.). A few spellings showed the merging of vowel 15 with vowel 19 after /w/ and /ʍ/ (/f/ as a dialect form in the NE, e.g. *fumper* 'whimper').

2.2.24 Vowel 16 in *e*

Vowel 16 was usually written ⟨**e**⟩ in words such as *bend, ettle* 'endeavour', *flegs* 'frights', *geld, kent* 'known', *set, sneck* 'latch', and *snell* 'severe'.

2.2.25 Vowel 17 in *a*

Vowel 17 was usually written ⟨**a**⟩ in words such as *alang* 'along', *back, canna* 'can't', *crack* 'chatter', *dang* pt. 'beat', *lat* 'let', *mak* 'make', *man, sang* 'song', *shak* 'shake', and *thrang* 'busy'.

2.2.26 Vowel 19 in *u*

Vowel 19 was usually written ⟨**u**⟩ in words such as *bums* 'buzzes', *burn* 'stream', *but, muckle* 'large', *smush* 'grime', *unco* 'strange', and *up*.

2.2.27 Other comments

As can be seen, "phonetic" representations of the dialect were the exception rather that the rule, even for such "marked" features as /f/ for ⟨**wh**⟩ and /jʌu/ for ⟨**ew**⟩. Ellis (1890: 155).

Commenting on the [aː] realization of vowel 12, Ellis wrote "The sound *auˑ* does not occur, but dialect writers have a habit of using 'au, aw' for *aaˑ*."

2.3 WRITTEN SCOTS FROM ULSTER

A selection of Rhyming Weaver[8] poetry taken from Hewitt[9] and the dialogue in the novels of W. G. Lyttle[10] paints a similar picture. Poets such as Thomas Beggs, David Herbison, Robert Huddleston, James Orr, Hugh Porter, and Samuel Thomson were clearly part of the same tradition as Ferguson and Burns.

---

8   Many of these artisans were often self-employed in the linen weaving industry. These independent thinkers published their poems in newspapers and books which were paid for by subscription. They often wrote in support of the 1798 rising of the United Irishmen and the American Revolution.

9   Hewitt, John (1974) "Rhyming Weavers and Other Country Poets of Antrim and Down", Blackstaff Press, Belfast

10 Lyttle, W.G, 1890, *Daft Eddy or the Smugglers of Strangford Lough*. Republished with appendix 1979, Newcastle NI, and Lyttle, W.G. 1896, *Betsy Gray or Hearts of Down*. Republished 1970 with other stories and pictures of '98, Newcastle NI.

[…] it would be fair to suggest that the Ulster vernacular bards were in much the same relationship to Burns as he had been to his predecessors, and were working free-handedly within the same tradition […] (Hewitt 1974: 6)

Apart from the occasional word of Gaelic [= Irish] origin, there is little evidence in the poems studied. (Connolly 1981: 13)

Unlike those who represented HE [Hiberno-English], Lyttle used orthographic conventions that were well known because they were derived from literary Scots. (Todd 1989: 134)

All follow the practices of the Scots revival in modulating the density of their use of Scotch according to subject-matter, style and form. The Scots vernacular revival also provided the Ulster poets with their characteristic verse forms, such as Standard Habbie and the Holy Fair stanza. As with their use of revival orthography, the verse forms came to acquire a symbolic or semiotic significance, and became a visual representation of revival Scots. (Herbison 2005: 80)

The Ulster poets saw in Burns's achievement a validation for their own linguistic and cultural identity. […] It drew on a shared cultural inheritance. The rural bards of the "Rhyming Weaver" tradition saw themselves as co-heirs with Burns of the Scots vernacular revival. (Herbison 2005: 81)

2.3.1 Use of *gh* and *ch*
All generally used ⟨**gh**⟩ /x/ in words such as *bright, laigh* 'low', *night*, and *saugh* 'willow' but towards the end of the period Thomas Given, who died in 1917, and W. G. Lyttle did use ⟨**ch**⟩ in words such as *dicht* 'wipe', *lauchs* 'laughs', *nicht* 'night', and *richt* 'right'.

2.3.2 Use of *wh*
All used ⟨**wh**⟩, the older Scots ⟨**quh**⟩ was not used in words such as *wha* 'who', *whan* 'when', *whase* 'whose', *whiles* 'sometimes', *whin* 'gorse', and *white*,

2.3.3 Use of *th* and *sh*
The fricatives /θ/ and /ð/ were spelled ⟨**th**⟩, and the possible interdental realizations /t̯/ and /d̯/ were never indicated. The fricative /ʃ/ was spelled ⟨**sh**⟩. The older ⟨**sch**⟩ was not used.

2.3.4 Use of ȝ
Examples of ⟨z⟩ or ⟨y⟩ for the older yogh ⟨ȝ⟩ were not found in the sample.

2.3.5 Use of *-na*
The negative particle ⟨-na⟩ was used by all, except by W. G. Lyttle, with, for example, ⟨-nae⟩ in *disnae* 'doesn't' and *wudnae* 'wouldn't' but *hae na* 'haven't', and Francis Boyle, who had an occurrence of *winnae* 'won't', The negative particle ⟨-na⟩ occurred in words such as *canna* 'can't', *dinna* 'don't', *disna* 'doesn't', *maunna* 'mustn't' and *wadna* 'wouldn't'.

2.3.6 Use of the apostrophe
All generally used an apostrophe to represent perceived "missing letters" in words such as *an'* 'and', *awa'* 'away', *mak'* 'make' *o'* 'of', *wi'* 'with' and for root-final ⟨l⟩ vocalization in words such as *a'* 'all', *ca'* 'call', *fa'* 'fall', and the suffix *-fu'* 'full' but in medial positions traditional graphemes were preferred in words such as *fause* 'false', *faut* 'fault', *gowd* 'gold', and *saut* 'salt'.

2.3.7 Deletion of terminal *-d*
All often rendered the elided terminal ⟨d⟩ in ⟨nd⟩ as an apostrophe in words such as *an'* 'and', *lan'* 'land', *roun'/roon'* 'round', and *stan'* 'stand'. An elided terminal ⟨d⟩ in words such as *auld* 'old', *bauld* 'bold', and *cauld* 'cold' was not indicated in the spelling.

2.3.8 Use of *ane, ance,* and *aince*
Ane, ance or *aince* 'one', 'once' were universally used, except for *yins* used by Thomas Given. W. G. Lyttle used both *ane* and *yin*. Many of the other authors who used *ane* would also have probably had a /jɪn/ pronunciation.

> It seems likely that Porter wrote ⟨ane⟩ but intended the word to be pronounced /jɪn/. (Connolly 1981: 141)

2.3.9 Weak verb past tense endings in *-ed, -'d, -led, -it,* and *-elt*
The past tense of regular verbs was often written ⟨-ed, -'d⟩ and ⟨-led⟩, though the Scots forms ⟨-it⟩ /ət/ and ⟨-elt⟩ /əlt/ were shown in spellings such as *crabbit* 'difficult', *hauntit* 'haunted', *plantit* 'planted', and *tummelt* 'tumbled'.

2.3.10 Present participles in *-in'*
The realization /ɪn/ for the gerund was often written ⟨-in'⟩ '-ing'.

2.3.11 Vowels 1, 8a, and 10 in *i(-e)*, *y(-e)*, *-ay*, *-ey*, and *-oi*

Vowels 1, 8a and 10 spelled with ⟨i⟩ or ⟨y⟩ with a mute ⟨e⟩ after a following consonant, for example, *ay* 'yes', *aye* 'always', *belyve* 'by and by', *pey* 'pay', *syne* 'since', and *whyles* 'sometimes'.

Standard English spellings ending in *-ay* were usually used, for example, *clay, may, pay, stay, way*.

> The most interesting example of this accidental re-spelling is Francis Boyle's ⟨Stay Brae⟩. To the modern reader this place name looks as if the first element was pronounced /ste/. However, there can be little doubt that Boyle's spelling represents the Scots adjective **stey**, (pronounced /staɪ/ […] (Connolly 1981: 19)

All used ⟨oi⟩ (vowel 10) in most words with /əi/ such as *join, point*, and *toil*.

> Ulster eighteenth century speech, as reflected in the rhymes, seems not to have made a distinction between ME oi and ui, and the problem of how this distinction, (apparently retained in Scots) came to be lost in Ulster, is as puzzling as the subsequent total abandonment in Antrim of /aɪ/ in /ɔɪ/ words. (Connolly 1981: 368)

2.3.12 Vowels 2 and 11 in *ee*, *ei*, and *ie*

Vowel 2 and 11 (root-final) usually ⟨ee⟩, but ⟨ei⟩ and ⟨ie⟩ also occasionally occur, for example, *agee* 'awry', *chiel* 'fellow', *een* 'eyes', *freet* 'superstition', *grief*, *neist* 'next', *reek* 'smoke', *speel* 'climb', *speerits* 'spirits', *theek* 'thatch', *wee* 'small', and *weel* adj. 'well'.

2.3.13 Vowel 3 in *ea* and *ei*

Vowel 3 was usually spelled ⟨ea⟩, for example, *bear, beasts, bread, clean, dead, dreadfu', fear, head, leal* 'loyal', *meat* 'food', *pleasin', sweat*, and *tea*. Thomas Given, who died in 1917, and W. G. Lyttle used ⟨ei⟩ in *heid* 'head'.

2.3.14 Vowels 4 and 8 in *ai*, *a-e*, and *ae*

Vowels 4 an 8 usually /e(ː)/, variously spelled ⟨ai, a-e⟩ or ⟨ae⟩, for example initial and medial *ain* 'own', *baith* 'both', *claith* 'cloth', *kail* 'cabbage', *laigh* 'low', *mair* 'more', *bane* 'bone', *gane* 'gone', *hale* 'whole', *nane* 'none', *quate* 'quiet', *stane* 'stone', *claes* 'clothes' and root-final *blae* 'blue-grey', *brae* 'hillside', *frae* 'from', *sae* 'so', and *strae* 'straw'.

2.3.15 Vowels 5 and 18 in *oa, o-e,* and *o*

Vowels 5 and 18 were usually written ⟨**oa**⟩, ⟨**o-e**⟩, and ⟨**o**⟩, usually as in Standard English cognates, in words such as *boast, com, cot* 'cottage', *gloamin* 'twilight', *groats, groset* 'gooseberry', *mony* 'many', *ony* 'any', *thole* 'endure', and *thorn.*

2.3.16 Vowel 6 in *ou, ow, oo,* and *u-e*

Vowel 6 was often written ⟨**ou**⟩ and ⟨**ow**⟩, as in Standard English cognates, but also ⟨**oo**⟩ or ⟨**u-e**⟩ in words such as *broo* 'brow', *croun/croon* 'crown', *doun/doon* 'down', *goun* 'gown', *loud, oor* 'our', *oot* 'out', and *toun* 'town'.

2.3.17 Vowel 7 in *oo, ui,* and *eu*

Vowel 7 was often written ⟨**oo**⟩ as in Standard English cognates in words such as *aboon* 'above' *food, loom, poor, stood.* Among the Scots forms using ⟨**ui**⟩ were *bluid* 'blood', *guid* 'good', *muir* 'moor' and *puir* 'poor' along with *dae* 'do', and *tae* 'to'. The verb and noun *use* remained so.

Before /k/ and /x/ vowel 7 was often written ⟨**eu**⟩ in words such as *neuk* 'corner' *sheugh* 'ditch' *pleugh* 'plough' and *teuk* 'took', though ⟨**oo**⟩ was common as were various methods of showing the /ʌ/ pronunciation such as *pl'ugh* 'plough', *luk* 'look', and *tuk* 'took', and the /u/ pronunciation in examples such as *hook, plough,* and *shough* 'ditch'.

2.3.18 Vowel 9 in *oy* and *oi*

Vowel 9 was usually written ⟨**oy**⟩ or ⟨**oi**⟩ in words such as *boy, corduroy,* and *noise.*

2.3.19 Vowel 12 in *au, aw,* and *a'*

Vowel 12 was written ⟨**au**⟩ usually initially and medially, ⟨**aw**⟩ usually finally, and ⟨**a'**⟩ usually for historic ⟨**l**⟩ vocalization (see above). The forms *auld* 'old' *bauld* 'bold', and *cauld* 'cold' were universal, other examples being *daur* 'dare', *fause* 'false', *faut* 'fault', *haud* 'hold', *maun* 'must', *sauld* 'sold', *saut* 'salt', *tauld* 'told' and *wauk* 'wake'. Interestingly, where that vowel occurred before ⟨**nd**⟩, ⟨**a**⟩ was used in words such as *han'* 'hand', *land,* and *stan'* 'stand' though spellings such as *bald* 'bold' and *sald* 'sold' may indicate that all these words had the same vowel.

2.3.20 Vowel 13 in *ow* and *ou*

Vowel 13 was variously written ⟨**ow**⟩ or ⟨**ou**⟩ in words such as *chow* 'chew', *fowk* 'folk', *gowk* 'cuckoo', *ower/oure* 'over', and *stow* 'pack'.

2.3.21 Vowel 14 in *ew* and *ue*

Vowel 14 was usually written ⟨**ew**⟩ in words such as *brew*, *new* and *view* but ⟨**ue**⟩ also occurred in words such as *blue*.

2.3.22 Vowel 15 in *i*

Vowel 15 was usually written ⟨**i**⟩ in words such as *ahint* 'behind', *bit, dinlin'* 'tingling', *hing* 'hang', *kilt* 'tuck', *lift* 'sky', *nit* 'nut', *rin'* 'run', and *whit* 'what'.

2.3.23 Vowel 16 in *e*

Vowel 16 was usually written ⟨**e**⟩ in words such as *cleg* 'horsefly', *denty* 'dainty', *efter* 'after', *gleg* 'sharp', *het* 'hot', *ken* 'know', *neb* 'nose', *snell* 'severe', and *yett* 'gate'.

2.3.24 Vowel 17 in *a*

Vowel 17 was usually written ⟨**a**⟩ in words such as *caff* 'chaff', *canty* 'cheerful', *drap* 'drop', *lang* 'long', *saft* 'soft', and *wat* 'wet'.

2.3.25 Vowel 19 in *u*

Vowel 19 was usually written ⟨**u**⟩ in words such as *burn* 'stream', *dub* 'puddle', *duds* 'rags', *grun'* 'ground', *lug* 'ear', *lummer* 'lumber', *muckle* 'much', *rung* 'baton', and *turn*.

2.4 WRITTEN SCOTS FROM SOUTHERN SCOTLAND

Writers from the Scottish border counties were also operating within the same tradition, as is shown in an analysis of traditional ballads recorded at the time, for example, in poetry by Robert Crawford, Jean Elliot, James Hogg, William Laidlaw and Thomas Pingle among others, found in Veitch.[11]

2.4.1 Use of *gh* and *ch*

All generally used ⟨**gh**⟩ for the older ⟨**ch**⟩ /x/ but towards the end of the period ⟨**ch**⟩ was increasingly used.

2.4.2 Use of *wh*

The older ⟨**quh**⟩ was replaced by ⟨**wh**⟩ in words such as *wha* 'who', *whan* 'when', and *what*.

2.4.3 Use of *th* and *sh*

The dental fricatives /θ/ and /ð/ were represented by ⟨**th**⟩, and ⟨**sh**⟩ /ʃ/ was used in preference over the older ⟨**sch**⟩.

---

11   Veitch, John. (1893) *The History and Poetry of The Scottish Border* Vol. II, Edinburgh/London: Wm. Blackwood and Sons. Chapters VII, VIII and IX.

2.4.4 Use of ʒ

No occurrence of ⟨z⟩ or ⟨y⟩ for the older yogh ⟨ʒ⟩ was found in the sample.

2.4.5 Use of the apostrophe

All generally used an apostrophe to represent perceived "missing letters" in words such as *an'* 'and', *awa'* 'away', *mak'* 'make' *o'* 'of', *wi'* 'with' and for root-final ⟨l⟩ vocalization in words such as *a'* 'all', *ca'* 'call', *fa'* 'fall' and the suffix *-fu'* 'full' but in medial positions traditional graphemes were preferred in words such as *cowt* 'colt', *gowd* 'gold', *rows* 'rolls', and *saut* 'salt'.

2.4.6 Use of *-na*

All used *no* 'not' and generally used ⟨-na⟩ for the negative particle equivalent to ⟨-n't⟩ in words such as *dinna* 'don't', *daurna* 'daren't', *haena* 'haven't', *maunna* 'mustn't', and *sanna* 'shan't'.

2.4.7 Deletion of terminal *-d*

Rendition of the elided terminal ⟨d⟩ in ⟨nd⟩ as an apostrophe occurred occasionally.

2.4.8 Use of *ane* and *ance*

Most used *ane* 'one' and *ance* 'once', although they probably pronounced them /jɪn(s)/, but Shairp used both *yin* and *ance*.

2.4.9 Weak verb past tense endings in *-ed, -'d, -led, -it,* and *-elt*

Most used ⟨-ed⟩ for the past tense of regular verbs /ət/ but ⟨-it⟩ and ⟨-'d⟩ also occurred in words such as *droukit* 'soaked', *dwined* 'withered', *ettled* 'endeavoured', *lookit, runkled* 'wrinkled', *ken'd* 'knew', *pu'd* 'pulled', and *row'd* 'rolled'.

2.4.10 Present participles in *-in'*

All wrote the present participle /ɪn/ ⟨-in'⟩.

2.4.11 Vowels 1, 8a, and 10 in *i(-e), y(-e), ai, oy,* and *oi*

Vowels 1, 8a and 10 were usually written ⟨i⟩ or ⟨y⟩ with a mute ⟨e⟩ after a following consonant in words such as *aye* 'always', *blythe* 'happy', *dwine* 'wither', *fine, kye* 'cattle', *lyart* 'grizzled', and *tryst* 'pledge'. All used ⟨-ay⟩ in words such as *hay, may, way* and ⟨oy⟩ and ⟨oi⟩ (vowel 10) in words such as *joy* and *toil*.

2.4.12 Vowel 2 in *ee, ei,* and *ie*

Vowel 2 was usually written ⟨**ee**⟩ but ⟨**ei**⟩ and ⟨**ie**⟩ also occasionally occur in words such as *bield* 'shelter', *briest* 'breast', *dreich* 'dreary', *green, fleech* 'coax', *friend, grief, weel/weil* (adj.) 'well', *weep,* and *weet* 'wet'.

2.4.13 Vowel 11 in *ee* and *e*

Vowel 11 (root-final) was usually written ⟨**ee**⟩ or ⟨**e**⟩ and no spellings indicating the local pronunciation /əi/ in words such as *be, flee, knee, me,* and *see* were found in the sample.

2.4.14 Vowel 3 in *ea*

Vowel 3 was usually written ⟨**ea**⟩ in words such as *beard, beast, clear, head, meal, shear,* and *tear.*

2.4.15 Vowels 4 and 8 in *ai, a-e,* and *ae*

Vowels 4 and 8 were variously written ⟨**ai**⟩, ⟨**a-e**⟩ or ⟨**ae**⟩, for example, initial and medial *ain* 'own', *bairn* 'child', *baith* 'both', *fain* 'content', *mair* 'more', *alane* 'alone', *hame* 'home', *gane* 'gone', and *stane* 'stone', root-final *brae* 'hillside', *frae* 'from', *gae* 'go', *nae* 'no', *sae* 'so', *wae* 'woe', and *claes* 'clothes'.

2.4.16 Vowels 5 and 18 in *oa, o-e,* and *o*

Vowels 5 and 18 were usually written ⟨**oa**⟩, ⟨**o-e**⟩, and ⟨**o**⟩ as in Standard English cognates, in words such as *bonny* 'pretty', *corn, gloamin'* 'twilight', *morn* 'morning', *mony* 'many', *ony* 'any' *road,* and *moss* 'marsh'.

2.4.17 Vowel 6 in *ou, ow, oo,* and *u-e*

Vowel 6 was variously written ⟨**ou**⟩ or ⟨**ow**⟩, occasionally ⟨**oo**⟩ or ⟨**u-e**⟩ in words such as *dule* 'sorrow', *doon* 'doun', *now, our, out, scoul* 'scowl', *soom* 'swim', and *south.*

2.4.18 Vowel 7 in *u-e, ui, oo,* and *eu*

Vowel 7 was variously written ⟨**u-e**⟩ or ⟨**ui**⟩ but also ⟨**oo**⟩ as in Standard English cognates in words such as *aboon* and *abune* 'above', *dune* 'done', *gude* 'good', *muir* 'moor', *puir* 'poor', and *toom* 'empty'.

The result of vowel 7 before /k/ and /x/ was often written ⟨**eu**⟩ in words such as *eneugh* 'enough' but also *look* and *took.*

2.4.19 Vowel 9 in *oy* and *oi*

Vowel 9 in words like *noise* and *boy* was not found in the sample.

2.4.20 Vowel 12 in *au*, *aw*, and *a'*

Vowel 12 was usually written ⟨**au**⟩ medial and ⟨**aw**⟩ initial and final, and ⟨**a'**⟩ usually for historic ⟨**l**⟩ vocalization (see above) in words such as *auld* 'old', *bauld* 'bold', *blaw* 'blow', *braw* 'fine', *craw* 'crow', *maun* 'must', *shaw* 'grove', and *snaw* 'snow'.

2.4.21 Vowel 13 in *ow* and *ou*

Vowel 13 was variously written ⟨**ow**⟩ or ⟨**ou**⟩ in words such as *bowe* 'bow', *douf* 'dull', *dowie* 'sad', *gowan* 'daisy', *grow*, *howe* 'hollow', *four*, *gowd* 'gold', *knowe* 'knoll', *lown* 'calm', *ower* 'over', and *row* 'roll'.

2.4.22 Vowel 14 in *ew* and *ue*

Vowel 14 was usually written ⟨**ew**⟩ in words such as *dew*, *few* and *slew* but also ⟨**ue**⟩ in words such as *blue*.

2.4.23 Vowel 15 in *i*

Vowel 15 was usually written ⟨**i**⟩ in words such as *sic* 'such', *night*, *rigg* 'ridge', *rin* 'run', *fit* 'foot', and *simmer* 'summer'. The graph ⟨**u**⟩ was also occasionally used for vowel 15 after /w/ and /ʍ/.

2.4.24 Vowel 16 in *e*

Vowel 16 was usually written ⟨**e**⟩ in words such as *den* 'ravine', *ken* 'know', and *skelp* 'slap'.

2.4.25 Vowel 17 in *a*

Vowel 17 was usually written ⟨**a**⟩ in words such as *aft* 'often', *amang* 'among', *crap* 'crop' *saft* 'soft', and *sang* 'song'.

2.4.26 Vowel 19 in *u*

Vowel 19 was usually written ⟨**u**⟩ in words such as *busk* 'dress', *cushat* 'pigeon', and *muckle* 'much'.

2.4.27 Other comments

No spelling evidence was found for the characteristic Southern Scots pronunciations of vowel 11 as /əi/ and root-final vowel 6 as /ʌu/, which give rise to the dialect being referred to as the *yow and mey* dialect 'you and me'. Furthermore, no spelling evidence was found for /-e/ in *awa'* 'away', *twa* 'two' and *wha* 'who', except for Elliot's *away* rhyming with *day*, or the pronunciations /θre/ for *frae* 'from' and /hjɛm/ for *hame* 'home' etc.

3
LANGUAGE PLANNING

3.1 THE 18TH AND 19TH CENTURIES

Those writing in the 18th and 19th centuries were well aware that a Scots-speaking readership would never pronounce the likes of *about*, *dead*, *sleight* and *night* as in Standard English but by the 20th century that could no longer be taken for granted and spellings such as *aboot*, *deid*, *slicht* and *nicht* had become more common. From the early 20th century knowledge of Scots literature began to dwindle and in the 1920s Craigie (1924: 14-16) commented that Scots language and literature no longer had any place in Scottish education.

As a result of that the vernacular came to be viewed as the local form of English and subsequently written Scots often diverged from the literary traditions of the 18th and 19th centuries, mostly through writers attempting to indicate local pronunciations based on the perceived sound-to-letter correspondences of the Standard English of the (educational) establishment, whereas previously such differences would have been subsumed in the traditional "pan-dialect" orthography of *Literary Scots*. Of course, there were writers who were well aware of the previous traditions, notably the "Lallans" poets.

> Although the 'Scots Renaissance' is inseparably associated with the portentous figure of Hugh MacDiarmid, the revivification of the Scottish poetic scene was gathering strength well before the publication of *Sangschaw* [...] (McClure 2003: 213)

That demise fostered a desire among interested parties to demand and initiate awareness- and status-building exercises.

> Since this is 'the national tongue' (Craigie 1924, pp.16f. *passim*), and 'has a national value' (Craigie 1924, p.11) and its effacement will imply 'a denationalization of the Scottish people' (Craigie 1924, p.20), and since its use is 'an assertion of Scottish identity' (McClure 1980a, p.18) it should be restored to spoken use and

given official status. That it can be so restored we may see if we look at the examples of Norwegian, Frisian, Catalan and various other languages which have had reputedly successful revival movements. If this restoration is not carried out, the Scots will end in the humiliating position of being unable to read their national literature without a glossary—a fear that has haunted us for a century and a half now (e.g. 1884 in Cockburn 1874, 2, pp.88–9; *Scottish Rev.* 1907, p.540)—the lexical riches of a 'rich, euphonious and expressive tongue' (Craigie 1924, p.25) will have perished, and the Scots will have been still further divorced from their native linguistic and cultural roots. (Aitken 1981a: 87)

Perhaps above all we should not underestimate the vital importance of such a user-friendly dictionary in helping raise the status of Scots and helping to alter the pupils' and the teachers' perceptions of their own speech. (Hodgart 1996: 29)

[...] it is surely an essential feature of any self-respecting culture that we teach our children to understand and appreciate their linguistic and literary heritage. If we continue to teach little or nothing about the Scots tongue, many of our finest writers of the past, or even the present, will be closed books to our children. (Hodgart 1996: 29)

Much more to the point: most Scots speakers cannot read (never mind write) Scots with any ease. (Millar 2005: 190)

Many of course were and had been interested in the Scots tongue. The 18th century "vernacular revival" perhaps helped produce Jamieson's *Etymological Dictionary of the Scottish Language*, published in 1808. That was followed in 1921 by Grant and Dixon's *Manual of Modern Scots*, a description of 19th century pronunciation, orthography and grammar based on the literature of the time. By 1931 the *Scottish National Dictionary* project was under way. As the 20th century continued, awareness- and status-building exercises began to take on the nature of language-planning exercises.

[...] the activity of preparing a normative orthography, grammar and dictionary for the guidance of writers and speakers in a non-homogenous speech-community. (Haugen 1961: 68)

Devising a normative orthography for Scots has been one of the
greatest linguistic hobbies of the past century. (Corbett 2003: 260)

Kloss (1952: 24ff) described the development of a *Mundart* (dialect) to a
Ausbausprache (standard language) as involving among other things the
standardization of its orthography. Kloss accepted that Scots had gone
some way towards achieving some of those but considered it a *Halbsprache*
(half-language).

Idiome, die weder in linguistischer noch in soziologischer Hinsicht
eindeutig als selbständig gelten können, die jedoch auf Grund
soziologischer und z.T. auch linguistischer Sonderentwicklung mit
Vorbehalt als Sprachen anerkannt werden können [...] (Kloss
1952: 36)[12]

Haugen, again, provides an answer. The growth of a language
entails four stages: selection, codification, elaboration and
acceptance. First of all, that is, one of the various existing speech
forms is chosen to become the basis of the national language;
secondly, its orthography and grammar are fixed by a series of
formal rules; thirdly, its range of uses is extended and developed
until it becomes an adequate vehicle for all the functions of a
national language; and finally the mass of the population is
persuaded to accept it for everyday use. (McClure 1980a: 19)

Only the first two stages, which deal with the orthographic nature of the
written form, are discussed here.

After selection, codification. It should be noted what this implies:
nothing less than the establishment of an agreed orthography for
every word in the language and a set of general spelling rules so
that new words can be accommodated; and a formal grammar
incorporating rules for all aspects of morphology and syntax.
(McClure 1980: 23)

The objective is to establish a standard written form of Scots and
this clearly cannot be based on localised dialect forms. (Purves
1979: 62)

---

12   'Varieties that can neither linguistically or sociologically be clearly identified as
     independent, but nevertheless on sociological grounds or partly, with reservations,
     because of particular developments may be considered languages [...]' [AE]

The question of standard Scots is a thorny one; to a degree the Central dialect, especially that of Edinburgh, has come to be regarded as some kind of literary standard, particularly in prose. In poetry, a more eclectic form, often referred to as Lallans, is sometimes used, with words from other dialects and other times. But neither of these can really be regarded as a standard for everyday and especially spoken language. (MacLeod 1993: 122)

Scots needs a standard spelling system for eventual use in newspapers and school text books. (Love 1995: 18)

[…] the Scots School Dictionary has been designed to make Scots more accessible from the point of view both of comprehension and of speaking or writing the language. Emphasis is on modern everyday language, including urban colloquialisms and slang (often neglected by earlier dictionaries). (Hodgart 1996: 30)

While dictionaries should not be regarded as the last word in standardization, they act as an important pointer to the way a language is going and provide some kind of yardstick. The Scottish National Dictionary Association accepts that dictionaries are always regarded to some extent as a guide to standard spelling and is well aware of its responsibilities in this area. (Hodgart 1996: 30)

The consensus o the November 1996 Collogue wis at "the definition of a standard spelling for a broad transcription of Scots should be the priority." (*Lallans* 56, 2004: 77)

Any standard should be based on the dialects of the Central Belt, where most speakers are. That of the Edinburgh area has a special place because of the amount of Scottish literature emanating from it over the centuries. (*SLD* 2002)

It follows that Scots orthography will only be standardised if Scots were to be used more widely in functions beyond the literary, and if a standard Scots spelling system were to be taught in schools so that writers could perform these functions adequately. (Corbett 2003: 261)

3.2 IDEOLOGICAL OBSTACLES TO PROGRESS TODAY

Acceptance of any proposed norm by the community is highly unlikely at present and likely to remain so.

> The debate is academic because, first, writing in unreformed Scots continues regardless, second, even if a consensus were to be reached (and neither in principle nor in detail is there any sign of one) there would be no way of enforcing it; third, the whole issue is of little moment to the Scottish populace as a whole, who evince a deplorable ignorance and indifference towards questions of language as to other aspects of the national culture. (McClure 1985: 206–7)

> Enthusiastic teachers, still alas a minority, report the need for English-Scots materials to help children write in Scots, especially in areas, in fact most places, where the language has already receded to a great extent. (MacLeod 1993: 120)

> It might be thought that the school pupil requires a much simpler treatment than the more sophisticated user, but in many ways both need guidance as to the right choice of word and how to use it. (MacLeod 1993: 121)

> [...] every writer who wishes to use it must learn it anew, and by his own efforts. Certainly, successive poets in the present century have built on each other's achievements [...] (McClure 1995: 23)

> In the absence of a distinct orthography for Scots, those wishing to write in the language have, since the 17th century, generally adopted the conventions of English spelling, modified to a greater or lesser extent according to the preferences of the individual writer. (McClure 1995: 37)

> If spoken Scots is a group of dialects, it is not much of an exaggeration to say that written Scots is a group of idiolects. (McClure 1995: 24)

> [...] that given a sufficiency of talented writers a language does not require a standard form to be the vehicle of major literature [...] (McClure 1995: 24)

It has been argued that an attempt to establish a standard Scots is unnecessary, as the language can be effectively written without it: this is unquestionably true. (McClure 1995: 25)

Teachers also seek help over the issue of orthography. Without a standard form they find it difficult to correct spelling [...] In my experience, pupils want to have rules of some kind, and many cannot 'see' how to spell a word they can say, even when they speak broad Scots. One pupil told me that he could not imagine how to spell a word because he 'didnae hae the picter'. Until the sight of Scots becomes more common, writing it will remain a struggle. (Niven 1998: 68)

[...] the lack of a standard for written Scots seems to be a deterrent rather than an opportunity for Scots writers—a claim which remains unsupported by evidence and which, moreover, can be contradicted by citing the writings of Tom Leonard, Alex Hamilton, James Kelman and others. Their representation of their variety of Scots has certainly thrived despite (or perhaps because of) the non-existence of a standard system of representation. (Hagen 2002: 148)

Some utilitarian Scots prose has recently been published, for example on the Scottish Parliament website[13] and by the Northern Ireland Department of Culture, Arts and Leisure,[14] though their transactional value has been questioned. As is shown by reactions to "Makkin yer voice heard in the Scottish Pairlament":

"Scottish" itself is questionable. [...] The better form here would be "Scots" or "Scottis". But I have the impression that whoever wrote this booklet knows very little about the history of the language. [...] Sometimes the poor author more or less gives up, being unable to find, or concoct, any Scots equivalent for the English he or she would naturally use. The result is a hotch-potch. [...] It does nothing for the Scots language, other than expose it to ridicule and bring it into contempt. It is frankly embarrassing. (Massie: *The Scotsman* 2004-01-31)

---

13 https://web.archive.org/web/20100424192614/www.scottish.parliament.uk/vli /language/scots/index.htm accessed 2021-10-30.

14 https://web.archive.org/web/20060219230642/www.dcalni.gov.uk/home /default.asp?lang=ulsterscots accessed 2021-10-30.

[…] poorly-written documents in some ill-thought-out linguistic mixter-maxter offered as "Scots", far from doing any service to the language, merely expose it to ridicule, and undercut both the real case for developing Scots and the efforts of those who have been engaged for years in credible attempts at doing so. Language development is not a task for amateurs; nor can it be achieved by slapdash, undirected efforts, however well intentioned. Why, then, is it being left to them? (McClure: *The Scotsman* 2004-02-07)

Comments on Scots documents published in Ulster are no less disparaging.

The net effect of an amalgam of traditional, surviving, revived, changed, and invented features is artificial dialect. It is certainly not a written version of the vestigial spoken dialect of rural county Antrim, as its activists frequently urge, perpetrating the fallacy that it's *wor ain leid*. (Besides, the dialect revivalists claim *not* to be native speakers of the dialect themselves!). The colloquialness of this new dialect is deceptive for it is neither spoken nor innate. Traditional dialect speakers find it counter-intuitive and false […] (Kirk 2000: 130)

REGARDING a notice published in the Belfast Telegraph on September 5 relating to the intention of the Department of Culture, Arts and Leisure to promote the formation of an Ulster-Scots Academy, we suggest that if the Department's concern for the welfare of Ulster-Scots is meant the living, every-day language of native speakers, that version is a travesty. […] Those of us who have or had Ulster-Scots as our first language have a deep and abiding affection for it. We find the Department's absurd version as offensive as it is bogus. (Cross: *The Belfast Telegraph* 2003-09-24)

Whatever feeling the translator may have for such pre-revival Ulster-Scots writers as Orr, Porter and Thomson, it is clear that he or she rejects them absolutely as literary models. One also suspects that the person responsible views his or her role as that of one empowered to undertake major structural reform rather than as a synthesiser or mediator of attested practice. […] From the above we can conclude that the orthographic practices in question not only differ considerably from any attested form of literary Scots, of whatever provenance, but contain diacritics borrowed from phonetic notation for the specific purpose of giving minor articulatory differences at the level of accent a presence in the written form of the idiom, [...] they have no place in a communicative text aimed at native speakers, whom they are likely merely to confuse. [...] their communicative value for native users of the Ulster variety is also severely diminished [...] the readiness of Northern Ireland officialdom to consign taxpayers' money to a black hole of translations incomprehensible to ordinary users is worrying. (Falconer 2005: 55–56)

4

PROPOSALS AND PRACTICES

4.1 GROUPS AND INDIVIDUALS PROMULGATING REFORM

Since the middle of the last century a number of proposals for a codified normative orthography have emerged alongside the publication of various dictionaries by the *Scottish National Dictionary Association* (SNDA)—this became *Scottish Language Dictionaries* (SLD) in 2002, and in January 2021 became *Dictionaries of the Scots Language* (DSL). The influence of the codifiers has been at best marginal, being confined to those who take an active interest in such matters. Examples of the proposed orthographies can be found in the Appendix.`

4.1.1 *The Scots Style Sheet* (1947)

That set of proposals was presented by a group of "Lallans" poets known as the "Makkar's Club". That was a modest two pages suggesting dropping the "parochial" or "apologetic apostrophe" and establishing conventions for representing vowel sounds. Those suggestions were clearly based on a more regularized application of 18th and 19th century conventions but also suggested ⟨**ch**⟩ for /x/, previously ⟨**gh**⟩, ⟨**ei**⟩ for vowel 3, and a new grapheme ⟨**aa**⟩ (vowel 12) was introduced for word-final ⟨**l**⟩ vocalization. (Mackie 1955: 30–31)

> These proposals closely followed the spelling ideas of Douglas Young and A.D. Mackie […] (Purves 1979: 62)

> A further innovation in [Douglas] Young's poetry, and one which at first sight makes his Scots *appear* to be more unalike that of his predecessors than it actually is, is his spelling practices. Several of the orthographic features which shortly afterwards were enshrined in the Scots Style Sheet, such as the digraph *aa* (previously unknown in Scots of any period), the consistent use of *ou* instead of the anglicism *oo* for the sound of [u] and *ow* for [ʌu], and the

abandonment of the apostrophe where Scots has lost (or never had) a sound which English retains, are a conspicuous feature of Young's writing. (McClure 2000: 121)

4.1.2 David Purves (1975)

Purves, a writer and editor, presented his proposals in *Lallans* issue 4, followed up in the *Scottish Literary Journal* Supplement issue 9, 1979. His aim was to "reconcile traditional spelling practices with the requirement that spelling should be consistent and should have a reasonably phonetic basis" (p.63), often citing precedents in the *Scottish National Dictionary* in order to justify some of his suggestions. Those were to some extent influenced by the conventions of older Scots. The representation of vowels often followed a more regularized application of 18th and 19th century conventions but also "rational spellings used by the mediaeval Makkars" such as *thai* 'they', *thair* 'their', *cum* 'come', *sum* 'some' (1997: 61), and *wes* 'was' (1997: 50). The "apologetic apostrophe" was eschewed, and ⟨ch⟩ was suggested for /x/, previously ⟨gh⟩. The traditional grapheme ⟨aw⟩ (vowel 12) was suggested for ⟨l⟩ vocalization in words such as *aw* 'all', *caw* 'call', and *faw* 'fall'.

> The objective is to establish a standard written form of Scots and this clearly cannot be based on localised dialect forms. How it is pronounced in practice will vary according to the dialect with which the reader is familiar. (Purves 1979: 62)

> Other spelling ideas […] have been taken from 'Mang Howes and Knowes' by Elliot Cowan Smith, 1926, and from 15th and 16th century writings in Scots. (Purves 1979: 62)

> In the courtly poems of the Makkars of the fifteenth and sixteenth centuries, the rather loose system of spelling used was far superior phonetically to the practices of later writers in Scots, […] (Purves 1997: 57)

4.1.3 Derrick McClure (1980)

McClure presented the basis of a phoneme-based system in the *Scottish Literary Journal* no. 12. McClure's suggestions were seemingly more of a *Gedankenspiel* illustrating the application of the phonemic principle rather than proposals that were expected to gain any support. McClure's suggestions were based on Catford's (1958) phonemic analysis of Scots dialects. McClure's (somewhat unconventional) choice of graphemes was often justified by their use in other European languages, not necessarily their current or previous use in Scots.

> This is an analysis only of the stressed vowel system in syllables of a certain structure: it says nothing about the vowels of unstressed syllables or stressed syllables of other types […] it is probably an over-simplification even on its own terms. However, it provides a useful and viable basis for a spelling system for Scots which accommodates some of the major dialect variations. (McClure 1980: 25)

> Spelling conventions unique to English, such as the use of *ee* and *oo* for the sounds [i] and [u], should be avoided wherever possible: this is not from mere Anglophobia but for the much more serious and valid reason that the whole purpose of establishing a spelling system for Scots is to underwrite its status as a language distinct from English, resulting from independent historical developments, and therefore not bound to adhere to conventions devised for English. The extent to which the orthographic conventions of other languages should guide the choice of symbols for Scots is an issue in which each case must be debated on its own merits: if the symbol chosen to represent a particular phoneme in Scots is the same as that used for the corresponding phoneme in another language, this may be a point in its favour; but a proposed spelling rule need not be rejected solely because such parallels are lacking. (McClure 1980: 25)

4.1.4 *The Scots Language Society* (1985)

The SLS published its "Recommendations for Writers in Scots" (and the accompanying word lists)[15] agreed at a meeting of Scots "makkars" in the School of Scottish Studies in Edinburgh. It is clear that Purves had substantial influence on that, especially some recommendations echoing Middle Scots. The desirability of employing spellings with traditional precedents was commented on. Here the "apologetic apostrophe" was eschewed, and ⟨**ch**⟩ was suggested for /x/, previously ⟨**gh**⟩. The traditional grapheme ⟨**aw**⟩ (vowel 12) was also used for ⟨**l**⟩ vocalization in words such as *aw* 'all', *caw* 'call', and *faw* 'fall'. Interestingly, it was also suggested "[…] that words used in Scots in common with English which have the same pronunciation […] should [not] be altered if the English spelling leaves no

---

15   *Lallans* 39, 40, 41, and 43.

doubt as to the pronunciation." That itself leads to spelling contradictions between "Scots" and "shared" vocabulary.

> Dis a leid that haes ae (reformed, simple, 'medieval' seistem for spellin the tae hauf o'ts wurds, an awthegither deiferent (onreformed, thrawart, 'Inglish' seistem for spellin the tither, hae onie chance o bein acceppit bi oniebodie outby the Lallans coterie? The norie at sic a fankle cuid be teatched as an aerlie or prymarie medium o leiteracie i scuils mairches on madness. (Allan 1995: 70)

4.1.5 Angus Stirling (1994)

Stirling came to the conclusion that "For Scots to function as a national language, it requires a fully regulated spelling system […]" (p.89). In order to achieve that, Stirling suggested it would be wise to "Design a new spelling system which is phonologically accurate and consistent, and can be applied to older texts for the purpose of making them more accessible." (p.90). Stirling failed to identify some underlying phonemes such as vowel 3 and the development of vowel 7 before /k/ and /x/, which he allocated vowel 14. He also failed to differentiate the vowels 1 long and 8a, 1 short and 10, 2 and 11, and 4 and 8. He then went on to suggest a system, apparently based on East Central Scots, using a hotchpotch of conventions from various sources such as Scandinavia, traditional Scots and Dutch. Stirling suggested introducing ⟨ä⟩ and innovative consonant clusters. It was often unclear where and how his vowel graphemes were to be applied.

> […] the spelling system involved is not normally Anglocentric; it may however seem Martian. Perhaps the most striking example of this is the spelling system of Stirling (1994), which is so enamoured of Scandinavian orthography that it does not recognize either the manifest differences in phonemic systems between these languages and Scots or the willingness of a Scottish writing and reading public to embrace what to them would be an utterly foreign system […] (Millar 2005: 191)

4.1.6 *The Aiberdeen Univairsitie Scots Leid Quorum* (1995)

The AUSLQ published its recommendations in its *Innin ti the Scots Leid* (Lovie 1995) based on Allan (1995). Allan was aware that any orthography substantially different from Standard English would have little chance of acceptance, but was working towards a two-stage "reform". Allan established the underlying consonants and vowel phonemes and allocated graphemes, sometimes misallocating the underlying vowel phonemes. Here the apologetic apostrophe was also eschewed, ⟨**ch**⟩ was suggested for /x/, previously ⟨**gh**⟩. The traditional grapheme ⟨**aw**⟩ (vowel 12) was also used for ⟨**l**⟩ vocalization in words such as *aw* 'all', *faw* 'fall', and *waw* 'wall'. Traditional consonant practice was generally followed but such forms as *houss* 'house', *louss* 'louse' did occur.

4.1.7 *The SNDA* (later *SLD*, now *DSL*)

The SNDA undertook an essentially descriptive approach (i.e. recording usage) and as such included many "historical, regional, accidental and idiosyncratic" variants (Macleod and Cairns 1993: vi). The choice of headwords in the dictionaries seems to be based on selection "from the numerous variants for which there is evidence in the parent dictionaries (SND and DOST)" or predictable spelling variants (Robinson 1985: xx, xviii, 1986: 23). Material shared with Standard English was not included. (Robinson 1986: 22)

> Since there is no standard spelling for Scots the lay person will find the dictionary *fykie* to consult. For the most part the headwords (provided by the parent dictionaries) are in fairly predictable spellings for Modern Scots, but the vagaries of the original corpora are evident; for instance, *lawnd* appears (and is referred to *land*), but *laund* does not, while *haund* does. Some words are entered under *ui* spellings, e.g. *muir*, others under *uCe*, e.g. *mune*. (Macafee 1985: 338)

> Thus for example the article **house** is also provided with the common modern variant *hoose* although this is completely predictable. Because the principal English and Scots *spellings* coincide (as ⟨house⟩), though their *pronunciations* differ (as [hʌus] and [hus] respectively) [...] (Robinson 1986: 21)

> Finally we provide guidance on acceptable spellings. Of course in no sense are we being prescriptive; but SND and DOST have already selected the mainstream spelling preferences of their respective periods by their choice of headwords; we confirm their choice and add other representative possibilities from the range found. (Robinson 1986: 27)

> The role of the lexicographer is to record language, i.e. to be descriptive rather than prescriptive. One of the aims of the SNDA however is to promote and encourage Scots and it is also well aware that, no matter how even-handedly its data are presented,

the dictionaries will in some ways be regarded as a standard. Editors have to be aware of users' need for guidance, even if they do not always base decisions on it. Methodologically the first task in dictionary compiling is one of selection and this could in itself be seen as a prescriptive role. The problem of keeping a balance is particularly difficult with a language such as Scots where the use of English as the language of authority over a long period has to some extent masked the need for standardization. (MacLeod 1993: 115–116)

It was only with the advent of the *Concise English~Scots Dictionary* (Macleod and Cairns 1993) and the *Scots Schools Dictionary* (Macleod 1996) that decisions about "recommended spellings" had to be made in the English-Scots section. Many of these were themselves contradictory but generally reflected traditional practice.

[…] usually only one spelling is given, or in some cases two or more, especially where there are regional variants […] Sometimes additional variants are given at the word's main appearance in the dictionary […] (Macleod and Cairns 1993: vi)

The choice of headwords is therefore a difficult one, and the main criteria applied in the Scots School Dictionary have been: will the spelling be a guide to the modern Scots pronunciation? Thus *moose* rather than *mouse*; does it conform to modern usage? Thus *souch* and *roup* (though *sooch* and *rowp* might have fulfilled the first criterion better). There is no easy answer to these problems and the solutions arrived at in this Dictionary are not meant to last forever. In some cases alternatives have been given, especially for regional forms, but the first head word is the one regarded as having the most general currency. (Hodgart 1996: 30)

As a general guide: if *SSD* includes more than one variant spelling used in general Scots (ie not identified with a particular region), the recommended form to use is the first of those listed. Note that some Scots words have settled on a single spelling, eg *heid* (never **heed*) 'head'. (SNDA 1996)

The situation is similar in Rennie (1999), which essentially dealt with grammar but spelling was often mentioned, based on traditional practice "and those [spellings] which have been in most general use this century" adding that "to impose a single spelling for every word at this stage in the history of the language would be an exercise in arbitrariness". On the SLD website[16] the apologetic apostrophe was also eschewed but an apostrophe could be used to indicate that two consecutive vowels were to be pronounced separately, e.g. *fa'in* 'falling' or to indicate a glottal realization of /t/, for example, *wa'er* 'water'; ⟨**ch**⟩ was suggested for /x/, previously ⟨**gh**⟩. Both the traditional grapheme ⟨**aw**⟩ (vowel 12) and the innovation ⟨**aa**⟩, along with ⟨**a**⟩, were suggested for ⟨**l**⟩ vocalization in words such as *a aa aw* 'all', *ca caa caw* 'call' and *fa faa faw* 'fall'. The modernism ⟨**oa**⟩ in *goat* 'got' and *oan* 'on' was presented as an option. The traditional negative particle ⟨**-na**⟩ was ignored and instead the modernism ⟨**-nae**⟩ suggested. The *Concise English-Scots Dictionary* (Macleod and Cairns 1993: vi-viii) stated that the "first headword from the *Scottish National Dictionary* (and therefore usually the *Concise Scots Dictionary* […]) is used" followed by a number of exceptions and the justification for choosing otherwise. The *Scots School Dictionary* (Macleod 1996: v), which was aimed at nine- to 14-year-olds, comments that "Scots has a very wide variety of different spellings […] In this little dictionary there has of course been no space for more than a very few different spellings". On pages vii–viii there is a superficial description of spelling conventions and their pronunciation. In the dictionary both *-na* and *-nae* are given for the negative particle. The SNDA *Recommendations for writing and transcribing Scots* (1999) were intended as an ongoing project and comments and suggestions were invited from interested parties for future versions. That commented that "Scots has (and has always had) a variant spelling system" and that "for everyday, modern Scots, the most *frequent* and *widespread* spellings of a word can be found in the *SSD*", also adding that "spurious spellings, created to distinguish a word from its English equivalent, but for which there is no evidence in Historical Scots" should be avoided. A similar approach was explained on the web-page *The Headword List A–C*[17] including a small sample of the headword list based upon the contents of the *Essential Scots Dictionary*.

> As every writer and reader of Scots is aware, Scots spelling is not fixed. It reflects regional differences and even differences in the formality level of the text. For practical reasons, it is desirable to

---

16   See https://web.archive.org/web/20061015063228if_/http://www.scotsdictionaries .org.uk/ScotsSpellingGrammar.htm accessed 2021-10-30.

17   https://web.archive.org/web/20061015063627/http://www.scotsdictionaries.org.uk /HeadWordList/About.html accessed 2021-10-30. Note that the first edition of the *Essential Scots Dictionary* (1996, Chambers; 1999, Polygon) appeared under the title *Scots School Dictionary*.

have a 'headword' under which variants can be embraced and this list is an attempt to provide a list of such headwords.

This list is NOT intended as a list of 'correct' or even 'recommended' spellings. It is simply a list of the most common spellings in our word collection. As these are the spellings that seem to be most common, it follows that these are the spellings which dictionary users are most likely to look up. This makes them the sensible choice for headwords in ordinary, everyday dictionaries.

Based upon the contents of the *Essential Scots Dictionary*, it is far from being an exhaustive list, but we hope it will be sufficiently comprehensive for practical purposes. However, contrary to our usual practice to date, some entries have been included that are shared with English. The reason for this is that we have found occasional variant spellings for these with little or no etymological or any other justification and the vast majority of Scots writers use a similar spelling to English and this is the one we have listed.

4.1.8 George Philp (1997)

Philp presented comments on his choice of spellings in his introduction to *Scorn, My Inheritance* (Graham 1997). There, among other recommendations was the consistent applications of ⟨**ui**⟩ for vowel 7, including the realization after /k/ and /x/, although Philp wrongly allocated this underlying phoneme to the Scots cognates of 'foot', 'put', and 'wood', which generally have vowel 15 in all dialects. Philp justified his spelling of the preposition formed by combining *for* and *by*, *forbye* on the grounds that "the learner" may pronounce it to rhyme with the town of *Corby* in Northamptonshire though a "learner" might as easily pronounce his spelling *forbye* /forbji/. Another "innovative" aid to the "learner" was the insertion of a hyphen in constructions such as *dae-in* 'doing' and *hae-in* 'having'.

Philp later reiterated in *Lallans* issue 71, calling his system *Scotscreive*, adding that it is founded on the sound of the *leid*. His seven "Pillars o Wisdom", which later became six, were that; (1) ⟨**ou**⟩ is used consistently for vowel 6. (2) Consistent use of ⟨**ow**⟩ for vowel 13, mentioning *growe* 'grow', *howe* 'hollow', and *lowe* 'flame' with word final ⟨**owe**⟩. (3) Lorimer's (1985) use of an acute accent for vowel 2 was followed for the Scots realization of ⟨**i**⟩ in Latinate words such as *addítion*, *consíder*, *mínister* etc., arguing that accents are found in Standard English "blessèd" and certainly in Gaelic. (4) Philp mentioned the Older Scots orthographic practice of using an ⟨**i**⟩ to lengthen the vowel it follows, so that ⟨**ei**⟩ = ⟨**ee**⟩ being used for vowels 2, 3, and 11, himself using exceptions with ⟨**ee**⟩ so presumably not applying it "across the board" but omitting to explain where ⟨**ee**⟩ is preferable to ⟨**ei**⟩. (5) Terminal ⟨**ie**⟩ was recommended for diminutives but mentioned that ⟨**y**⟩ need not necessarily be abandoned altogether in other words. Terminal ⟨**ie**⟩ was also to be used, with added acute to "preserve the written Scots form", in *gíe* 'give', *híe* 'high', *príe* 'taste', and *thíe* 'thigh' and in *companie* and *countrie* "to rhyme with *bee*". (6) Consistent use of ⟨**ey**⟩ for vowel 8a. The seventh pillar, reserving ⟨**ee**⟩ for Northern realizations of vowel vowel 7 and vowel 4 before /n/, was dropped because ⟨**ee**⟩ "is widely used throughout Scotland", presumably for vowels 2 and 11. Philp hoped that *Scotscreive* would be eye-friendly, consistent, and uncontrived.

4.1.9 Philip Robinson (1997)

Robinson presented suggestions for the Ulster dialect in his *Ulster-Scots A Grammar of the Traditional Written and Spoken Language*. Robinson himself was of the opinion that "Ulster-Scots" constituted a language in its own right. Those are the most esoteric of proposals which have had any influence so far. The motivation seemed to be less an interest in developing the established tradition and more a desire to invent a new one emphasizing a political and ethnic distinctiveness.

> Anyone with half an ear knows that some Ulster speech contains usage and constructions which seem consistently different from Scots or northern English or Irish usage of English.
>
> Why would one want to assert its existence the answer would seem to be to assert a native version of Ulster Protestant identity, which would mirror that version of Irish identity in which the possession of a distinct language is central. [...] Language and culture emerged as a political axe to grind in the 1980's from within the maze prison, where initially, republican inmates took to learning Irish [...] the claim that the Ulster-Scots language and heritage cause has been set rolling only out of a sense of cultural rivalry among some Protestants and unionists, keen to counter-balance the onward march of the Irish language movement [...] (Brett: 1999)

While most argue that Ulster-Scots is a dialect or variant of Scots, some have argued or implied that Ulster-Scots is a separate language from Scots. The case for Ulster-Scots being a distinct language, made at a time when the status of Scots itself was insecure, is so bizarre that it is unlikely to have been a linguistic argument. It may reflect, in emblematic cultural terms, an ideological division within unionism between a British political

identity (within the UK) and an 'Ulster' political identity, the latter
finding its most extreme form in a movement for an independent
Northern Ireland, or, as its advocates put it, an independent Ulster.
(Mac Poilin 1999: 116)

Robinson's specious justification for language status begins "Ulster-Scots
or 'Ullans' is a close relative of the language called Scots" (1997: 1) and
implies the academic credence of such a stance with "Ulster-Scots has been
described as a 'variant' of Scots [...]. However, many Scots language
academics have observed that Ulster-Scots differs from its sister tongue:
Ulster-Scots has its own range of dialects, along with its own distinctive
literary tradition, vocabulary and grammar; all of which differ in some
respects from Lallans. In simple terms, the relationship between Ulster-
Scots and Lallans could be compared to the relative positions of Irish and
Scottish Gaelic." (1997: 1) Robinson failed to name those "language
academics" and I am only aware of "language academics" describing its
similarity or "sameness".[18]

> It must be emphasised that in their strongest rural forms these
> dialects are Lowland Scots dialects. Those of Antrim and North
> Derry are barely distinguishable from Ayrshire dialects. (Milroy
> 1982: 27)

> Ulster Scots is, as Johnston (1977b) points out, clearly a dialect of
> Central Scots. The bulk of the Scots Planters are known to have
> come from the west of Scotland (West Central and South-West
> Scots: both are Central dialects, with the addition of lawless
> elements expelled from the Borders (Southern Scots). (Macafee
> 2001: 121)

Robinson does mention that native speakers referred to their variety as
broad Scotch or Scots and quotes numerous sources describing the
language (1997: 19). None of them refer to it as "Ulster-Scots" but simply
as Scotch or Scots. After unilaterally declaring "Ulster-Scots" a language
Robinson then provides it with an ancient pedigree, perhaps to emphasize
its autochthonous status:

---

18   See *Aw Ae Oo – Scots in Scotland and Ulster*, Eagle 2005. Available at https://web.archive
     .org/web/20170401082720/http://scots-online.org/articles/contents/awaeoo.pdf
     accessed 2021-10-30.

> For 1000 years, almost since the watershed between the prehistoric
> and historic eras, Germanic, Celtic and Romance languages have
> interfaced around the land fringe of the Irish Sea Basin. Ulster
> Scots is one of the direct descendents of the west Germanic
> elements as far as north-east Ireland is concerned. (1997: 3; 2007:7)

> So it is that Ulster-Scots in east Ulster may trace some of its earliest
> Germanic linguistic precedents to Old Norse in the 8th to 10th
> centuries rather than to Old English or Anglian of the 6th to 7th
> centuries, as is the case with Lallans in Scotland. (1997: 4)

In order to accommodate such fanciful claims within the linguistic reality
on the ground it is pointed out that "[...] Ulster-Scots as spoken today is
dominated by the Scots forms introduced during this plantation period.
[...] Consequently, a considerable body of Ulster-Scots documentary
material survives from the early decades of the 1600s." (1997: 4) Of course
much of that "Ulster-Scots" material would have been written by people
who were born and educated in Scotland, but apparently after stepping off
the boat their language spontaneously changed from Scots (or *Lallans* as
Robinson prefers to term it) into "Ulster-Scots". Any self-respecting *language*,
of course needs its literary tradition and "Ulster-Scots literature, as a
tradition in its own right had survived some 400 years [...]" (1997: 10) but
Robinson seems to contradict that stance by mentioning that the "Scots
literary tradition of Scotland was integral to the Ulster-Scots literary
tradition, while Ulster-Scots writers contributed significantly to this broader
Scots renaissance in their own right." (1997: 9). That is of course undeniably
true, and the "rhyming weavers" saw themselves as part of the same Scots
tradition as their contemporaries in Scotland (Herbison 2005: 81).
Robinson claims to have indulged in a "detailed exploration of 18th and
19th century Ulster-Scots literature." (1997: 7) but seems not to have
compared what was found with contemporary sources from Scotland.

> Without a systematic treatment of the contrast between Ulster
> Scots and Scottish varieties, it is impossible for the reader to gauge
> the degree to which Ulster Scots can be understood as a fully-
> developed language in Robinson's sense, or to the degree to which
> it is best described as a variety of Scots. (Kallen 1999: 160)

Robinson sensibly provided a disclaimer that "It has been written by an
Ulster-Scot, not by a linguist." (1997: 11) Robinson took a "reinvent the
wheel" approach to orthography, no doubt motivated by a desire to empha-

size the distinctive and independent nature of the *language* "Ulster-Scots". Traditional consonant practice was generally followed but older conventions such as ⟨**quh**⟩ (⟨**wh**⟩) and ⟨**sch**⟩ (⟨**sh**⟩) were suggested along with ⟨**ch**⟩ for /x/, previously ⟨**gh**⟩. Diacritics such as ⟨**à**⟩, ⟨**á**⟩, ⟨**è**⟩, ⟨**ò**⟩, and ⟨**ó**⟩ were used to indicate either a particular realization of the preceding consonant, vowel quality or duration and ⟨**ä**⟩ apparently for a possible /ɪ̈/ (/æ̈/) (Gregg 1972: 121) realizations of vowel 15. The "apologetic apostrophe" was eschewed and the innovation ⟨**aa**⟩ (vowel 12) was suggested for ⟨**l**⟩ vocalization in words such as *aa* 'all', *caa* 'call', and *faa* 'fall'. The modernism ⟨**oa**⟩ was used in *boadie* 'body', *loast* 'lost', and *moarn* 'morning' etc. Robinson provided a long explanation of vowel spellings based on often random and confusing correspondences with the vowels in Standard English words. The traditional negative particle ⟨**-na**⟩ was ignored and instead the modernism ⟨**-nae**⟩ was suggested.

> Robinson leaves the reader to work out a series of correspondences between Ulster Scots and something referred to simply as "English", a term which can mean many things to many people. (Kallen 1999: 158)

4.1.10 *The Scots Spelling Comatee* (2000)

That committee was established after a public meeting hosted by the *Scots Language Society* and the *Scots Language Resource Centre* in the A. K. Bell Library Perth on 10 November 1996. The committee published its *Report an Recommends o the Scots Spellin Comatee* in *Lallans* issue 56.[19] That is the most freely available comprehensive exposition on the subject to date. The recommendations were based on a series of principles used to serve as a test for assessing particular spelling proposals and a series of rules based on an analysis of forms used in the *Scots School Dictionary* and traditional precedents. Those generally followed traditional vowel and consonant practice but suggested ⟨**ch**⟩ for /x/, previously ⟨**gh**⟩ and the innovation ⟨**aa**⟩ (vowel 12) for ⟨**l**⟩ vocalization in words such as *aa* 'all', *caa* 'call', and *faa* 'fall'.

4.2 APPROACHES TO ORTHOGRAPHIC REFORM

Assuming that the aim of establishing a normative orthography is to facilitate language "elaboration and acceptance" by the wider community,

---

19 Also available at https://web.archive.org/web/20211030125719/https://evertype .com/scots/ScotsSpellinCom.pdf accessed 2021-10-30 and at https://web.archive .org/web/20060620105026/http://www.zyworld.com /tallini/tribalisation/ScotsSpellinCom.doc accessed 2021-10-30.

how well have the proposals presented above achieved that? Haugen (1974: 109) assumes the necessity of choosing one of the various existing speech forms to become the basis of the national language, thus imposing a new norm on those who do not speak the chosen variety and by implication defining their speech as "sub-standard". Another possibility is, of course, a pan-dialectal orthography which is phonologically accurate (as against phonetically), thus being able to represent differing dialect pronunciation (diaphonemic) based on a consistent correspondence of graphemes to underlying phonemes. Such an orthography does not prescribe a standard pronunciation, but enables the reader to pronounce the written word according to their own dialect. The pan-dialectal approach will be discussed in this paper, including considerations of etymology and the regular spelling of morphemic elements.

> A rational approach to spelling reform must recognize the various phonological, morphological and syntactical patterns in the current orthography, and must increase either the regularity of the existing patterns or the range of one group of patterns at the expense of others. To base spelling reform on the argument that orthography should by nature be phonemic, morphemic or anything else is both unrealistic and unsupportable. There is no valid basis, either diachronic or synchronic, for claiming that the current orthography should be anything in particular than what it is. Some people may desire that it be phonemic or morphemic, but this is somewhat different from the claim that the orthography, by nature, should be that way.
>
> To argue that the existing orthography is irregular and then to propose a phonemic alphabet for English as a cure is to present a *non-sequitur*. The existing irregularities are in syntactic and morphological patterns as much as the phonological ones, so a phonemic alphabet, while presumably correcting the phonological deviations, creates even greater irregularities in the other patterning systems. (Venezky 1970: 122–123)

> The phonetic differences which are really significant for the alphabet-maker are those which affect the number of phonemic *distinctions* a speaker makes or which relate to the actual *words* in which he uses each of his phonemes. The precise phonetic value he gives his phonemes (or, better, their allophones) in each of the various phonetic contexts in which they occur is only of minor importance. (Allerton 1982: 59)

In the case of a phonemic difference between dialects, the extra distinction possessed by the one dialect may be an original one that has been preserved or a new one that it alone has developed. In either case it should be possible to represent in the orthography the maximal number of distinctions, even though no one dialect has all of them. (Allerton 1982: 63)

A phonemic system is one in which each phoneme of the language is consistently represented by one orthographic symbol. A 'symbol' in this sense need not be a single letter [...] (McClure 1980: 25)

Regardless of the method by which they have been taught, or have taught themselves, to read, many literate people attribute sounds to the letters of the alphabet. This is to put the cart before the horse, for, as should be perfectly clear by now, letters do not "have" sounds, but merely symbolize them [...] (Pyles and Algeo 1982: 60)

The nature of the Scots tongue in its diverse forms and of the Roman alphabet are such that a perfect representation of actual speech (or what is presented in fiction as such) is simply impossible, and even a tolerably accurate one is extremely difficult to achieve. (McClure 1997: 183)

[...] we see that there is no such thing as a pure phonemic writing system. Indeed, there is considerable variation within phonemic writing systems as to the amount of morphological information required. (Rogers 2005: 14)

The reactions to some of the transactional Scots published so far indicate that it would be sensible to ensure the co-operation of native speakers and linguists, or at least detailed use of linguistic research, when developing a "standard".

Linguists who disclaim normative interests seem, in fact, to be less concerned to evade the practical consequences of their work than anxious to shun the company of people whose interest in linguistic prescription is suspect—people who like to set themselves up as an elite to take charge of programmes of linguistic standardisation and reform. By withdrawing, however, linguists only ensure that every enterprise of linguistic planning will be dominated by ignorant enthusiasts and incompetent pedants. (Haas 1982: 2–3)

4.2.1 Maximalist approaches

The suggestions above for "standardizing" Scots orthography can be seen to fall into what may be considered two camps—the maximalist and minimalist.

> The maximalist position […] is that the existing conventions of Scots spelling require not to be improved in detail, but to be fundamentally reformed. (McClure 1995: 28)

Here it is often argued that Scots needs an orthography geared for and adapted to the Scots sound system, and that this itself has to be systematic and consistent whereby each phoneme has one symbol in order to make it easy to learn. Depending on the choice of symbols, this will also give Scots the appearance of being a distinct language and thus increase its prestige. Commenting on written Scots as it usually appears today, McClure (1995: 29) writes:

> The fact is certainly that in its written form it does not *look* like a language, but like a distortion of another language. To most people who are not linguists, this is sufficient to set the seal on its inferior status—the status of 'a form of a language', or a 'dialect' in the popular sense of the word.

No great leap of imagination is required to realize that an orthography substantially different to that of Standard English is simply a ploy to achieve the "look" of a language and can readily be dismissed as such. The resulting increase in prestige is likely to occur only among those who hold the language in high esteem anyway, rendering such an exercise pointless.

> […] preoccupation with the appearance rather than the substance of written Scots, and with its prestige rather than its actual qualities, is symptomatic of the effort to procure an independent status for Scots not because it is in fact independent, but because it should be considered to be so. (Hagen 2002: 146)

Furthermore, it is argued that the conventions of Middle Scots have to be re-employed to avoid modern inconsistencies borrowed from Standard

English in order to give the orthography an historical Scottish identity, although that itself defies historical reality.

> [...] since the Union of the Crowns, Scots has been spelled increasingly with the English conventions of its (including our) time. (Stirling 1994: 90)

> It fails to take account of the fact that Scots spelling did not develop independently of English spelling and that Scots too has borrowed on a large scale from Latin and French without assimilating foreign spellings. Scots was also subject to the effects of the Great Vowel Shift, but did not revise its own spelling conventions accordingly. (Hagen 2002: 143)

4.2.2 Minimalist approaches

The minimalist approach tends to reflect the linguistic reality on the ground, where Scots and Standard English forms are frequently mixed, and the education system ever teaching Scots as an autonomous alternative to Standard English is highly unlikely. By building on what is familiar, native speakers may be more likely to accept and adopt the proposed conventions. An orthography with conventions broadly compatible with those of Standard English will enable the inevitable mixing of Scots and Standard English forms, which, for example, are often used in poetry to form a rhyme, to mell together as a homogenous language.

> The minimalist approach focuses on the fact that English is and will remain an established language of Scotland (that it can or should be entirely superseded by Scots is not seriously proposed). [...] The traditional English-based orthography for Scots should in general be retained, though obvious anomalies in individual words should be removed. (McClure 1995: 28)

> However, since they [Scots speakers] presumably are already literate in Standard English and familiar with its spelling rules, they are unlikely to appreciate having to learn a new system [...] (Hagen 2002: 152)

> For the layman any deviation from the traditional standard spelling he has learned in school is disturbing and unwelcome. He may commit errors himself or be insecure in his production, but he is sensitive in reception because his speed of perception is reduced

by unfamiliar word images. From receiving a message he may entirely fail to recognise it or he may misread it. Even if it corresponds exactly to his own pronunciation, he may find it confusing. Writers who make use of what has been called 'eye-dialect' are clearly calling attention to a pronunciation but not necessarily one that is stigmatized. (Haugen 1977: 275)

Here the intention is, as Stirling suggested, to "select aspects from the spelling of modern Scots and refine them" (1994: 90)—which Stirling himself rejected, preferring instead to "reinvent the wheel". The spelling of modern Scots analysed here are those of the 18th and 19th century revival described above. Those practices will be analysed in order establish how far they were phonemically and morphologically based, "phonemically" being here understood as capable of representing various dialect realization using the same graphemes but not necessarily one grapheme per phoneme.

Attempts to write Scots "phonetically" often entail writing perceived details that are orthographically redundant resulting in obsessive application of the perceived sound-to-letter correspondences of Standard English. That is especially true when writing "dialects", where the resulting orthographic barriers make the written "dialects" appear much more different from each other than they sound, implying less mutual comprehension in the spoken language than actually exists. If written Scots is seen to be independent and not beholden to and created for non-speakers, much redundant orthographic detail can be avoided. The idea is that an abstract phonemic (and morphemic) spelling system is less phonologically prescriptive, thus being far more unifying in written representation than a pseudo-phonetic one, consequently avoiding homogenization of pronunciation.

It is assumed that the suggested graphemes will be taught or learnt as an autonomous system and it made clear that spellings being shared with Standard English does not necessary imply that they are pronounced the same. For example, it is usually accepted that the same letters or letter combinations are pronounced differently in different languages, for example, in Standard English ⟨**oo**⟩ is pronounced [uː] or [ʊ] rather than as [oː] or [oʊ] as in Dutch, and in German ⟨**eu**⟩ is pronounced [ɔɪ] and not [øː] as in Dutch and French. On the other hand, different graphemes may be pronounced the same in different languages. French ⟨**ch**⟩, Italian ⟨**sci**⟩ and Standard English ⟨**sh**⟩ are all pronounced /ʃ/. Why should it be any different with regards to Scots and English or dialects thereof?

The guiding principle in any transcription must be that it should convey the information which its reader needs, no more and no less. Conveying more information than needed is to overwrite the dialect, and less than is needed is to under-write it. The writer must gauge his prospective audience's previous experience and temper his transcription accordingly. He must be able to judge which rules of reading his audience knows and can therefore assume without entering them in the transcription. Whatever decision he makes, it will therefore reflect a judgement concerning his readers. If the dialect is badly underwritten, it will reflect a negative judgement concerning the dialect and its speakers: this is an unimportant variety of the language. If it is greatly overwritten, it is a compliment to his readers, but it will probably be felt as pedantic and possibly even as snobbish. (Haugen 1977: 275–6)

Speech, after all, is regularly non-fluent, with numerous break-downs and minor repairs, as any genuine transcription reveals: by contrast, literary representations are invariably polished and idealized, reflecting only a selection of salient markers. Literary dialect is thus never unplanned spontaneous speech. Of all oral genres, perhaps oral narrative is the most sustained in literature. (Kirk 1997: 199)

Since political union Scots has been influenced by exposure to the conventions of Standard English. Therefore, in order to understand and appreciate the phonemic and graphemic conventions, of traditional—"traditional" from here on meaning the more widespread practices of the 18th- and 19th-century revival—Scots orthography it is necessary to understand those of Standard English.

English is, and has long been, of a mixed character, made up of words derived from different sources; and to a great extent this difference of origin is reflected in the spelling. Several classes of words retain more or less exactly a type of spelling which is distinctive of the language from which they are derived; and while they are consistent with each other, they are at variance with those which have similar sounds, but come from a different source. (Craigie: 1927: 1)

For practical purposes, it is sufficient to recognise three main types of spelling, the first of which includes the native types, and those

which are most closely related to them, while the second covers
the large contribution from the classical and Romanic tongues in
which different principles can be clearly observed, and the third
comprises the medley of exotic forms which either in sound or
spelling are most remote from the natural English standard.
(Craigie 1927: 4–5)

As it is, this feature of English spelling that presents the greatest
number of anomalies […] The impression of irregularity conveyed
by these exceptions is naturally increased by the frequent
occurrence of a limited number of common words in which
spelling and sound are obviously at variance. (Craigie 1942: 2–3)

[…] the simple fact is that the present orthography is not merely a
letter-to-sound system riddled with imperfections, but instead, a
more complex and more regular relationship wherein phoneme
and morpheme share leading roles. (Venezky 1970: 11)

The nature of the base form of a word tends to be phonemic—not
in the one-letter one-sound system that has become the Holy Grail
of many educators and linguists, but in a more graphemically
economical fashion whereby position, environment, and overt
markers allow the same symbol to perform several distinct
functions, and whereby several symbols represent the same sound.
(That *homo sapiens* is somehow most at ease with a one-letter one-
sound system has often been assumed, but no evidence has ever
been produced to substantiate this limitation on man's mental
capacities). (Venezky 1970: 120)

More irregular spellings in English are due to borrowings than to
any other cause. Yet such borrowings cannot be classed as entirely
irregular, since their spelling often marks their foreign identities.
(Venesky 1970: 121)

In the absence of a distinct orthography for Scots, those wishing
to write in the language have, since the seventeenth century,
generally adopted the conventions of English spelling, modified to
a greater or lesser extent according to the preferences of the
individual writer: the theoretical unsoundness of this procedure
has been obscured by a widespread failure to realise the true nature
of the relationship between the two tongues (actually cognate

dialects, but taken to be the 'correct' and 'vulgar' form of the same language). (McClure 1985: 203)

This chaotic mingling of conventions characterised Scots spelling until the present century. Written Scots *looked* very much like English, but the written form bore little resemblance to the spoken—even by the standards of conventions governing phoneme-to-grapheme relationships in English!—and suggested a somewhat modified version of English rather than a distinct speech form with a phonological system which had been developing independently of the southern dialect for many centuries. (McClure 1985: 204)

It is perfectly possible to devise a spelling system for Scots, or several feasible systems, which would be far more regular, consistent, and etymologically sound than those in current use (or, for that matter, than English orthography); but those very qualities would result in a written language radically unlike the Scots to which readers are now accustomed. (McClure 1985: 208)

It has been pointed out that attempts to regularize the hybrid nature of English orthography, and by inference that of Scots, may often cause more problems than they solve. (Craigie 1944).

5

CONSONANTS

5.1 ORTHOGRAPHY IN THE 18TH AND 19TH CENTURIES

The consonant graphemes of the 18th- and 19th-century revival match those known from Standard English but many of those also occurred in Middle Scots.

Below is a selection of Middle Scots spellings, from later in the period, taken from the *Dictionary of the Older Scottish Tongue*. They may not all be the most wide spread or common, but they were all certainly used and known at the time.

> beu**k**, dy**k**e, **k**eep, see**k**, ma**k**; ba**ck**, se**ck**, mu**ck**le; **ch**ief, wra**tch**;
> beu**ch**, drei**ch**, eneu**ch**, fe**ch**t, hau**ch**, li**ch**t, skei**ch**, teu**ch**, we**ch**t;
> **gn**aw; **kn**ee, **kn**ife, **kn**owe;
> au**ld**, bau**ld**, bie**ld**, cau**ld**, fau**ld**; be**nd**, bu**nd**, free**nd**, gru**nd**,
> hu**nd**er, se**nd**;
> **qu**air, **qu**ean; fi**sh**, **sh**e, **sh**euk (NOTE: ⟨sch⟩ also occurred); ky**the**,
> **th**at, **the**, **th**ir; a**th**ort, drou**th**, len**th**, mou**th**, **th**ole, **th**ree; **wh**a,
> **wh**an (NOTE: ⟨**quh**⟩ also occurred but its use was in decline).

5.1.1 The consonant system of Scots

	Bilabial	Labio-dental	Dental	Alveolar	Post-alveolar	Palatal	Velar	Labio-velar	Glottal
Plosive	p b			t d			k g		ʔ
Nasal	m			n			ŋ		
Flap				r					
Fricative		f v	θ ð	s z	ʃ ʒ	ç	x		h
Affricate					tʃ dʒ				
Approx-imant				ɹ		j		ʍ w	
Lateral Approx.				l, ɫ					

Another inherent feature in the orthography is the distinction between functionally simple and functionally compound consonant units. One of the most general, although not entirely regular, spelling-to-sound rules is that the vowel spellings *a, e, i, o u* are mapped into one form before a single consonant unit which is followed by a vowel and into another form in all other environments. In the vocabulary of the direct letter-to-sound school, these forms are the LONG and SHORT pronunciations of the vowels [...] What is important is first that, the rule mentioned above, and, as will be shown soon, almost all spelling-to-sound rules, be based not upon letters or graphemes as such, but rather upon functional spelling units, and second, that functionally simple and functionally compound units be distinguished. (Venezky 1970: 35-36)

A knowlege of phoneme arrangements which are not allowed in English words is a necessary prerequisite for analyzing many spelling-to-sound correspondences. [...] The elision of sounds in consonant clusters can be predicted, not only across morpheme boundaries, but also in initial and final positions. (Venezky 1970: 44-45)

Even more significant was the Anglo-Norman influence on English consonant doubling. The convention of repeating a consonant to indicate a preceding short vowel, which is so widespread in current English, has a long and complicated history. In part it grew out of a sound simplification of geminate consonants in late Old English, where the double symbol was retained in the traditional spelling system. Similarly, Latin geminate consonants which were simplified in Old French were often represented by medieval scribes with the double symbol which they were familiar with in Classical Latin orthography. Thus in both English and French the convention of using a double symbol to represent a single consonant was well known. The association with preceding short vowels is in origin English, beginning in the late Old English period when long vowels were shortened before a combination of two following consonants. (Scragg 1975: 49-50)

5.1.2 Orthographic single and double consonants

Traditionally single consonant graphemes are usually written after single and double vowel graphemes and where the root word has a final silent ⟨e⟩

in words such as *beast*, *heid* 'head', *toun* 'town', *sooth*[20] 'south', *ane* 'one', *byre* 'cowshed', and *syne* 'ago'.[21] Consonant graphemes are usually doubled following a single vowel grapheme in the first stressed syllable in disyllabic words such as *blatter* 'beat', *fremmit* 'strange', *biggit* 'built', *dizzen* 'dozen', *donnert* 'stunned', and *butter*.[22] Purves (1979: 64) and the SLS (1985) also mentioned that. Allan (1995: 83) accepted Standard English doubling conventions except following a digraph or ⟨y⟩ giving the example *maiter* 'matter'. Allan (p.84) also mentions doubling of word-final ⟨f⟩, ⟨k⟩ becoming ⟨ck⟩, ⟨l⟩ and ⟨s⟩. SLD (2002) also generally follow Standard English conventions but then ignores them when changing an 'English' spelling to indicate the Scots vowel in words such as *bul* 'bull', *jaicket* 'jacket', *maitter* 'matter', and *seeck* 'sick' (Macleod and Cairns 1993, Macleod 1996). That was apparently followed for the headword list based upon the contents of the *Essential Scots Dictionary* in the example *aipple*, 'apple'.[23] Robinson (1997: 48) only made certain recommendations for particular consonants but did write "[…] the author has attempted to minimize spelling variations between equivalent words in the two languages [English and 'Ulster-Scots']." Those variations were often more than "minimal". The *Scots Spelling Comatee* (2000) recommended following Standard English consonant rules, also mentioning the doubling of ⟨k⟩ to ⟨ck⟩, ⟨f⟩, ⟨l⟩, ⟨s⟩ and ⟨z⟩ after a single-letter vowel.

In some monosyllabic words such as *ebb* 'shallow' the following consonant is doubled following an initial single vowel. Traditionally the following graphemes are not usually doubled: ⟨c⟩, ⟨h⟩, ⟨j⟩, ⟨k⟩, ⟨q⟩, ⟨v⟩, ⟨w⟩, ⟨x⟩, ⟨y⟩.

5.2 TRADITIONAL ORTHOGRAPHIC MAPPINGS

The traditional mappings of most of the consonant phonemes, as expected, match Standard English.

5.2.1 Mapping of /p/ and /b/, and of /t/ and /d/

The plosives /p/ and /b/ map to ⟨p⟩ and ⟨b⟩, /t/ and /d/ map to ⟨t⟩ and ⟨d⟩.

---

20 Some clustered consonant graphemes of course represent single consonant phonemes e.g. ⟨ch⟩ /tʃ/ and /x/ or /ç/, ⟨ng⟩ /ŋ/, ⟨sh⟩ /ʃ/, ⟨th⟩ /θ/ and /ð/, ⟨wh⟩ /ʍ/, ⟨dg(e)⟩ and ⟨tch⟩ for /dʒ/ and /tʃ/.

21 All headword forms in the SND.

22 All headword forms or derivatives thereof in the SND.

23 https://web.archive.org/web/20061015063701/http://www.scotsdictionaries.org.uk /HeadWordList/A.html accessed 2021-10-30. In the 2004 ESD, the headword is *aipple*, *epple* (p. 2).

Für früheres *d* findet sich *th*: *mither* (msch. moder, muddir) [...] *pouther* 'powder' [...] *shouthers* 'shoulders' [...] *souther* 'löten' [...] Intervokalisches *d* vor *ɼ* wurde in Mundarten zu *d̠* [...] auch wenn ein dem *d* vorher gehendes *l* ausgefallen oder vokalisiert wurde (*souther, shouther!*) gilt dieses Gesetz. (Steiger 1913: 48-49)[24]

Conversely *d* becomes *th* [ð] in s. and m.Sc., e.g. *lether, poother, shouther, sowther*, Eng. ladder, powder, shoulder, solder. (SND III: 1, s.v. "D")

It may be argued that the intervocalic grapheme ⟨**d**⟩ before /r/ might easily be interpreted /ð/ in words such as *ledder* 'ladder', *pouder* 'powder', *shouder* 'shoulder', and *sowder* 'solder'[25] by those with such a realization.

5.2.1.1 Dental realization of /t/ and /d/

The dental realizations /d̠/ and /t̠/, which may occur, especially before /(ə)r/ in Irish- and Gaelic-influenced dialects of Ulster and Scotland were never indicated in the sample of traditional Scots writing analysed above or any of the recommendations or suggestions above—except Robinson (1997), who suggested ⟨**dh**⟩ and ⟨**th**⟩[26] for /d̠/ and /t̠/ as in *dhrap* 'drop', *shoodher* 'shoulder', *butther* 'butter' and *sthrae* 'straw'. Robinson further conflated that by also suggesting representing the dental realizations by ⟨**è**⟩ as in *dannèr* 'wander' *eftèr* 'other' *shooldèr* 'shoulder', *watèr* 'water', and *Ulstèr* 'Ulster', thus applying a diacritic to a vowel, not in order to indicate modification of its sound but to indicate modification of a previous consonant.

The main Irish substitutions are, of course, the Irish blade *T*, spelt *th* and blade *D*, spelt *dh*, for the English alveolars *t* and *d*, especially before *r*, e.g. *bitther, dhrunk, dhrowned*, giving a thick sound to English ears [...] one cannot tell whether one is dealing with *t* or *th* [Θ/ð]. (Braidwood 1975: 29)

---

24 'Earlier *d* is replaced by *th*: *mither* (Middle Scots. moder, muddir) [...] *pouther* 'powder' [...] *shouthers* 'shoulders' [...] *souther* 'solder' [...] In dialects intervocalic *d* before *ɼ* became *d̠* [...] This rule holds even where an elided or vocalized *l* preceded the *d* (*souther, shouther!*).' [AE]

25 All headword forms in the SND.

26 That has been used in Hiberno-English dialect writing, for example, *thrue* 'true', *thrick* 'trick' (Connolly 1981: 378, 388) *scondher* 'undercooked' and *dhrum* 'drum'. (Todd 1989: 130, 132).

> Dental plosives do, however, occur in the North as allophones of
> /t/ and /d/. They are found not only adjacent to /θ, ð/ [...] but
> also to some extent in the vicinity of /r/ [...] (Wells 1982: 445)

Since those dental realizations only occur before /(ə)r/, the clusters ⟨**dr**⟩, ⟨**der**⟩ and ⟨**tr**⟩, ⟨**ter**⟩ would act as sufficient markers in a normative orthography. One may assume that the only reason for marking that in any other way is simply to exaggerate the difference to Standard English. Robinson suggests the spellings *butther* 'butter' and *watèr* 'water' but some speakers realize a /t/ between vowels as /ʔ/, which Robinson suggests should be written ⟨**tt**⟩. That would imply the spellings *butter* and *watter*. Robinson also suggested *tràictèr* 'tractor' the ⟨**à**⟩ representing a consonant quality two letters previously. The traditional spellings *butter* and *watter* accommodate both realizations equally well without the need for confusing diacritics. Those forms also indicate the vowel quality, and the ⟨**a**⟩ in *watèr* may be interpreted as /e/, whereas the ⟨**tt**⟩ in *watter* clearly indicates /a/. Native speakers with such realizations will produce them unconsciously in words such as *attercap* 'spider', *bedral* 'bedridden', *better*, *bowster* 'bolster', *craitur* 'creature', *draucht* 'draught', *straik* 'strike', and *traivel* 'travel'.[27]

> A number of clusters ending /t d/ lose their second element when
> they appear at the end of a syllable. Such a development in a
> natural one throughout English when a consonant begins the next
> word; Scots carries it further into citation forms, so that the coda
> consists of the consonant that preceded the alveolar. The effect
> seems to appear first in clusters of /kt/ and, to a lesser extent, /xt/
> and /st/ [...] The clusters /pt/ and /ft/ join the list of permissible
> inputs for this rule [...] Towards the end of the period, a tendency
> to restore the /t/ in /st xt ft/ starts to work [...] leading to forms
> with 'excrescent /t/' as well as restored forms [...] (Johnston
> 1997a: 101)

> It is worth noting that an accurate spelling-pronunciation of many
> words of this class would be difficult to achieve in English. For
> instance, *debt* and *doubt*, on the analogy of *apt* or *clubbed*, might have
> /pt/ or /bd/ but it is not likely that they could be pronounced
> /bt/. (Scragg 1975: 55)

---

27   All headword or frequent forms in the SND.

5.2.1.2 Simplification of original clusters in /ld/ and /nd/

The clusters /ld/ and /nd/ are often simplified to /l/ and /d/. In derived forms such as past tenses simplification may not occur.

> The tendency is particularly strong in the whole Mid-Northern group, where /nd ld/ are simplified both finally and inter-vocalically, whether a morpheme boundary is present or not (Dieth 1932: 124). In North Northern, West and South-west Mid, western Border dialects and variably in the Lothians, a more restricted rule applies, where /nd/ simplifies to /n/ in all positions, but /ld/ becomes /l/ only finally, especially when a consonant begins the next word (Wilson 1923: 15–16). This form of simplification is variable in Edinburgh and Angus, and is becoming increasingly common over the rest of the Mid-Scots region. (Johnston 1997b: 502)

> Both Scots and English dialects have a tendency to drop *d* after *n* and *l*. This frequently leads in Ulster to its erroneous "replace-ment" in words which never had it […] *scunder* (see SCUNNER). (Macafee 1996: xxix)

Purves' (1979: 70) approach was:

> The 'd' is not usually pronounced and there is no reason why it should be represented in the spelling of many words. […] It may be necessary to retain 'd' in [certain words] since the 'd' may be pronounced in derived forms […]

That was also reiterated by the *Scots Language Society* (1985). Allan (1995: 77) also suggests elision on the basis that it was so widespread. SLD (2002) suggested both ⟨**nd**⟩ and ⟨**ld**⟩ as well as elision. Robinson (1997) suggested word-final elision for ⟨**nd**⟩, modifying it to ⟨**nn**⟩ after a single vowel grapheme as in *hann* 'hand', *blinn* 'blind', and *mynn* 'mind' but also mentioned that some speakers may "reinstate" the ⟨**d**⟩ in past tense forms (Robinson 1997: 124). Robinson suggested ⟨**nn**⟩ for medial /nd/ simplifica-tion but also ⟨**nnèr**⟩ to indicate a possible dental realization /ṇ/ before /r/ thus applying a diacritic to a vowel in order to indicate a modification of the previous consonant. Only Robinson suggested orthographically indica-ting simplification of ⟨**ld**⟩. The *Scots Spelling Comatee* (2000) recommended ⟨**nd**⟩ on the basis that it is easier to ignore a letter that is there than to pronounce one that is not present, and included forms such as *finnd* 'find', apparently to emphasize the Scots vowel realization.

[...] remove obvious anomalies (such as the prescribed retention of *d*'s which for centuries have corresponded to nothing in the pronunciation in words like *fin, en* and *lan,* [...] (McClure 1980: 26)

McClure's claim, as shown in Johnston (1997b: 502), is incorrect, some dialects not simplifying and others often only when unemphatic, the SND confirming the existence of "*d*'s" in *find, hinderend,* and *land.* As such simplification varies across dialects. The often internally contradictory conventions of some suggestions are a recipe for chaos in a normative orthography. As simplification is a realization of the underlying /nd/ and /ld/, it would be sensible to include the full form in a normative orthography. Those who simplify will do so unconsciously anyway. For a reader it is easier to "ignore" a letter that is written than to pronounce one that is not. Furthermore, it is even more difficult not to write a consonant which, for some, is pronounced.

All but the Style Sheet and McClure made a recommendation for the conjunction spelt **and** in Older Scots and written either **and** or **an'** in the modern Scots literature analysed. That conjunction is now seldom pronounced with a /d/ and the tendency was to suggest **an** except Philp who used **and** and Stirling who suggested **ann.** The SNDA suggested **and** and **an** in the Scots School Dictionary but only **an** in the English to Scots section, **an** also being used in the *Grammar Brownie.* Consistency would suggest the etymological spelling **and** for a normative orthography, also conveniently distinguishing that from the indefinite article **an.** Nevertheless, context should make it clear whether **an** represents the conjunction or indefinite article.

5.2.1.3 Simplification of original clusters in /kt/ and /pt/

In some dialects clusters including /t/ are simplified (Grant and Dixon 1921: 7–8). In the clusters; /kt/ and /pt/ are simplified to /k/ and /p/.

In conservative speech, the loss of stops is often categorical in final stop-stop and sonorant-stop sequences, e.g. [kɛp] *kept,* [hɑːn] *hand,* [əʉl] *old.* (Harris 1985: 59)

The combination /st/ in codas may be simplified to /s/ as a sporadic chance in Caithnessian, Angus and Perthshire dialects [...] This change is probably an extension of the general Scots simplification of stop + /t/ (in *act, accept*), which is attested from Older Scots times onwards [...] (Johnston 1997b: 509)

That has been sporadically indicated in traditional writing as *ac'* or *ack* 'act', *fac'* or *fack* 'fact', and *temp'* or *temp* 'tempt' etc. Purves (1979) and the SLS (1985) suggested spelling the /kt/ simplification with ⟨**k**⟩ as in *expek*, *objek*, and *respek*. Allan (1995) seemed to suggest much the same, including simplification of /pt/ to ⟨**p**⟩. Robinson (1997) suggested simplification of /pt/ to ⟨**pp**⟩ e.g. *app* 'apt', *slepp* 'slept', *tempp* 'tempt' etc. but never mentioned simplification of /kt/ to /k/. In the headword list based upon the contents of the *Essential Scots Dictionary* examples such as *act*, as against *abstrack* 'abstract' and *affeck* 'affect', occurred. The only example where possible simplification of /pt/ may occur was *accept*.[28]

In some dialects the /t/ in the word final cluster /st/ is simplified to /s/, most probably an outcome of the simplification of consonant clusters in connected speech, much as in Standard English "just now" /dʒʌs naʊ/. Pronounced individually and emphatically, the /t/ would remain in such words. The SND includes the following as headword forms: *beast, best, feast, interest, lest* (v.) 'last', and *nest*. Loss in the plural forms like *beasts* is probably the result of assimilation caused by the difficult-to-pronounce cluster /sts/. Assimilation also occurs in the medial clusters /xt/ and /st/ before final /(ə)n/ and /(ə)l/. The SND includes the following as headword forms: *frichten* 'frighten', *saften* 'soften', *tichten* 'tighten', *thristle* 'thistle', and *whistle*. Assimilation also occurs in *aften* 'often'. Only Robinson (1997) suggested indicating that orthographically, for example, *affen, beess, bess, feess, intèress, less* and *ness*, also *whussles*, but *whustlin* (from 'whistle'. Since native speakers assimilate unconsciously, its representation is arguably unnecessary in a normative orthography, perhaps even in words such as *aften* 'aften', *listen*, and *whistle* where the /t/ never occurs but is etymological.

5.2.2 Mapping of /g/

The plosive /g/ traditionally maps to ⟨**g**⟩ but may also be ⟨**gh**⟩ in a few words such as *ghaist* 'ghost' (SND IV: 286 s.v. "GHAIST"). Allan (1995: 78) suggests using ⟨**g**⟩ for that. The etymological spelling of the cluster ⟨**gn**⟩ is usually adhered to (Grant and Dixon 1921: 13). That has been simplified to /n/ in most dialects but /gn/ still persists in some peripheral ones. Regularizing the ⟨**gh**⟩ in words such as *ghaist* to ⟨**g**⟩ may have some merits but that is clearly not the case with the cluster ⟨**gn**⟩, the realization, /gn/, by some speakers, would necessitate its retention in a pan-dialectal normative orthography.

---

28 https://web.archive.org/web/20061015063701/http://www.scotsdictionaries.org.uk /HeadWordList/A.html, accessed 2021-10-30. In the 2004 ESD the headwords are *abstrack, accep, ack, affeck* (p. 1).

5.2.3 Mapping of /k/

The plosive /k/ traditionally maps to both ⟨c⟩ and ⟨k⟩. A double ⟨k⟩ grapheme is traditionally represented by ⟨ck⟩. Only Purves (1979) and the *Scots Language Society* (1985) suggested ⟨kk⟩ for that, Purves (2000: 52), apparently, justifying that on the basis of such traditional exceptions as *makkin* 'making' and *takkin* 'taking',[29] though his original inspiration was probably the Older Scots practice. The *Scots Language Society* also suggested that "It is not suggested that words used in Scots in common with English which have the same pronunciation [...] should be altered if the English spelling leaves no doubt as to the pronunciation." That implied the use of ⟨ck⟩ in shared words, resulting in confusing and contradictory spelling conventions where some words in the language are spelled according to revived Older Scots practice and others following those of modern Standard English (Allan 1995: 70). Purves and the *Scots language Society* also suggested ⟨k⟩ after initial ⟨s⟩. Purves (2000: 52), suggested that specifically Scots words should be spelled ⟨sk-⟩, justifying such a stance on English exceptions such as *skulk*, *skull* and *skunk*. Macleod (1996) was not particularly consistent with the use of initial ⟨sc⟩ or ⟨sk⟩. Robinson suggested spellings such as *bak* 'back', *blak* 'black', *brick*, *clack* 'clock', *quäck* 'quick', *muckle* 'much', and *pickle* 'a few'.

> Although ⟨c⟩ could still unambiguously represent /k/ before back vowels and consonants (as it still does in *cat, cot, cut, climb, crumb*), there was no agreed way of distinguishing the sound graphically before front vowels. The use of ⟨k⟩ appeared sporadically from the ninth century but it was not until the thirteenth that it was fully established in words like *king* and *keen* [...] (Scragg 11975: 45)

> The representation of /sk/ in Middle English varied between ⟨sc⟩ and ⟨sk⟩, modern usage being etymological, e.g. words in ⟨sk⟩ are generally of Norse or Dutch origin (from Norse: *skin, sky, skate* (fish), *skull* (noun); from Dutch: *skate* (verb), *sketch, skipper*) and those in ⟨sc⟩ are French (*scarce, scorn, scullery*) or Greek (*sceptic, scope*).[30] (Scragg 1975: 46)

---

29 The ⟨kk⟩ in those examples is simply the outcome of Scots spellings resulting from *mak'* and *tak'* , later *mak* and *tak* which eschew the apologetic apostrophe, where the only "logical" way of indicating the vowel /a/ would be to double the ⟨k⟩; *makin* and *takin* could indicate /e/. The root forms *mack* and *tack* never gained any currency.

30 Departures from the etymological principle have ⟨sc⟩ before back vowels and consonants (e.g. Norse *scant, scrape*, Dutch *scour*) and ⟨sc⟩ before front vowels (French *skew, skim*, Greek *skeleton*). Loanwords from other languages which retain the spelling of the parent language have produced more anomalies, e.g. *school* (educational) and *science* from Latin, *schooner* and *school* (of fish) from Dutch. [Original footnote]

In Sc. orthography C [k] is used: (1) at the beginning of a syllable before the vowels *a, o, u,* e.g. *ca', caur, collie, coom, couk, cutty,* (2) before the consonants *l, r, w,* e.g. *clyte* [kləit], *crine* [krəin], *cweel* [kwil]. Note also *scr* as in *scrieve* [skriːv] and *scl* as in *sclate* [sklet]. […] *Ck* at the end of a syllable after a short vowel is a digraph = [k], e.g. *vrack, geck, bick, bock, ruck.* (SND II: 1 s.v. "C")

In origin and orthographic representation it is, gen. speaking, the same as in Eng., *i.e.,* it usu. appears as *c* before back vowels, *l* and *r*; as *k* before front vowels and *n*; as *ck* when intervocalic after a short vowel, and final. (SND V: 356 s.v. "K:")

5.2.3.1 Use of ⟨c⟩ and ⟨sc⟩ versus ⟨k⟩ and ⟨sk⟩

An analysis of spelling tendencies indicated that initial ⟨c⟩ and ⟨sc⟩ are usually used before the vowels /a/, /aː/, /ɔː/, /oː/, /ʌː/, and /u/, the allophones of vowel 7 /o/, /ɪ/, /e/, /i/, root-final /ʌu/, /l/, and /r/. The SND includes the following as headword forms: *caw* 'call', *caddie* 'messenger boy', *carle* 'fellow', *caird* 'card', *cairt* 'cart', *cleid* 'clothe', *creash* 'grease', *cloot* 'cloth', *croun* 'crown', *coff* 'buy', *cowp* 'overturn', *cowt* 'colt', *scant* 'scarce', *sclaff* 'slap', *sclate* 'slate', *scaud* 'scald', *scaur* 'scar', *scone, scoor* 'scour', *scowth* 'scope', *scunner* 'disgust', *scowder* 'scorch', *scrieve* 'scribble' *scruif* 'scruff', and *scuip* 'scoop'.

An analysis of spelling tendencies indicated that initial ⟨k⟩ and ⟨sk⟩ are usually used before the vowels /ɛ/, /e/, /i/, /ɪ/, the diphthongs /ɔi/, /ai/, the consonant /n/ and in many words of Norse origin. A few exceptions before /e/ occur. The SND includes thefollowing as headword forms: *keek* 'peep', *kebbock* 'a cheese', *kelter* 'tumble', *ken* 'know', *kye* 'cows', *kyte* 'stomach', *kythe* 'appear', *kail* 'cabbage', *knife, skail* 'spill', *skaith* 'damage', *skelf* 'splinter', *skelp* 'slap', *skeel* 'skill', *skirl, skive* 'prowl', *skime* 'gleam', *skite* 'slip', *skire* 'bright', *skol* 'bowl', *skraich* 'screech' *skrink* 'shrink' and *skull.*

Regularization to ⟨k⟩ and ⟨sk⟩ would certainly produce a large number of unfamiliar, non-traditional spellings. A less radical option would be to regularize based on the tendencies described above, especially where such forms have widespread currency in the literary record. Of course exceptions will exist, but judicious analysis of the literary tradition could identify those that were never commonly written according to the tendencies described above.

5.2.3.2 Realization of original /kn/

The etymological spelling of the cluster ⟨kn⟩ is usually adhered to. (Grant and Dixon 1921: 8, 12, 20). That has been simplified to /n/ in most dialects but /kn/ or /tn/ still persist north of the Tay. In Avoch /kr/ may occur. The SND includes the following as headword forms: *knee, knife, knock* 'hill', and *knowe* 'knoll'. (Grant and Dixon 1921: 8, 12, 20)

5.2.4 Realization of /t/, /k/, and /p/ as /ʔ/

The glottal stop /ʔ/ is often the realization of /t/ between two vowels and word final in many dialects, sometimes also for /k/ and /p/ in words such as *butter, maiter* 'matter', *whit* 'what'.

> The Central Scots version is similar to the well-known, widespread rule in most British dialects, especially urban ones (Wells 1982: 322–6). This type of Glottalling affects /k/ less often than /t/, and /p/ even less often, and usually results in a complete replacement of the stop. (Johnston 1997b: 501)

> Most have glottal stops for /t/ in medial and final positions (as in *water, what*) [...] (Milroy 1982: 27)

> In the speech of many [...] individuals, unvoiced plosives pronounced with a simultaneous glottal stop [...] With some speakers [t'] loses its alveolar closure and only the glottal stop remains [...] this feature is not universal [...] (Gregg 1958: 401)

In the sample of traditional writing analysed above the glottal stop was never indicated.

> Glottalling as a Scottish phenomenon was first noticed in Glasgow in 1892 (Macafee 1994a: 27), though it is unclear whether it was an independent native development or an importation from England, or even whether the London development is of Scottish origin. (Johnston 1997b: 500–501)

Robinson (1997) suggested using ⟨**tt**⟩ where /ʔ/ is a possible realization of /t/, but overlooked the inherent contradiction in that and proposed ⟨**tèr**⟩, where ⟨**è**⟩ indicates a dental realization of /t/, suggesting the spelling *watèr* 'water'. On that basis *mettle* 'metal' is suggested. SLD (2002)[31] suggested using an apostrophe *wa'er* 'water' but that could cause no end of confusion when word-final, as in *fi'* 'foot', *ca'* 'cat', since /ʔ/ is an actual realization that is neither silent nor 'missing', and traditional spellings such as *watter, fit* and *cat* would be adequate, since native speakers who realize /t/

---

31   See https://web.archive.org/web/20061015063228if_/http://www.scotsdictionaries .org.uk/ScotsSpellingGrammar.htm, accessed 2021-10-30.

between two vowels or word-final as /ʔ/ would do so unconsciously anyway, which would imply following established practices in a normative orthography.

5.2.5 Mapping of /m/ and /n/

The nasals /m/ and /n/ traditionally map to ⟨m⟩ and ⟨n⟩. An interdental allophone /n̪/ may occur before /(ə)r/in Ulster. That was not indicated in the sample of writing from Ulster analysed above. Robinson (1997) suggested representing interdental /n̪/ by ⟨è⟩ in words like *unnèr* 'under', *thunnèr* 'thunder', and *wunnèr* 'wonder'. Interdental realizations are produced unconsciously by native speakers, the following /(ə)r/ being a sufficient marker of their occurrence, arguably rendering their representation in a normative orthography unnecessary.

5.2.6 Mapping of /ŋ/

The velar nasal /ŋ/ traditionally maps to ⟨ng⟩ but it also occurs in the grapheme cluster traditionally written ⟨nk⟩ /ŋk/ in words such as *bank*. Because Scots has /ŋ/ where Standard English would usually have /ŋg/, attempts to indicate that have included *fing'er* (Robinson 1997) and *fingir* (Purves 2000: 52) but those are no clearer to the uninitiated than *finger*. Native speakers of Scots would unconsciously produce /ŋ/ anyway, rendering ⟨ng⟩ the obvious, unambiguous choice for a normative orthography.

> ng in Scots [...] is pronounced as in English 'sing', not as in English 'single'. (Macleod and Cairns 1993: x)

> There is no natural way of spelling such a Scots pronunciation so that it is distinguished from the Standard English one ... (Macafee 1996: xxii)

5.2.7 Mapping of /r/ and /ɹ/

Alveolar /r/ and /ɹ/ traditionally map to ⟨r⟩, the obvious, unambiguous choice for a normative orthography.

5.2.8 Mapping of /f/ and /v/

The fricatives /f/ and /v/ traditionally map to ⟨f⟩ and ⟨v⟩ but also ⟨ph⟩ /f/ in words of Greek origin. The bilabial realizations /ɸ/ and /β/ of /f/ and /v/ which may occur in the Irish-influenced dialects of Ulster were not indicated in the sample of traditional Scots writing analysed above and orthographic indications of such realizations have never been suggested.

The phonemes /f v/ may be realised as bilabial [ɸ β] in Ulster Scots, particularly around back sounds, where 'broad', plain Irish /f v/ would be realised this way in that language [...] also uncovered a case of this [...] near the Highland Line, so that (South?) Gaelic influence can probably be invoked. (Johnston 1997b: 509–510)

[.] *p* is occas. aspirated to *ph*, *f*, finally after *m* as in BUMPH, CLOMPH, *gamph* (GAMP), HUMPH, *n.*¹, SUMPH, TRUMPH. (SND VII: 1 s.v. "P")

For word-final /f/ Purves (1979) suggested ⟨f⟩ in all words, including monosyllabic words following a single vowel such as *af* 'off', *caf* 'chaff', *glif* 'fright', *nyaf* 'dwarf', and *sklif* 'scrape'. The SND includes the following as headword forms: *aff*, *caff*, *gliff*, *nyaff*, and *skliff*.

Both ⟨f⟩ and ⟨v⟩ are unambiguous choices for a normative orthography, bilabial realizations will be produced unconsciously by native speakers, rendering their representation unnecessary. It would also seem sensible to follow the established use of word-final ⟨ff⟩ where it occurs. Likewise, ⟨ph⟩ in words of Greek origin and for the aspirated plosive ⟨p⟩ forms of *bump*, *gamp* 'gape', *hump*, *sump*, and *trump* etc. as *bumph* [bʌmf], etc.

5.2.9 Mapping of /θ/ and /ð/

The dental fricatives /θ/ and /ð/ both traditionally map to ⟨th⟩, word final /ð/ usually being mapped to ⟨-the⟩. The SND includes the following as headword forms: *blithe* 'cheerful', *kythe* 'appear' *laithe* 'loathe', and *teethe*. Noun and verb forms are often distinguished by using ⟨th⟩ /θ/ and ⟨the⟩ /ð/ in, for example, *laith* (n.) 'loath'—*laithe* (v.) 'loathe', *skaith* (n.)—*skaithe* (v.) 'damage' and *teeth* (n.) 'teeth'—*teethe* (v.) (SND). Robinson (1997) suggested indicating the widespread initial th-debuccalization to /h/ in a few words by placing an accent over the following vowel giving *thànks*, *thìng* and *thìnk*. Robinson (1997) suggested spelling the elided colloquial form of the relative pronoun that as *at*,³² the as *thà* but *tha*³³ when /ð/ is retained, similarly *thàim* and *thaim* 'them'. Robinson explained that as follows:

---

32   This may also represent an alternative form borrowed from Norse.
33   The emphatic realization [ðə] is usual in all Scots dialects and the traditional spelling the has always been *the*. Although /ə/ can be represented by any vowel letter Robinson's use o ⟨a⟩ in *tha* could be interpreted as indicating *[ðɑ], an unattested pronunciation, but is more likely a respelling for the sake of being different. Robinson's examples on pp. 64-65 indicated that the form *thà* occurred only after a consonant. Strangely *the* is recommended in such adverbial phrases as *theday* 'today', *thenicht* 'tonight' and *themorra* 'tomorrow' although their elements would usually be interpreted and written separately as *the day* etc.

[...] the behaviour of these three words is not consistent in Ulster-Scots. *That*, *tha*, and *thaim* lose 'th' and become *at*, *thà* and *thàim* only when the preceding word ends with a consonant rather than a vowel sound. The loss of 'th' does *not*[34] occur at the beginning of a sentence, or [if] the preceding word in a sentence ends with a vowel sound. (1997: 37)

Perhaps the most distinctive marker of "Ullans" writing to the casual reader, and one which has become remarkably common in revivalist Scots writing in Northern Ireland, is the respelling of the definite article as *tha*. While such strategies are often adopted in eye dialect and are equally valid in Scots and English, the use of the spelling in revived Ulster Scots has the idiom-specific rationale of distinguishing it from *the*, used for unstressed 'they' in some dialect writing. Such use of *the* is open to criticism, since confusion in English writing between *you're* and *your*, *there*, *their* and *they're*, or *'ve* and *of* can be associated with illiteracy. Conversely, the semantic differentiation of homophones through spelling can be associated with an idiom's historicity, intellectual standing and *Ausbau*. [...] While the *schwa* in the unstressed form of the definite article [ðə] or [ə] could be spelt with any vowel, the specific spelling choice of *tha* is at odds with the history of the language, since it was used in Middle Scots for both 'they' and *thae* 'those', and by no means all writers of Ulster Scots respell 'they' as *the*. Based on statistical frequency, it would be more economic to retain the traditional spelling of the definite article, instead changing 'they' to *tha*. If spelt with an apostrophe, such an approach would also have the advantage of being pandialectal, since 'they' is often rendered *thai* or *thay* in mainstream Scots. If the apostrophe were used with the English spelling, the difference between third person plural pronoun and definite article would be adequately marked, and there would be no need for any further reforms. (Eagle and Falconer 2004: 100)

Intervocallic /ð/ generally does not delete [...] but may do quite frequently in Ulster Scots [...] The equivalent of /ð/-deletion for the voiceless sound is /θ/ > /h/. This can be found in initial and intervocallic positions, including before /r/ (that is, in *thing*, *nothing*, *three*) in many Scots dialects [...] (Johnston 1997b: 507)

34 Where Robinson 1997 uses an underscore it has been set in italics here and passim.

Even the Ulster Scots dentalisation of /t/ and /d/, which Robinson's orthography highlights, is a feature which overlaps with many
southern Irish English varieties (see Ó Baoill 1990; Ó hÚrdail
1997). (Kallen 1999: 161)

Such characteristics of colloquial speech are never usually represented in
writing except in descriptive dialogue. Since such elisions are mastered by
native-speakers unconsciously, their representation in writing may cause
more confusion that clarification. The full forms of the words would be
transparent enough in a normative orthography.

Umgekehrt finden wir ein *d* statt *th*; *fader* [...] Ein intervokalisches
đ aus ae. *d* fiel mit ursprünglichem ae. *đ* zusammen und nahm
dieselbe Entwicklung wie dieses: es wurde in den meisten Teilen
Schottlands und den Nordlands zu *d* [...] (Steiger 1913: 49)[35]

The process that underlies /θ ð/-Stopping, the difference between
Northern *idder* and Mid Scots *ither*, and perhaps even the
Glaswegian /ð/-Rhotacisation rule, has its roots deep in the Older
Scots period, and in part it may even go back into Old North-
umbrian. (Johnston 1997a: 102)

Traditionally in Aberdeenshire, /d/ appeared for /ð/ intervocali-
cally in words like *mother, father, bother,* particularly in coastal
localities, though this is sharply recessive now (Dieth 1932: 109).
There seems to be a general interchange between stops and
fricatives in all English to some extent where an /r/ follows
immediately or in the next syllable; *father,* after all, goes back to
Old English *fæder.* The tendency towards generalising one type or
the other one, usually the fricative at the expense of the stop, is
furthest advanced in localities in North Britain, however (Zai 1942:
195, Wilson 1926: 29). Dialects which face the Solway Firth or
Irish Sea have a tendency to have dental stops in this position from
either original stop or fricative. (Johnston 1997b: 506)

Since the Northern realization /d/ is environmentally predictable in
words such as *brither* 'brother', *ither* 'other', *mither* 'mother',[36] the intervocalic

---

35   'Conversely we find a *d* instead of *th*; *fader* [...] An intervocalic *đ* from Old English *d* fell
     together with the original Old English *đ* and developed the same way: In most parts of
     Scotland and the Northlands it became *d* [...]' [AE]
36   All headword forms in the SND.

grapheme ⟨**th**⟩ before /r/ could easily be interpreted as /d/ by those with such a realization. For the Southern and Central Scots realization of /d/ as /ð/, see ⟨**d**⟩ above.

5.2.10 Mapping of /s/ and /z/

The fricatives /s/ and /z/ traditionally tend to map to ⟨**s**⟩ or ⟨**se**⟩ when not a plural marker. In words of Romance origin ⟨**c**⟩ generally occurred before ⟨**e**⟩ and ⟨**i**⟩, for example *censor, ceevil* 'civil', *cedent*, and *ceil* 'ceiling' (SND II: 1 s.v. "c").

> As in E., **s** is generally written initially with *s*, sometimes with *c* in *romance* words before *e*—medially by *ss* and *s* (especially in derivatives), finally by *ss, se* and *ce. se* and *ce* are used as in corresponding E. words, but less regularly. (Grant and Dixon 1921: 24)

> [...] as the breathed fore-blade fricative [s], gen. written *s, -ss-* medially, or *-ss, -se* finally, or when in contact with an unvoiced consonant; (2) as the voiced equivalent [z] when orig. *s* is final after a vowel or voiced consonant or medially between voiced sounds but in Sc. final [s] is retained when it becomes medial before an inflection, as in *houses* ['husɪz], *gallowses* ['gɑləsɪz], and in WISE [wɔis], esp. when used in peculiarly Sc. senses; *dose* is pronounced [doːz] in Sc. on the analogy of other Fr. borrowings *close, rose*, etc. (SND VIII: 1 s.v. "s")

> Medially it [/z/] is generally written *s*, but *z* and *zz* are used by writers who wish to indicate the exact pronunciation. Finally *z* is written *s* (1) in words like *is, his, was, has*, which originally had an **s** sound: (2) in the plural terminations *s* and *es* after voiced sounds: in other cases *se* and *ze* are used. (Grant and Dixon 1921: 25)

In traditional writing ⟨**z**⟩ for /z/ seldom occurred, but it often represented the older yogh; in the manuscripts ⟨ȝ⟩ and ⟨z⟩ fell together, and with the introduction of printing ⟨z⟩ was used for both.[37] In Older Scots the spelling ⟨**lȝ**⟩ was used in words such as *spoilȝie* 'spoil', *spuilȝeid* 'spoiled', and *caperkeillȝie* 'capercaillie', and ⟨**nȝ**⟩ in words such as *disdenȝe* 'disdain', *Spanȝe* 'Spain', *meinȝe* 'people', *cunȝe* 'coin', and *seinȝie* 'synod' (Smith 1902: xxiv-xxv). With time the ⟨**z**⟩ that had replaced ⟨ȝ⟩ was no longer perceived as accurately representing the modern Scots pronunciations /l(j)i/ and /ɲ/~/ŋ/ so alternate spellings replacing ⟨**lz**⟩ and ⟨**nz**⟩ with ⟨(**l**)**y**⟩ and ⟨**n**⟩

---

37   See note 3 above on p. 13.

and ⟨**ng**⟩ arose, such as *bailzie/bail(y)ie* 'bailiff', *brulzie/brulyie* 'brawl', *spulzie/spulyie* 'spoil', *gaberlunzie/gaberlunyie* 'beggar', *cu(i)nzie/cunyie* 'coin', and *feinzie/feingie* 'feign' (Grant and Dixon 1921: 16–17). That may also be found in personal names such as *Dalziel/Dalyell*, *Menzies/Mingis*, and *MacKenzie* which now seems to be universally pronounced with /z/ rather than as *MacKenyie* (or *MacKengyie*? SND X:297 gives "[†məˈkɛnji]").

Robinson (1997: 42–44) confused the historical yogh in ⟨**lʒ**⟩ /ʎ/ with initial /j/ or a yod-glide from the Older Scots use of ⟨**ʒ**⟩ for /j/ in words such as *ʒeir* 'year' and *ʒow* 'you', referring to that as a "yogh sound" and describing a non-phenomenon he calls "yoghing".

> Like care must be shown in the interpretation of the later use of *y* (consonant) and *z* for the scribal ʒ, the representative of O.E. ᵹ. (Smith 1902: xxix)

> Old Scots had a sound—the so called *l mouillé*—which was unknown to English though found in French. According to Murray this sound, represented by the digraph *lz*, survived in to the nineteenth century [...] but has now become a simple [l] or an [l] followed by a [j] sound [...] (Tulloch 1980: 189)

> Scots also had the sound of French *gn* in *digne* [ɲ] spelt *nʒ*, *nz* or *ny*. [...] The [ɲ] sound developed into [ŋ] giving for example the older pronunciation of *Menzies* as *Mingies*. (Tulloch 1980: 190)

Whether the traditional terminal spelling ⟨(**e**)**s**⟩ for the plural, present inflections and in many other words is rendered /s/ or /z/ is the outcome of a phonological rule. The pronunciation /s/ usually occurs after /f/, /k/, /p/, /t/, /θ/, and /x/, e.g. *hooses* 'houses', *leafs* 'leaves', *wifes* 'wives', *lochs*, and *threaps* 'argues', etc. The pronunciation /z/ usually occurs in plural endings and after a vowel sound or /b/, /d/, /g/, /l/, /m/, /n/, /r/~/ɹ/, /v/, /ð/, and /ŋ/, for example, *dous* 'doves', *haunds* 'hands', *steams*, *gie's* 'give us/me', *his*, *hers*, *thairs* 'theirs' etc. (Grant 1921: 25). Only Robinson (1997) made suggestions that indicated either a /s/ or /z/ realizations in some words. The suggestion that ⟨**z**⟩ be used where ⟨**s**⟩ traditionally occurred being a characteristic "eye dialect" representation.

> The use of *z* instead of *s* in the spellings of *is*, *was* etc., [...] are fairly frequent illustrations of this. (McClure 1997: 176)

Sometimes Robinson uses spellings which appear to be straight-forward phoneticisations, e.g. the use of ⟨z⟩ "corresponding to 's' and 'ys' in words like *iz* ('us' and *sez* ('says'" (21.) Phonetic spellings of this kind are equally plausible for most dialects of English and understandable to outsiders simply because there is nothing particularly Ulster Scots about them. (Kallen 1999: 158)

Purves (1997) and the *Scots Language Society* (1985) suggested terminal ⟨-ss⟩ for /s/ except following a consonant where ⟨-se⟩ is suggested, giving examples such as *kiss, horse, mense, fauss, houss, crouss, uiss, poliss, promiss, gress*. Purves also suggested ⟨-se⟩ for /z/ giving examples such as *surpryse, ryse, brose, rouse*, and *lowse* (v.).

Allan (1995) suggested there was a good case for ⟨z⟩ in *aixerceize* 'exercise' and *bapteize* 'baptize' etc.[38]

As the realization /s/ or /z/, in for example plural markers, is conditioned by phonetic environment and realized unconsciously by native speakers, traditional practice would best be followed in a normative orthography. As would the use of ⟨se⟩ and ⟨ss⟩ exemplified in the SND headword forms *brose* [broːz], *crouse* [krus] 'cheerful', *dose* [doːz], *fause* [faːs, fɔːs, faːs] 'false', *groose* [grus] 'grouse', *horse* [hɔrs, hors], *lowse* [lʌuz] 'loosen' [lʌus] 'loose', *mense* [mɛns] 'courtesy', *rise* [raɪz], *rose* [roːz], *rouse* [ruːz] 'provoke', *gress* [grɛs], and *kiss* [kɪs]. The grapheme ⟨ʒ⟩, for practical reasons, does not readily offer itself, therefore the use of ⟨y⟩ and ⟨ng⟩ in words such as *brulyie* 'brawl', *gaberlunyie* 'beggar', *senyie* 'synod' and place names such as *Cadyou* 'Cadzow', *Cullain* 'Culzean', *Diyel* 'Dalziel', *Drumelyer* 'Drumelzier', *Fingan* 'Finzean', and *Kirkguneon* 'Kirkgunzeon' may be sensible. A case may be made for the retention of ⟨z⟩ where it is well established in names such as *Menzies* (*Mingis*).

5.2.11 Mapping of /ʃ/

The fricative /ʃ/ traditionally maps to ⟨sh⟩. Only Robinson (1997) suggested ⟨sch⟩ instead of ⟨sh⟩ for /ʃ/, apparently using ⟨sch⟩ where ⟨sh⟩ was traditionally used, reserving ⟨sh⟩ for words where the underlying /s/ was realized /ʃ/, a feature of many Scots dialects but not universal. Robinson also applied that ⟨sh⟩ to words such as *harnish* 'harness', *shoo* 'sew', and *veshel* 'vessel' where /ʃ/ was usual in Scots but not in the Standard

---

38 The Oxford English Dictionary recommends an etymological basis for this choice for standard English, using the *-ize* type of spelling for words using the Greek suffix *-ιζειν*, and retaining the *-ise* type of spelling for loanwords from French in *-mise* and *-prise*. Should such a criterion be selected for a normative Scots orthography, *exerceese* would not have a *z*. [ME]

English cognates. The alveolar realization /c/ for /ʃ/ that may occur in the Irish-influenced dialects of Ulster was not indicated in the sample of traditional Scots writing analysed above.

> The Old Scots spellings *sch* for English *sh* and *quh* for English *wh* survived in documents into the eighteenth century but were then replaced by their English equivalents. (Tulloch 1980: 198)

> [...] the digraph *sh*, also written *sch*, which survived as a spelling into the early 18th c. and is occas. still used *arch.*, representing the unvoiced afterblade fricative [ʃ], rarely the voiced equivalent [ʒ] in FUSHION, PUSHION [...] (SND VIII: 1 s.v. "s")

The unambiguous choice for a normative orthography would arguably be ⟨**sh**⟩.

The fricative /ʃ/ also occurs in the cluster traditionally written ⟨**nch**⟩ /nʃ/. The SND includes the following as headword forms: *dunch* 'bump', *hainch* 'haunch', *inch* 'small island', *kinch* 'a kink', *lench* 'launch', *painch* 'paunch', *stainchel* 'a bar', and *stench* 'staunch'.

Since the representation ⟨**nch**⟩ is so well established, innovations such as ⟨**nsh**⟩ would seem unnecessary in a normative orthography.

5.2.12 Mapping of /ʒ/

The fricative /ʒ/ traditionally maps to ⟨**s**⟩, individually and in the clusters ⟨**-sian**⟩ and ⟨**-sion**⟩, and to ⟨**sh**⟩ as described above in words such as *ephesian* 'pheasant', *fushion* 'vigour', *pushion* 'poison'. and *veesion* 'vision'.

By analogy with words such as *craitur* 'creature', *lectur* 'tecture' and *pictur* 'picture' also ⟨**s**⟩ in *leisur* 'leisure', *meisur* 'measure', and *pleisur* 'pleasure' (see the section on morphemes below).

The alveolar realization /z/ for /ʒ/ that may occur in the Irish-influenced dialects of Ulster was not indicated in the sample of traditional Scots writing analysed above. Once again, in order to maintain familiarity, the unambiguous choice for a normative orthography would arguably be to follow established practice.

5.2.13 Mapping of /ç/ and /x/

The fricatives /ç/ and /x/ were often written ⟨**gh**⟩ but ⟨**ch**⟩ was also used. The latter inherited from Middle Scots (Aitken 2002: Vol. XII, liv) as in the following examples from DOST: *dochter* 'daughter', *laich* 'low', *micht* 'might', and *nicht* 'night'.

> [...] commonly written *ch* [...] (SND I: xxiii §73)

The Scots realizations is unambiguously indicated by ⟨ch⟩ and because it never occurs initially cannot be confused with ⟨ch⟩ for /tʃ/ (below). Where most dialects have /xt/, /θ/ may occur in Northern dialects in words such as *dochter* 'daughter' and *micht* 'might' (SND I: xxxv §138).

The fricative /ç/ usually occurs word-initially or following a front vowel. The fricative /x/ usually occurs following a back vowel (SND I: xxiii §73) in words such as *laich* 'low', *lauchter* 'laughter', *loch*, *nicht* 'night', and *pech* 'pant'. Initial /ç/ occurs in words such as *hue*, *huge*, *heuk* 'hook', and *human*, and attempts to represent that orthographically are likely to produce unrecognizable forms. Since the initial /ç/ is conditioned by environment, the traditional spellings are arguably a sufficient marker. All suggested ⟨ch⟩ for medial or final /ç/ and /x/. The *Scots Language Society* (1985), Allan (1995: 80) and the *Scots Spelling Comatee* (2000) suggested dropping the silent ⟨gh⟩ in *through* and *though*. The grapheme ⟨ch⟩ certainly offers itself as an unambiguous choice for a normative orthography. The case for omission in words such as *throu* 'through' and *tho* 'though', which no longer have the fricative, has its merits but in words such as *burgh*, for want of an unambiguous alternative, would probably have to remain ⟨gh⟩.

5.2.14 Mapping of /h/

The fricative /h/ traditionally maps to ⟨h⟩, except in Southern Scots before /o/, where it is realized /ʍ/ (Tulloch 1980: 252). Omission of initial /h/ does not occur in Scots except, in the unemphatic reduced form of *hae* /ə/ 'have', as in constructions such as *haed hae haen* [hədə'hɪn] 'had have had' (Gregg 1972: 130) and in the unstressed forms of pronouns such as *he*, *him* and *her*. That may also occur in many words of Romance origin spelt with initial ⟨h⟩ such as *honest* and *honour*, but older speakers may still omit it in words such as *herbs* and *hospital*. Robinson (1997) suggested ⟨è⟩ and ⟨ò⟩, as in *hè* 'he', *hònest*, *hòor* 'hour', and *hòspittle*[39] 'hospital', to indicate the silent ⟨h⟩.

> [...] the stressed form is [...] **hɐz**? [...] [hus] the unstressed forms are **əs, əz**. (Wright 1905: 273)

> [...] *h* appears and is pronounced [h] initially before all vowels except (1) in the pronouns he, him, his, h*er(s)*, and in parts of the verb hae, *q.v.*, when these are in unstressed position [...] (2) in many words of Romance orig., where the usage now gen. follows that of Eng. Older speakers are still heard to say *'erbs, 'ospital*, [...] (SND: IV:471 s.v. "H")

---

39 Presumably the ⟨tt⟩ in *hòspittle* is to represent /ʔ/, which could equally be /t/ in Ulster.

[...] the omission of *h* [in spelling] from those third-person pronouns (particularly pointless in that the loss of [h] in these words when unemphatic is universal in all "Englishes") are fairly frequent illustrations of this [eye dialect]. (McClure 1997: 176)

The use of ⟨h⟩ as a diacritic in ⟨ch⟩ and ⟨sh⟩, indicating that ⟨c⟩ and ⟨s⟩ have a pronunciation different from that normally expected of those consonants,[40] was not new to English when ⟨ch⟩ was introduced from French, for ⟨th⟩ had earlier been used alongside ⟨þ⟩ [...] Both ⟨ch⟩ in French and ⟨th⟩ in English derive from Latin orthography, use of ⟨h⟩ as a diacritic in Latin being made possible by the disappearance of the sounds represented by ⟨h⟩ from the language in the late classical period. As a result of the establishment in English of diacritic ⟨h⟩ in ⟨ch⟩ and ⟨th⟩, other consonant groups were formed on the same pattern. The grapheme ⟨gh⟩ [...] ⟨wh⟩ has a rather different history, for it began in Old English as an initial consonantal combination ⟨hw⟩ corresponding to /xw/. Assimilation of the group to a single voiceless consonant /ʍ/ had taken place by the Late Old English period, and Middle English scribes, associating the sequence ⟨hw⟩ for the single phoneme with the use of ⟨h⟩ as a fricative marker in other graphemes, reversed the graphs to ⟨wh⟩. (Scragg 1975: 46–47)

The grapheme ⟨**h**⟩ is arguably the obvious choice for a normative orthography, even for the realization /ʍ/ before /o/, which is environmentally conditioned and unconsciously mastered by native speakers. Since its elision generally only occurs in unemphatic forms, the full forms of such words would be sensible in a normative orthography.

5.2.15 Mapping of /tʃ/

The affricate /tʃ/ traditionally maps to ⟨**ch**⟩ when word-initial or after /r/ and ⟨(**t**)**ch**⟩ when word-medial and -final. The realizations /tɕ/ for /tʃ/ that may occur in the Irish-influenced dialects of Ulster were not indicated in the sample of traditional Scots writing analysed above. The SND includes the following as headword forms: *airch* 'arch', *catch*, and *eetch* 'an adze'. In some Scots dialects /tʃ/ occurs when a ⟨t⟩ is followed by /j/ sound, for example in a northern form of *taw* [tɑː, tɔː] realized [tjɑːv, tʃɑːv] (SND IX:463 s.v. "TYAUVE").

---

40   i.e. ⟨h⟩ as a fricative marker, allowing for the fact that ⟨sh⟩ is historically a simplification of ⟨sch⟩. [Original footnote]

Purves (1979: 69) was also aware of that "[ch] is a velar fricative, except when used at the start of a word [...] or when it follows 'n', 'r' or 't' [...]", as was the SLS (1985). Allan (1995: 82) suggested always using ⟨**tch**⟩, except after a consonant. SLD (2002) suggested ⟨**ch**⟩ word-initially and either ⟨**tch**⟩ or ⟨**ch**⟩ word-finally, offering no reason for choosing one or the other, although (Macleod and Cairns 1993: x, Macleod 1996: vii) preferred ⟨**ch**⟩ word-initially and ⟨**tch**⟩ word-medially and finally. The *Scots Spelling Comatee* recommended initial ⟨**ch**⟩, otherwise ⟨**tch**⟩, except after /r/.

The grapheme ⟨**ch**⟩ is, arguably, an unambiguous choice word-initially, and since the realization /tʃ/ after /r/[41] is predictable, no further innovation would seem necessary. The grapheme ⟨**tch**⟩ certainly offers itself in other positions, especially where simple ⟨**ch**⟩ may be confused with the fricative /x/, though even here the fricative /x/ is arguably being marked by a preceding ⟨**ei**⟩ in words such as *abeich* 'aloof', *dreich* 'dreary' and *heich* 'high'.[42] The preceding ⟨**ea**⟩[43] and ⟨**ee**⟩ marking /tʃ/, although a few examples of ⟨**ee**⟩ before /x/ also occur as headwords in the SND, for example, *eechie* in the phrase *eechie nor ochie* 'neither one thing or another', *feech* 'an exclamation of disgust' and *wheech* 'whizz'.

5.2.16 Mapping of /dʒ/

The affricate /dʒ/ traditionally maps to ⟨(**d**)**g**(**e**)⟩, ⟨**j**⟩, ⟨**g-**⟩.

> The letter [g] [...] when assibilated, that of the consonant diphthong [dʒ], occasionally [ʒ], sometimes also written *dge, ge, j*. The distinctions correspond in the main to those of Eng. [...] (SND: IV: 217 s.v. "G")

The realizations /dz/ for /dʒ/ that may occur in the Irish influenced dialects of Ulster were not indicated in the sample of traditional Scots writing analysed above. The SND includes the following as headword forms: *breenge* 'rush', *cadge* 'beg', *gauge, gentie* 'graceful', and *jalouse* 'surmise'. Attempts to regularize to any particular grapheme may produce unfamiliar forms, so it may well be best simply to judiciously study the literary record and adopt the most widespread form of a particular word.[44]

---

41 For ⟨**nch**⟩ see §5.2.11 above.
42 All headword forms in the SND.
43 See vowels 2 and 3 below.
44 That does not necessarily include the vowel conventions in any particular word.

5.2.17 Mapping of /j/

The approximant /j/ traditionally maps to ⟨y⟩.

> As the voiced front fricative consonant [j] representing (1) an
> earlier palatal guttural, as O.E. ʒ-, as in YAIRD, YELD, YESTREEN,
> YETT, FORYETT, YON, though in n. and s.Sc. it tends to be
> dropped before [i] [...] (SND X: 246 s.v. "Y")

Note that ⟨y⟩ also often represents the diphthongs /əi/, /ai/ (Vowels 1, 8a
and 10) and is used word-finally in adverbs and adjectives. It is not usually
indicated in writing where it occurs as part of other vowel clusters.
Traditional practice, once again, offers the best solution.

5.2.18 Mapping of /ʍ/

The labial velar approximant /ʍ/ traditionally maps to ⟨wh⟩.

> *w* also occurs in the consonant digraph *wh* [...] (SND X: 1 s.v. "W")

> The Old Scots spelling [...] *quh* for English *wh* survived in
> documents into the eighteenth century but were then replaced by
> their English equivalents. (Tulloch 1980: 198)

That is often realized /f/ or /ɸ/ in Northern dialects, in Angus /ʍ/
before interrogatives otherwise /f/. In Northern dialects it may be /w/ in
recent loan words. In the sample of traditional Scots writing analysed above
⟨wh⟩ was usually used, even the Northern writers seldom respelt to ⟨f⟩ in
order to indicate the realization /f/. Examples: *wha* 'who', *whippit*
'whipped', *white*, *whalp* 'whelp'. Some options, spelt ⟨f⟩, representing the
northern /f/ realization were offered in Macleod and Cairns (1993) and
Macleod (1996), only Robinson (1997) suggested using the older ⟨quh⟩,
but only for pronouns and adverbs; in other words ⟨wh⟩ was suggested.
The grapheme ⟨wh⟩ is, arguably, the unambiguous choice, the realization
/f/ is predictable and need not be represented in a normative orthography.

5.2.19 Mapping of /w/

The labial velar approximant /w/ traditionally maps to ⟨w⟩ The cluster
/wr/, traditionally written ⟨wr⟩, has been simplified to /r/ in many
dialects. In some Northern dialects it may be realized /vr/. The SND
includes the following as headword forms: *wrack* 'wreck', *wrang* 'wrong',
write, and *wricht* 'wright'. Some options spelt ⟨vr⟩, representing the northern
/vr/ realization, were offered in Macleod and Cairns (1993) and Macleod

(1996). The grapheme ⟨w⟩ is the unambiguous, obvious choice, the realization /vr/ is predictable and need not be represented in a normative orthography.

> [...] the retention of [w] before [r] in words like *write* [...] (Tulloch 1980: 186)

5.2.20 Mapping of /l/ and /ɫ/

The lateral approximants /l/ and /ɫ/ both map to ⟨l⟩. The usual realization is a dark /ɫ/ but in areas where Gaelic was relatively recently spoken, including Dumfries and Galloway, it may be a clear /l/. Differentiation between clear and dark *l* has never been indicated in writing. In Ulster an interdental allophone /l̪/ may occur. For the word-ending traditionally written ⟨-le⟩ Purves (1979) and the *Scots Language Society* (1985) suggested ⟨-il⟩, Purves was perhaps influenced by Middle Scots practice and also doubled ⟨l⟩ after doubled vowels in *weill* 'well' but not in *sail*. The *Scots Spelling Comatee* (2000) recommended ⟨-le⟩ but pointed out that ⟨-el⟩ often occurred after ⟨nn⟩ or ⟨v⟩. The grapheme ⟨l⟩ is the unambiguous, obvious choice for a normative orthography, as is word-final ⟨-le⟩, particularly as a frequentative suffix, or ⟨-el⟩ in words such as *guddle* 'grope', *muckle* 'much', *jabble* 'agitate a liquid', *stumple* 'walk heavily or clumsily', *tousle* 'ruffle', *traivel* 'travel', and *vennel* 'alley',[45] though here a judicious study of the literary record may be necessary in order to establish the most widespread form in a particular word.

---

45   All headword forms in the SND.

6
VOWELS

The underlying phonemes of stressed vowels based on Aitken (1981b: 132–133). For vowel 1, short is indicated with s, long with L. For a historical treatment of Scots vowels, see Aitken (2002).[46]

Aitken's number	8a, 10, 1s	1L	2	11	3	4	8	5	18	6
Underlying phoneme	əi	aˑe	i	i	i, e(ː)	e	eː	oː	ɔ	u

Aitken's number	7	7 -k, -x	9	12	13	14	15	16	17	19
Underlying phoneme	ø	(j)u, (j)ʌ	oi	aː, ɔː	ʌu	iu, ju	ɪ	ɛ	a	ʌ

> […] many spelling-to-sound patterns which can be described only clumsily in direct spelling-to-sound terms are more adequately described in phonological terms. (Venezky 1970: 45)

Many of the vowel graphemes used in the 18th and 19th centuries were inherited from Middle Scots, as the selection below, from later in the period, taken from the *Dictionary of the Older Scottish Tongue* shows. They may not all be the most wide spread or common, but they were all certainly used and known at the time.

> **fine, fire, knife, like, wife** but also **byre, dyke, fyle, syne, wyte; byle, pyne, spyle** (NOTE: forms such as **bile, pine,** and **spile** also occurred);
> **bield, chief, dreich, skeich, neist, speir, sweir;**
> **freend, greet, keep, seek, weet;**
> **bere, here;**

46 With regard to the chart here, note that Aitken included those spelled ⟨eu⟩ under vowel 14 although separate treatment is justified for many of them by their differing etymology (Anglo–Saxon long ō, vowel 7 before /k/ and /x/) and resulting phonetic realizations.

hie; dee, ee, dree, free, see, tree, three;

be, he, she, we;

beir, heid, deid, deif (NOTE: forms such as bere, hede, dede, and defe also occurred);

gear, leave, quean, season (NOTE: forms such as gere~geir, leve~leive, queen~quein and seson~seisoun also occurred);

ane, bane, hale, hame, lane, stane;

brae, sae, frae, gae;

braid, mair, saip (NOTE: forms such as brade, mare, and sape also occurred);

day, say;

gey, quey, Mey, pey;

afore, note, poke, thole, troke;

coal, coat, loan;

athort, body, box, corn, on;

about, broun, cou, dou, doun, drouth, house, mouth, nou, out, sou, toun;

buird, guid, fuid, fluid, fluir, muir, puir, pruive;

beuch, beuk, eneuch, heuk, leuk, neuk, sheuk, teuch, teuk;

noise; boy, coy;

baw, caw, faw, waw, blaw, braw, craw, slaw, snaw;

faut, saut, auld, bauld, cauld, fauld, hauch;

awa, twa, wha;

bowt, gowf, howff, howk, howp, lowp;

flowe, growe, howe, knowe, lowe, rowe;

dew, few, new;

bird, brig, drink, fit, hill, kist, licht, pit, simmer, wid 'wood', will, wirm;

bed, bend, ebb, fecht, ferm, gled, hert, ken, lenth, seck, send, wecht;

back, laft, lang, mak, tak, strang, want;

bull, bund, drumly, dub, full, grund, hunder, pull, unce

6.1 VOWEL LENGTH IN SCOTS

Vowel length in Scots is usually conditioned by the *Scottish Vowel Length Rule*, also known as *Aitken's Law* (Aitken 1981b: 131–157)

> All vowels are short before a following /p, t, tʃ, k/ […] All vowels except /ɪ/ and /ʌ/ are long before a following final /v, ð, z, r/ or # […] But a peculiar Ulster development has then resulted in […] the use of long allophones of /e, ɛ, a, ɔ/ in any monosyllable

closed by a consonant **other** than /p, t, tʃ, k/. We might refer to this extra development as Ulster Lengthening [...] (Wells 1982: 439)

Ulster Scots, [...] is a recognizable dialect of Lowland Scots [...] by, among other things, its typically Scots pattern of conditioned vowel length [...] (Harris 1984: 116)

The conditioning of vowel length by phonological environment negates its representation in a normative orthography. The phonological environment itself acting as the vowel length marker, which native speakers would instinctively recognize.

6.1.1 Schwa /ə/

Schwa /ə/ usually occurs in unaccented syllables as a substitute for any vowel.

[...] but it may be heard also in Sc. Before **r** in accented position, instead of **ɪ** or **ʌ** and is then tense as a rule. Examples: *third, bird*; **θərd, bərd**. (Grant and Dixon 1921: 54)

In some of the Northern dialects another flat vowel may be heard [...] it takes the place of **ɪ** in words like *put, foot, hit, him* [...] (Grant and Dixon 1921: 55)

Since none of the traditionally available vowel letters is capable of representing /ə/ any better than any other, arguably the best solution would be to retain the traditional spelling, or identify a prevalent one through judicious study of the literary record.

Some varieties retain the Irish and Scottish Gaelic epenthetic /ə/ between liquid consonants such as /l/, /r/, or /n/ and nasals in words such as *girl* and *film*.

[...] in Glaswegian words like *warm* are often pronounced with an epenthetic vowel between [r] and the syllabic consonant [m]. The intrusion of a helping vowel makes the word disyllabic so that it is pronounced [war(ə)m]. (Hagen 2002: 265-266)

Since the insertion of an epenthetic schwa in mastered unconsciously by those who have it, representation in a normative orthography is not necessary.

Similar to the above are words with a varying phonetic structure usually depending on emphasis.

> Characteristically the words in this class include auxiliary verbs, personal and relative pronouns, coordinating and subordinating conjunctions, some adverbs, and a few individual lexemes [...] The list of members of this class is variable, within Scots as within the entire range of dialects , creoles and pidgins collectively referred to as "English" (or "Englishes"); but the class itself is always present. [...] The far-reaching implication of this well known fact is that a completely phoneme-based spelling [...] would be impractical, if not impossible: many words would have two or more distinct written forms, of which the distribution could not be predicted with accuracy. (McClure 1997: 174)

> Furthermore, some historical Scots spellings could be as liable as modern English ones to suggest pronunciations other than those in actual use: *thair* and *thaim* can readily be associated with [ðer] and [ðem]; but on the other hand *wes* is the commonest MSc spelling for the preterite of *be*, and the invariably contemporary pronunciation (emphatic or not) is [wɪz], never with [ɛ] or [i]. Nonce spellings may present difficulties of interpretations to readers who cannot easily "auditorise" the dialect which the writer is mentally hearing as he writes; and a more serious objection is that they are liable to merge into mere eye-dialect, departures from standard spelling (or simple mis-spellings) which may suggest that the dialect represented is in general non-standard but convey no clear indication of **how** the pronunciation of an abnormally-spelt word differs from the standard. (McClure 1997: 175–6)

> Weak forms have been characteristic of Scots as of all dialects derived from Old English throughout its history, and neither Scots, standard literary English, nor any other dialect has found it necessary to devise special spellings for them. To make this a regular device in written Scots, besides, could convey a suggestion that weak forms as a linguistic feature are unique to Scots, which is absurd; or could arouse suspicions that the authors **imagine** that they are unique to Scots, or even a particularly interesting or distinctive feature of it [...] which would reflect no credit on their understanding of linguistic facts. (McClure 1997: 181)

[…] since weak forms by their nature contain an obscure vowel, for which no letter of the Roman alphabet is self-evidently more appropriate than any other, it cannot be possible in all cases to produce an unambiguous spelling on the sound-to-symbol principle: the conventional spelling may be just as suitable, or as unsuitable, as any alternative, thus removing any warrant for the change. (McClure 1997: 181–2)

That was often overlooked but the following suggestions and practices arose.

[…] some current writers employ the spellings, *fer, fir, fur* for the word *for*, which is used in common with English. Since the vowel here is unstressed and hardly differentiated, such spellings serve no useful purpose. (The *Scots Language Society* 1985)

The *Aiberdeen Univairsitie Scots Leid Quorum* and Allan (1995) recommended retaining "established spellings". SLD did not mention that but (Macleod 1996) included some emphatic and unemphatic variants. Robinson (1997) suggested unemphatic forms for some words and emphatic forms for others. The *Scots Spellin Comattee* recommended using the "familiar vowel letters". Arguably, the emphatic forms may seem less ambiguous in a normative orthography.

6.1.2 Use of diacritics

Diacritics have not traditionally occurred in Scots although R. L. Stevenson in *Underwoods* tentatively used diacritic ⟨ü⟩ for vowel 7 but generally preferred ⟨ui⟩, commenting tongue-in-cheek:

[…] and just to prove that I belong to my age and have in me the stuff of a reformer, I have used modification marks throughout. Thus I can tell myself, not without pride, that I have added a fresh stumbling-block for English readers, and to a page of print in my native tongue, have lent a new uncouthness. *Sed non nobis.* (Stevenson 1905: 152–153)

Lorimer's (1985: 467) unintrusive use of accents was clearly intended as a guide to pronunciation for those unfamiliar with spoken Scots and not necessarily intended as an orthographic innovation. Those either indicated syllable stress or vowel 2 /i/[47] written ⟨í⟩ or ⟨ý⟩ in Latinate words such as

---

47   ⟨â⟩ was also used to indicate vowel 12 in *congregâtion* and *creâtor* etc.

hýpocríte, mínister and *peredítion*, as in words such as *kíng, síck, stír, wísdom* and in words in which an accent-less spelling would represent /i/ to those familiar with Scots anyway, for example, *bíeld* 'shelter', *fíeld, gíe* 'give', and *saitisfíe* 'satisfy' etc. The word-final use in words such as *gíe* [giː] is presumably to avoid confusing the pronunciation with the likes of *pie* [pʌɪ]. Philp used ⟨í⟩ for vowel 2 as Lorimer did, commenting on its value as an aid to the learner (Graham 1997: xi). Robinson (1997) seems to have adopted the concept but got carried away.

> This orthographic double-take is opaque, counter-intuitive, and confusing. In attempting to replace conventional symbolism with something, in intention, mimetically realistic, it ends up offering only more and worse symbolism. (Kirk 1998: 127)

> [...] the use of the grave accent on a vowel to indicate the quality of a preceding dental runs counter to the reader's intuition, since analogy with other languages would encourage one to assume that it affected either the quality of the vowel or the general stress of the word. The present writers have encountered no neophyte readers capable of working out for themselves, for example, that the grave on the letter ⟨a⟩ in a word such as *tràictèr* 'tractor' refers to a linguistic phenomenon two letters before, though that is of course not to say that such people do not exist. In the "Ullans" system, the grave can also refer to the pronunciation of ⟨th⟩ as [h] or ∅. Kallen (1999: 159) refers to "the awkwardness of these proposals". Since the grave is always placed on the first vowel after the letter that it modifies, there is no way in which the interdental quality of the final ⟨t⟩ in the word *get* in a phrase such as "get real" can be marked. There are many such examples. (Eagle and Falconer 2004: 105)

Robinson most often used diacritics above vowels to represent the quality of the preceding consonant as described above, but also included the umlaut ⟨ä⟩, perhaps inspired by Gregg's use of /ӕ/ in phonetic transcriptions, for what may be an Ulster Scots realization /ɪ/ of vowel 15, though /ë/ also occurs, especially in Donegal (Gregg 1972: 121). Robinson, never applies that systematically, for example *bäg* 'big' but *biggin* 'building' and *pän* 'pin' but *yin* 'one', the assumption perhaps being that the second in each pair is not recognizably English, so no modification of the vowel is deemed necessary. Robinson was perhaps unaware of the history of the *umlaut* in, for example, German and the potential necessity of an alternative rendering owing to its unavailability on British keyboards.

> German has one diacritic, the **umlaut**, as in ⟨ä ö ü⟩. The umlaut derives from a small ⟨e⟩ written over the main symbol; although the umlauted forms are normal and required in all types of German, if the writer is unable to write an umlaut (perhaps using an English typewriter), writing ⟨ae oe ue⟩ is a recognized alternative. (Rogers 2005: 176)

Further diacritics were ⟨**á**⟩ in words such as *awá* 'away' and *twá* 'two' to indicate long vowels but in *roád* and *boát* it represents a possible disyllabic pronunciation [roːəd, boːət]. Robinson also used ⟨**â**⟩, ⟨**í**⟩, and ⟨**ŷ**⟩ to indicate syllable stress but he may also have intended that ⟨**í**⟩ represent vowel 2.

6.2 VOWELS 1, 8A, AND 10
Vowels 1, 8a and 10, variously /əi/, /ɛi/, /ae/ and /aˑe/, /aɪ/.

> The PRICE words are distributed in two distinct phonemic categories in the Scotch-Irish area (as in Scotland), with [əi(ː)] in some words and [ɑ(ː)e] in others. The choice between these two diphthong types is partly conditioned by phonetic environment, e.g. [əi] before voiceless consonants, [ae] before vowels, thus [lɔik] *like* , ['raeət] *riot*; but in many environments both are possible. (Wells 1982: 443)

> The distribution of the diphthongs [ae] and [əi] generally follow the conditions of Aitken's Law:[48] [ae], in which both morae are long, occurs only in 'long' environments, and [əi], in which both morae are short, usually only occurs in 'short' environments. (Harris 1984: 121)

> Most dialects have either [ɛi~ ëi] [...] or [əi] [...], usually distinct from all other diphthongs, but, in some Caithnessian, merging in some environments with [ɛi] [...] Forms [...] such as [ʌi] or even [ɔi] [...] are not unknown in Scotland, but are most often found in specific environments favourable to backing, such as post-labially [...] or after /r/ [...] (Johnston 1997b: 493)

---

48   That is, the Scottish vowel length rule. [AE]

An uncentralised [ɛi] is common in parts of Fife, Wigtownshire, Ulster and the Tweeddale area [...] (Johnston 1997b: 494)

Following /w/ and /ʍ/, the diphthong /ɔi/ is used to the exclusion of /ɑe/ regardless of what follows [...] (Montgomery and Gregg 1997: 620)

6.2.1 *Scots Style Sheet* recommendation

The *Scots Style Sheet* only suggested ⟨y⟩ for the diphthong in words such as *wynd* 'wind' (v.), *mynd* 'mind', and *hyst* 'hoist' in order to differentiate it from vowel 15 in words such as *wind* (n.), *bind* (v.), and *find*, and the traditional practices were presumably adhered to in others.

6.2.2 Purves' recommendation

Purves (1979) also commented on a similar distinction between vowels 1 short, 8a and 10 and vowel 1 long, suggesting that ⟨y⟩ and ⟨y-e⟩ can be used to represent both, but only ⟨ey⟩ for the short diphthong. Purves also reiterated that distinction (2000: 51–2), claiming that the distinction need not be indicated in English but is important in Scots in words such as *fire* and *alive* and *tyme* 'time', *wyfe* 'wife', and *wynd* 'narrow lane'.

6.2.3 McClure's recommendation

McClure (1980) suggested ⟨iy⟩ in words traditionally written *bite*, *bide* 'remain', and *fire* etc. citing a near-precedent in Middle Scots and a near-parallel in Dutch. McClure was aware that ⟨y⟩ might do. McClure suggested ⟨ey⟩ in words traditionally written *May*, *Tay* and *hay* etc. commenting, that that is in some dialects, a distinct phoneme from the previous one but that etymological consideration should prevail over phonetic ones and "*ey* should be reserved for the diphthong derived from former /ai/ in open syllables, and *iy* for both the open and the close diphthongs derived from /iː/" (p. 28).

6.2.4 *Scots Language Society* recommendation

The *Scots Language Society* suggested ⟨y⟩ and ⟨y-e⟩ medially in words such as *tryst*, *wynd*, *wyfe* 'wife', *dyke*, *syne* 'ago', *clype* 'tell tales' etc. and ⟨ey⟩ initially or finally in words such as *eydent* 'diligent', *cley* 'clay', *stey* 'steep', and *wey* 'way'.

6.2.5 *Aiberdeen Univairsitie Scots Leid Quorum* recommendation

The *Aiberdeen Univairsitie Scots Leid Quorum* and Allan (1995) suggested ⟨y⟩ and ⟨i-e⟩ in *ay* 'yes' *ky*, 'cows', *dry* and *fwe* differing from the diphthong spelt

⟨y⟩ and ⟨y-e⟩ in *gyte* 'mad', *mynd* 'mind', *nyne* 'nine', and *wyfe* 'wife'. Word-initial and -final ⟨ey⟩ was also suggested in words such as *eyle* 'oil', *eydent* 'diligent', *cley* 'clay', *pey* 'pay', and *wey* 'way'.

6.2.6 *SLD* recommendation

SLD differentiated the diphthongs 8a, 10, 1 short /əi/ and long /aɪ/,[49] suggesting spellings such as *gyte* 'mad', *byke* 'wasp's nest', *jine* 'join', *wife*, *pint* 'point', and *gey* 'very' for the short diphthong and *kye* 'cows', *guise*, and *rise* for the long diphthong. In the headword list based upon the contents of the *Essential Scots Dictionary* the same tendency was indicated in words such as *agley* 'squint', *aside* 'beside', *aweys*[50] 'everywhere' along with *ay(e)* 'yes' and *aye* 'always', the former perhaps indicating a preferred differentiation of the two as *ay* 'yes' and *aye* 'always'.[51]

6.2.7 Robinson's recommendation

Robinson's (1997) proposals were based or correspondences with Standard English, suggesting ⟨y⟩ in words such as *mynn* 'mind' and provided spellings such as *syne* 'ago', *gye* 'very', *tryst* but also *dive*, *drive*, *ride*, and *side* and also in words such as *bine/bynn* 'bind' (v.) where vowel 15 would be usual in Scots (c.f. Gregg 1958). Interestingly, no occurrences of that diphthongization was indicated where Standard English cognates usually have ⟨oi⟩[52] (vowel 10), though Gregg (1958) gives [bəil] 'boil' (n.) and Braidwood (1964: 62–63) adds [dʒəin] 'join' and [spəil] 'spoil'.

> Another possible alteration in linguistic habits may have been brought about by a conscious or unconscious rejection of certain pronunciations which had both been typical of northern and southern Hiberno-English. Industrialization increased the North's prosperity and its links with England and resulting political events began to polarize what had at one time been a relatively homogenous country. This brought into being what may be described as a "Northern consciousness", probably in the last quarter of the nineteenth century. This may have well led to a repudiation of forms such as /aɪ/ in *join* […] (Connolly 1981: 405)

---

49 See https://web.archive.org/web/20061015063228if_/http://www.scotsdictionaries .org.uk/ScotsSpellingGrammar.htm, accessed 2021-10-30.

50 This is an 'eye dialect' running together of two words, *aw* and *weys* 'all ways'.

51 https://web.archive.org/web/20061015063701/http://www.scotsdictionaries.org.uk /HeadWordList/A.html, accessed 2021-10-30. In the 2004 ESD the headwords are *a weys*, *a'weys* 'in all directions' (s.v. *a'*); *agley*, *aglee* (p. 2); *aside* (p. 3); *ay*, *aye* 'yes'; *aye*, *ay* 'always' (p. 4).

52 See Johnston (1997: 495–6).

6.2.8 *Scots Spelling Comatee* recommendation

The *Scots Spelling Comatee* recommended internal ⟨y⟩ in words peculiar to or with a connotation peculiar to Scots such as *wynd*, *syne* 'ago', *tyne* 'lose', *tyke* 'dog', *wyfe* 'wife', *byde* 'remain', *fyle* 'defile', in those words where Standard English cognates have ⟨**oi**⟩ (vowel 10) such as *jyne* 'join' and *pynt* 'point' and to indicate the diphthong in *mynd* 'mind', *kynd* 'kind', and *rynd* 'rind' etc. along with *eydent* 'diligent', *gey* 'very', and *kye* 'cows'.

6.2.9 Discussion of vowel 1

Traditionally vowel 1 (long and short) was usually represented by either ⟨i-e⟩ or ⟨y-e⟩, the latter in words which were apparently "particularly" Scots such as *blithe* 'cheerful', *bide* 'stay', *fire*, and *wife*; *byre* 'cow shed', *dyke* 'wall', *hyne* 'far off', *kye* 'cows', and *syne* 'ago',[53] arguably making any other innovations redundant. However, ⟨i⟩ may represent vowel 1 before consonant clusters, particularly ⟨**nd**⟩ and ⟨i-e⟩ in words such as *hind* 'farm-servant', *kind*, *mind*, *mint* 'to intend', *rind* 'hoarfrost', and *strind* 'lineage' but also vowel 15 /ɪ/ in words such as *ahint* 'behind', *blind*, *find*, *flint*, *hinder*, *lint* 'flax', *rind* 'tallow', and *strind* 'streamlet'.[54] The use of ⟨y⟩ would perhaps make the diphthongized pronunciation clearer giving *hynd*, *kynd*, *mynd*, *mynt*, *rynd*, and *strynd*, etc.

2. *e* appears in combination with another vowel to indicate a diphthong: (1) *ei*, *ey* [ei, əi], e.g. *fey*, *gey*, *pey*; *eident*, *gleid*, and, in s.Sc., *key*, *mei* (me); (2) *ie*, *ye* [ɑe], usually in words common to Sc. and Eng., e.g. *lie*, *pie*, *cried*; also *fye* (ne.Sc. form of *whey*), *kye*. (SND III: 192 s.v. "E")

3. as the diphthong developed mostly from O.E. *ī*, *ȳ*, O.N. *í*, *ý*, O.Fr. *i*, viz. [əi, s.Sc. ëi], written *i-e*, *y-e*, †*ay*, †*ey*, but finally, and in n.Sc. before voiced fricatives, [ɑe] as in *buy*, *dry*, KYE, and among old speakers in n.Sc. in a rounded form [ʌi] as in *bide*, *hoyne* s.v. HYNE, *mine*, *five*, *pipe* [bʌid, mʌin, etc.] (SND V: 246 s.v. "I")

in stressed syllables as a diphthong developed chiefly from O.E. *ī*, *ȳ*, O.N. *í*, *ý*, O.Fr. *i*, sounded [əi, s.Sc. ɛi], but finally in monosyllables and, esp. in m.Sc., before *r* and voiced fricatives as [ɑe], in such words as BY, *dry*, KYE, *my*, BYRE, FLYTE, FYKE, HYTHE, KYLE, SYBOW, TYNE, WYTE, etc. This coincides in most cases with *i* in similar positions (see I, letter, **3.**) and alternates

---

53 All headword forms in the SND and frequent spellings in DOST.
54 All headword forms in the SND..

arbitrarily with it and occas. with *ei-* in spelling, *y* being thought of as gen. more archaic, e.g. *byde*, BIDE, *pyne*, PINE, *tyke*, TIKE, *quhyte*, WHITE, *ydent*, EIDENT, *ingyne*, INGINE. *y* also develops from Mid.Eng. *oi, ui,* unrounded as in *jyner*, joiner, *dytt*, DOIT, *n.*[1], *myen*, MOYEN. (SND X: 246 s.v. "Y")

The choice between ⟨**i-e**⟩ or ⟨**y-e**⟩, perhaps being dependent on a judicious decision as to whether a word is considered "particularly" Scots or not.

6.2.10 Discussion of vowel 8a

Root-final vowel 8a originally had the same realisation as vowel 8 /e/. However, by the Middle Scots period vowel 8a became diphthongized to /əi/, though traditionally represented by ⟨**-ay**⟩, still indicated in the usual pronunciation of the name MacKay, which to a modern reader could be interpreted as /e/. Here an alternative grapheme ⟨**-ey**⟩, offers itself in words such as *gey* 'very' and *quey* 'heifer', which in a regularized orthography could also be applied to words such as *Mey* 'May', *pey* 'pay', and *wey* 'way' etc.[55] making any other innovations redundant. Words such as *day, lay,* and *say*[56] retained the original vowel /e/ (see §6.4).

Some suggested differentiating *ay* 'yes' and *aye* '(always', and that seems to be fairly well established in traditional literature.

The spelling of this and the preceding word in Sc. is irregular, but *ay* = yes, and *aye* = always, seem to predominate. Both words in Sc. are markedly diphthongal but not identical in pronunciation. *N.E.D.* and *Un. Eng. Dict.* prefer *ay* = always, and *aye* = yes, the first of which rhymes with the *ay* series of Eng. words like *say, day,* etc., while the second does not. The *Concise Eng. Dict.* spells *ay* = yes, and *aye* = ever, always.] (SND I: 109 s.v. "AYE")

6.2.11 Discussion of vowel 10

Vowel 10 was traditionally represented by ⟨**oi**⟩, which to a modern reader could be interpreted as /oi/, /ɔi/, /oe/.

As in Eng. this diphthong came to be pronounced [əi] in the 16th c. and this has remained in Sc. when the sound returned to [ɔi] in Eng. in the 18th c. (SND VI: 455 s.v. "O")

---

55 The spellings cited may also be found in DOST.
56 All headword forms in the SND.

However, the traditional graphemes ⟨**i-e**⟩ and ⟨**y-e**⟩ offer themselves as alternatives. The SND preferred ⟨**i-e**⟩ as in the headword forms such as *avide* 'avoid', *bile* 'boil', *jint* 'joint', and *sile* 'soil' but *anoint, join, point, toil,* and *voice.*

Depending on how past tenses are formed (see §7.3) the options ⟨**i-e**⟩ and ⟨**y-e**⟩ raise issues of clarity. The form ⟨**i-e**⟩ when applied in words such as *bile* 'boil' and *jine* 'join' might pose morphemic problems when forming the past tense in ⟨**-t**⟩, resulting in clumsy *bilet* or *bilt* and *jinet* or *jint* (the latter indicating vowel 15), alternatively *bile't* and *jine't* unless ⟨**-d**⟩ was used giving *biled* and *jined*. The alternative ⟨**y-e**⟩ would perhaps provide clearer, giving either *bylt*[57] or *byled* and *jynt* or *jyned*. The forms *jint* 'joint' and *pint* 'point' may also indicate vowel 15, the alternatives *jynt* and *pynt* avoiding that. Other innovations are arguably redundant but a judicious choice may be necessary word-initially the SND using both ⟨**ey-**⟩ and ⟨**i-e**⟩ in the headwords *eyntment* 'ointment', rather than *intment*, and *ile* 'oil', though even *eyl* suggests itself. Similarly, should it be *eident*[58] 'diligent' suggesting vowel 2, or, *ident* or *eydent* ['əidənt]?

6.3 VOWELS 2, 11, AND 3

Vowels 2 and 11 (root-final) are identical in all dialects except Southern Scots and Ulster dialects influenced by it, where vowel 11 is usually diphthongized to /əi/. In Ulster, when final, /e/ may also occur.

> [...] **ɛi** is heard in Sth. Sc. in final position, where **i** is the rule in Mid. Sc. [...] (Grant and Dixon 1921: 57)

> [...] for Old English *ea* before [ç] or [x] Scots has [iː]. Thus Scots has *Hieland* [...] where English has *Highland*. Before [g] Old English *ēō* gives [iː] in Scots, producing *fleeing* [...] as the Scottish equivalent of *flying* and also *dree* 'endure' [...] from Old English *drēōgan* [...] (Tulloch 1980: 185)

> Its most common spelling in [Older] Scots is ⟨eCe⟩ medially and ⟨e⟩ finally, though ⟨eeC⟩ and the Norman influenced ⟨eiC⟩ are nearly as common from the earliest manuscripts, and even ⟨ie⟩ may appear this early in words that have this spelling now in standard English, such as *thief, priest, field, shield, siege* [...] (Johnston 1997a: 71)

---

57 Elision of final ⟨**-e**⟩ is common practice when adding word final morphemes, cf. *come* ⟩ *coming.*

58 The SND headword form.

The diphthongisation […] after /w ʍ/, so that *wheen* becomes *fyne*, is the most restricted of the various Post-Velar Diphthongisation rules affecting front vowel classes in the north-east. (Johnston 1997b: 456)

The bulk of the Scots Planters are known to have come from the west of Scotland (West Central and South-West Scots: both are Central dialects, with the addition of lawless elements expelled from the Borders (Southern Scots). (Macafee 2001: 121)

Scots also retained vowel 2 in many words of Latinate origin where that became diphthongized in Standard English.

Words of Romance origin retain this vowel [i] in Sc. (Grant and Dixon 1921: 41)

[…] which, with lengthening, produces *ceevil*, as in Scots and Ulster dialect […] (Braidwood 1964: 53)

6.3.1 *Scots Style Sheet* recommendation

The *Scots Style Sheet* suggested ⟨e-e⟩, ⟨ee⟩, ⟨ei⟩, ⟨ie⟩, and ⟨i⟩ "according to old usage" but were clearly also assuming many words with vowel 3 also belonged to this class. Examples given were *heed, deed*,[59] *ee* 'eye', *yestreen* 'yesterday evening' *die, hie* 'high', *ambition, king* and *tradition*.

6.3.2 Purves' recommendation

Purves (1979) suggested ⟨ee⟩, ⟨ei⟩, and ⟨ie⟩ where it "is the established usage in common with English" (p.66) although his intention was to minimize the use of that digraph "borrowed from English" (p.64), examples of such included ⟨ee⟩ in *leek* and *been* but also *ee* 'eye', *leeve* 'live' (v.), and *wee* 'small'. Purves also assumed many words with vowel 3 belonged here, suggesting internal ⟨ei⟩ in those and words such as *reik* 'smoke', *seik* 'sick', *steik* 'stitch', and *theik* 'thatch', and that this was also employed in Latinate words such as *releigion* 'religion' and *poseition* 'position' etc. Word-final ⟨ie⟩ was suggested in words such as *die, drie* 'endure', *flie* 'fly', *hie* 'high', Purves also suggesting it for "words with identical pronunciations and different meanings" (p. 67) such as *bien* 'comfortable', *spier* 'enquire', and *fier* 'companion'.[60]

---

59   The examples given *deed* and *heed* , with vowel 2, contrast with *deid* 'dead' and *heid* 'head' with vowel 3, though no explanation was given as to why.

60   Contrasting the last two with words with vowel 3 *speir* 'spear' and *feir* 'fear'.

6.3.3 McClure's recommendation

McClure (1980) suggested ⟨**ei**⟩ on the grounds of its being well established from Middle Scots but that applied equally to this and vowel 3 at the time (Aitken 2002: 57, 76, 100).

6.3.4 *Scots Language Society* recommendation

The *Scots Language Society* (1985) suggested ⟨**ee**⟩, ⟨**ei**⟩, and ⟨**ie**⟩, retaining ⟨**ee**⟩ where it is firmly established in, for example, *ee* 'eye', with ⟨**ei**⟩ word-internally, also allocating this to many words with vowel 3 and words of Latinate origin which retained this vowel and ⟨**ie**⟩ word-finally in monosyllabic words such as *brie* 'liquid', *die*, *gie* 'give', and *grie* 'agree' etc.

6.3.5 *Aiberdeen Univairsitie Scots Leid Quorum* recommendation

The *Aiberdeen Univairsitie Scots Leid Quorum* (1995) suggested ⟨**ei**⟩ internally and ⟨**ee**⟩ word-finally including some words with vowel 3.[61]

6.3.6 *SLD* recommendation

SLD suggested ⟨**ei**⟩, ⟨**ie**⟩, and ⟨**ee**⟩, giving the examples *dreich* 'dreary', *scrieve* 'scribble', and *flee* 'fly'.[62] Those were also applied to many words with vowel 3, for example, *heid* 'head' and *deef* 'deaf' in Macleod and Cairns 1993 p.vii. In some words of Latinate origin which retained this vowel ⟨**ee**⟩ was suggested. The headword list based upon the contents of the *Essential Scots Dictionary* provided forms such as *abreed* 'apart', *abreist*[63] 'abreast', *ajee* 'to one side', *atweel* 'certainly', *atween* 'between', and in Latinate words both *airtificial* and *artifeecial* 'artificial' along with *ambeetious* 'ambitious', *anxeeitie* 'anxiety', and *appeteet* 'appetite'.[64]

6.3.7 Robinson's recommendation

Robinson (1997) did not make specific recommendations but tended to use ⟨**ee**⟩ or ⟨**ae**⟩, perhaps, to represent the /e/ realization which Robinson claims may occur in some dialects.[65] Robinson also used ⟨**ei**⟩ in words such as *bein* 'been', *eild* 'age', and *heich* 'high', ⟨**ie**⟩ being used in words such as

---

61 Although here ⟨**ea**⟩ was often recommended.

62 See https://web.archive.org/web/20061015063228if_/http://www.scotsdictionaries .org.uk/ScotsSpellingGrammar.htm, accessed 2021-10-30.

63 This may indicate vowel 3 but the SND only lists [brist Sc., but ne. + brijt] under *breist* from Anglo–Saxon *brēost*.

64 https://web.archive.org/web/20061015063701/http://www.scotsdictionaries.org.uk /HeadWordList/A.html, accessed 2021-10-30. The 2004 ESD does not have the headword *abreed* or the variant *airtificial*.

65 No evidence for that was found in the material consulted, except for *been* [ben] and *seen* [sen] in Ballymoney and *eel* [el] and *heel* [hel] in Newtownards in the LAS Vol. 3 (Mather 1986).

bield 'shelter', *gie* 'give', and *nieve* 'fist', while ⟨ee⟩ also occasionally occurred in words with vowel 3. Robinson (p.33) assumed that traditional spellings in Latinate words such as *meenister* 'minister' as used by Ulster writers were the result of their simply following "Scots" convention and probably assumed the current Mid Ulster English realization to be "Ulster Scots".[66]

6.3.8 *Scots Spelling Comatee* recommendation

The *Scots Spelling Comatee* (2000) recommended ⟨ei⟩ in words traditionally pronounced "ee" in Scots but "i" in Standard English, giving examples such as *eimage* 'image', *tradeition* 'tradition', *seik* 'sick', *steik* 'stitch', and *weik* 'wick', and ⟨ee⟩ in identical and close cognates and word-finally,[67] while ⟨ie⟩ was recommended in identical Standard English cognates. Many words with vowel 3 were included here but the recommended spelling was usually ⟨ea⟩ or ⟨ei⟩. None of the recommendations clearly identified the underlying phonemes of vowels 2 and 11, and none, except Allan, (1995: 88) mention the Southern Scots diphthongization of word-final vowel 11.[68]

None clearly identify the underlying vowel 3 in many words with /i/, although Allan (1995: 88) commented on the Fife realization [deːd] for *deid* 'dead'.

6.3.9 Discussion of vowel 2

For vowel 2 various traditional graphemes offer themselves: ⟨ee⟩, ⟨e-e⟩, ⟨ie⟩, and ⟨ei⟩, though closer analysis of headword forms in the SND shows that their application was not completely random. Certainly ⟨ee⟩ predominated,[69] in words shared with Standard English, but also in many cognates where Standard English has ⟨e⟩ such as *freet* 'fret', *weel* 'well', and *weet* 'wet' and in Latinate words such as *bapteese* 'baptize', *ceevil* 'civil', *leeberal* 'liberal', *leeshence* 'licence', *obleege* 'oblige', *peety* 'pity', and *speerit* 'spirit'. The digraph ⟨ee⟩ also occurred in words such as *abreed* 'abroad', *beek* 'bask', *beet* 'repair', *breer* 'briar', *cleek* 'hook', *deek* 'peep', *leed* 'language' and *neep* 'turnip'. The familiar ⟨e-e⟩ also occurred, in words shared with Standard English but also in words such as *fere* 'comrade'. The grapheme ⟨ie⟩ seemed to prevail in words shared with Standard English such as *chief*, *grief*, and *field*

66 Fenton (2000) provides examples such as *artyfeecial, conteenyal, obleege, poseetion* etc. Fenton also provides examples with ⟨i⟩ where /i/ would be expected, for example, *minister* and Gregg (1958) usually has /ɛ̈/ in such words, although this may simply be a result of a shift towards Standard (Ulster) English.

67 With familiar exceptions such as *gie* 'give' and *hie* 'high'.

68 Giving as an example *tea*. This is a late introduction to the language, the ⟨ea⟩ having no etymological relevance. Originally [teː], and still so in many dialects, then [tiː] and hence [tɔi] in Southern Scots.

69 An anglicized spelling that appeared late in the Middle Scots Period. (Aitken 2002: lvi)

but also before /f/, /l/, and /v/ in words such as *bield* 'shelter', *bonspiel* 'curling match', *chield* 'fellow', *lief* 'beloved', *nieve* 'fist', *scrieve* 'scribble', *shiel* 'a hut', and *stieve* 'rigid'. The grapheme ⟨ei⟩ seemed to prevail before /x/, /r/, and /st/ in words such as *dreich* 'dreary', *heich* 'high', *neist* 'next', *skreich* 'shriek', *skeich* 'frisky', *sneist* 'supercilious', *speir* 'inquire', *sweir* 'reluctant', and *weir* 'guard'. The ⟨ei⟩ in *deil* 'devil' perhaps derives from an apostrophe-less *de'il*.

(2) (a) In an accented open syllable followed by a mute *e*, *e* has the sound [iː] as in Eng., e.g. *bene, bere, dede, eme, fere, tene*, but is frequently shortened with change of quality, esp. in em.Sc.(a). (SND III: 192 s.v. "E")

(3) *ee* [iː], often as a variant spelling for [*ei* or *ie*] below […] and in Gen.Sc. for Romance [i], e.g. *eemage, feenish, leeshance, obteen, peety*. (SND III: 192 s.v. "E")

Since the 18th c. the spelling *ee* or, less commonly, *ie* has been largely adopted for this sound; (SND V: 246 s.v. "I")

Many suggested a more rigorous application of the grapheme ⟨ei⟩ on the grounds of its "pedigree" in older Scots, albeit along with the more prevalent ⟨e-e⟩ among others.[70] Since the 18th and 19th centuries the grapheme ⟨ei⟩ has become associated with vowel 3 in words such as *beir* 'bear', *breid* 'bread', *deid* 'dead', *heid* 'head', and *leid* 'lead *n.*'.[71] Wider use of that grapheme for vowel 2 may, for a modern reader, produce somewhat unfamiliar and "complicated" forms such as *heiliegoleirie*, where *heeligoleery* might be easer on the eye and easier to "analyse". A decision to use either ⟨ee⟩, ⟨e-e⟩, ⟨ie⟩, or ⟨ei⟩ may depend on a judicious study of prevailing forms and application of the tendencies described above. The SND certainly provides a guide here, and if a form exists which has been regularly used and conforms to the chosen "rules", its acceptance as the "norm" cannot be dismissed lightly. It cannot be argued that coping with various graphemes for the same sound is beyond the scope of human ingenuity. Most adult English-speakers certainly have no problem with *dead* and *bead* or *bough* and *rough* etc.

---

70 Both ⟨ei⟩ and ⟨e-e⟩, along with ⟨ey⟩, were used in Older Scots. (Aitken 2002: lvi)
71 All the cited examples are given as headword forms in the SND.

6.3.10 Discussion of vowel 11

As vowel 11 only occurs root-final, it poses less of a problem, the traditional form being ⟨**ee**⟩, arguably rendering any innovation redundant.

6.3.11 Discussion of vowel 3

Vowel 3, remained distinct as /ɛi/ in Caithness, but has merged with either vowel 2 or 4, pronounced variously /i/ or /e(ː)/ in other dialects, the choice varying across both dialect and individual words. In Ulster /e/ is common (Braidwood 1964: 58–60) and in some conservative areas /iː/ occurs in what would normally be short environments.[72] In most Scots dialects the pronunciation /ɛː/ may occur before ⟨r⟩.

> With regards to Scots the evidence of the present day Scots dialects, which vary between [eː] and [iː], strongly suggests that Scots was going through the same transition as English at about the same time. In the mid Scots area, the eastern branch north of the Forth has the older [eː] against [iː] south of the Forth. West mid Scots (whence most of the Ulster settlers) has [iː] in all but a few words. Kintyre, where many of the Lowland Scots were settled immediately prior to crossing to Antrim, balances between [eː] and [iː], according to *SND*, but it cites only *chaip, daith* for the [eː] pronunciation against *deif, heid* etc., and this in fact is the position in the west mid Scots of today […] (Braidwood 1964: 60)

> […] J. Wilson, *Lowland Scotch* (London, 1915), has drawn up such a list (p. 39) of items with /e/ for the Stratherne dialect of Perthshire which he later contrasts with the list for the central Ayrshire dialect in his book *The Dialect of Robert Burns as Spoken in Central Ayrshire* (London, 1923). The latter list is almost identical with the comparable items for the SI [Scotch-Irish] dialect of G. [Glenoe] which again underlines the kinship of SI with south-western Scots, specifically Ayrshire and hinterland. (Gregg 1972: 127)

> […] the use of ⟨i⟩ as a diacritic of vowel length in breid and leid. (Scragg 1975: 37)[73]

---

72 This has been found in Scotland as well.
73 Commenting on the orthography in a circa 1520 version of the Lord's Prayer. *Breid* 'bread', *leid* v. 'lead'.

There are several dialect areas in Scotland [...] where the MEAT-
MEET merger has either not taken place or not been completed.
(Harris 1985: 249)

[...] although the predominant spelling, ⟨eCe⟩ medially, ⟨e⟩ finally,
matches that of MEET, ⟨ei⟩ is not so common so early on, becoming
so only in the course of the fifteenth century, while ⟨eeC⟩ is very
rare. Instead, one finds English-like ⟨ea⟩ spellings, especially before
/r/ and labials from the beginning, and ⟨aCe⟩, ⟨aiC⟩ occasionally,
starting in the mid- to late fifteenth century. It seems that ⟨ee/ei⟩
spellings are therefore associated with the /eː/ value traditionally
held by MEET, if not /iː/ itself [...] (Johnston 1997a: 73)

[...] from Standard-like [i(ː)] [...] to [e‑(ː)~ɪ(ː)], [e(ː)] or [ɛ(ː)] [...]
diphthongs like [ɛɪ] or [eɪ] [...] usually resulting from Northern
Diphthongisation, and even [e‑ə~eə] [...] common in North Mid
A and sporadically elsewhere. (Johnston 1997b: 456)

The sequence /er/ from this or any other source undergoes Pre-
Rhotic Vowel Lowering to /ɛr/ in Ulster Scots [...] the /r/ is /ɹ/
in the Irish case [...] (Johnston 1997b: 458)

The *Scots Style Sheet*, Purves (1979), McClure (1980), the *Scots Language
Society*, the *Aiberdeen Univairsitie Scots Leid Quorum* (1995) and the *Scots Spelling
Comatee* failed to identify this vowel as an underlying phoneme.

6.3.12 *Scots Style Sheet* recommendation
The *Scots Style Sheet* allocated individual items to vowels 2 or 4, suggesting
spellings such as ⟨**ei**⟩ in *deid* 'dead' and *heid* 'head' and perhaps ⟨**ai**⟩,
although no specific examples were given.

6.3.13 Purves' recommendation
Purves (1979) allocated individual items to vowels 2 or 4 suggesting
spellings such as ⟨**ei**⟩ *breid* 'bread', *deif* 'deaf', *dreid* 'dread', *heid* 'head' and
threid 'thread', ⟨**ai**⟩ in *daith* 'death' and ⟨**ae**⟩ in *rael* 'real', *baet* 'beat', *claen*
'clean', *chaep* 'cheap', *dael* 'deal' and initially before ⟨**r**⟩ in *aerlie* 'early' and
aern 'earn' etc., Purves commenting that the "infiltration" of ⟨**ea**⟩ "into
Scots has been particularly damaging to Scots orthography" (p.63), citing
precedents in the SND for his alternatives.

6.3.14 McClure's recommendation

No examples of words with this phoneme were cited by McClure (1980).

6.3.15 *Scots Language Society* recommendation

The *Scots Language Society* cited only *deid* 'dead' and it is assumed such words were allocated to either vowel 2, 4 or 8, suggesting ⟨ei⟩ and ⟨ai⟩.

6.3.16 *Aiberdeen Univairsitie Scots Leid Quorum* recommendation

Allan (1995: 88) commented on the Fife realization [deːd] for *deid* 'dead', suggesting ⟨ei⟩ in *heid* 'head' and ⟨ae⟩ in *baet* 'beat', *saet* 'seat', and *aet* 'eat' in words with Standard English cognates in ⟨ea⟩ but ⟨ea⟩ in *plea, plead* and *spear*. The *Aiberdeen Univairsity Scots Leid Quorum* also appeared to allocate items to vowels 2 or 4 suggesting ⟨ae⟩ in the examples *baet* 'beat', *great* 'great', *saet* 'seat', and *aet* 'eat', reserving ⟨ei⟩ for "the sound in *feel*" adding that "words shared with English will be spelt with *ee* or *ea* as is familiar" providing the examples *heid* 'head' and *plead* among others that had an underlying vowel 2 or 11. The spellings *breid* 'bread', *eleivent* 'eleventh', *feart* 'afraid', *meat* but also *maet, pleise* 'please', *saicont* 'second', and *seivin* 'seven' were also suggested in the *Innin* (Lovie, 1995).

6.3.17 *SLD* recommendation

SLD apparently allocated words with this underlying phoneme to vowels 2 or 4, giving such examples as *breid* 'bread', *deid* 'dead', *eat, heid* 'head', *leaf*, and *seat*.[74] Macleod (1996) also includes forms such as *deef* 'deaf' and *mait* 'meat'.

6.3.18 Robinson's recommendation

Robinson (1997) described that on the basis of Standard English ⟨ea⟩, suggesting ⟨ei⟩ in words such as *breid* 'bread', *deid* 'dead', *leiven* 'eleven', *heid* 'head', and *seiven* 'seven', ⟨ee⟩ in *deef* 'deaf', ⟨ai⟩ in *baird* 'beard', *clain* 'clean', *daith* 'death', *mait* 'meat' and ⟨a-e⟩ in *sate* 'seat'.

6.3.19 *Scots Spelling Comatee* recommendation

The *Scots Spelling Comatee* apparently recommended ⟨ea⟩ in Standard English cognates pronounced the same as in Scots giving the example *lean* and apparently ⟨ei⟩ in others. The use of ⟨ae⟩ was suggested for regional variants of words with ⟨ea⟩ in Standard English in words such as *aet* 'eat' and *maet* 'meat'.

---

74   See https://web.archive.org/web/20061015063228if_/http://www.scotsdictionaries
     .org.uk/ScotsSpellingGrammar.htm, accessed 2021-10-30.

6.3.20 Further discussion of vowel 3

The merger of Vowel 3 with either vowel 2 or 4 occurred in the early Scots period[75] and was subsequently written using the graphemes for those vowels. In the 18th and 19th centuries the vowel was traditionally represented by ⟨ea⟩ though occasional forms with ⟨ei⟩ such as *deid* 'dead' and *heid* 'head' occurred, those having gained in popularity by the 20th century.

(2) *ea* [now mostly [iː] but, in Sh., mn.Sc. (b) and em.Sc. (a) and prob. Gen.Sc. in 18th cent., [eː], and in Ags., in certain words, often in association with a front consonant, [eˡː], e.g. *beat, deaf, death.* [...]. This spelling, alternating with the less frequent *ai*, represents mostly, as in Eng., O.E.*ǣ, ēa, ē, e* in open syllables, e.g. *ream, quean, swear, tear, threap*; (SND III: 192 s.v. "E")

(4) *ei* [iː], from O.E. *ǣ* (Anglian *ē*), *ēa, ēo, ē* in open syllables; Gen.Sc. except for conditions under 3 (2), e.g. *breid, deid, deil, dreich, eik, eild, ein* (eyes), *heid, reid*; (SND III: 192 s.v. "E")

The merger of vowel 3 with vowels 2 or 4 makes it difficult for most speakers to identify vowel 3 as an underlying phoneme. The traditional grapheme ⟨ea⟩ theoretically suffices as a marker of the Caithness /ɛi/ and the /i/ or /e/ realization of other dialects, though arguably the influence of Standard English literacy may interfere with such an interpretation, especially where /ɛ/ occurs in such words has *dead, deaf, head* and *thread* etc. Here ⟨ei⟩ certainly offers itself as a less ambiguous alternative, although it is also used in some words with vowel 2. That could certainly also be applied for all occurrences of vowel 3 but may seem unfamiliar to many where the traditional ⟨ea⟩ for /i/ is also familiar from Standard English. Certainly the traditional ⟨ea⟩ could be employed here. The *Scots Spelling Comatee* suggested that those wishing to indicate an /e/ realization could use ⟨ae⟩, as did Philp (Graham 1997: xi), although an unconventional use of that grapheme in an initial or medial position, the grapheme would leave most words, in which it was applied, recognizable. As ⟨ee⟩ is traditionally applied to vowel 2 and 11, its use here would be misleading, and arguably that also applies to ⟨ai⟩, which is usually associated with vowel 8 and to some extent vowel 4. A consistent regularization would imply the use of ⟨ei⟩ for all occurrences of vowel 3, a less radical approach accepting various application of ⟨ei⟩ and ⟨ea⟩ in words such as *beir* 'bear', *breid* 'bread', *deid*

---

75 The usual spelling was ⟨e-e⟩, the mergers with vowel 4 were rarely reflected in spelling. (Aitken 2002: lvi)

'dead', *dreid* 'dread', *heid* 'head' and *leid* 'lead *n.*', and *beal* 'fester', *beard*, *beast*, *cheat*, *dearth* 'dearness', *deave* 'deafen', *east*, *lead v.*, *meal*, *meat*, and *peat*,[76] perhaps with the addition of ⟨**ai**⟩ (or ⟨**ae**⟩) depending on the writer's dialect. Certainly the latter would leave the written form familiar to those acquainted with traditional written Scots.

6.4 VOWELS 4 AND 8

Vowels 4 and 8 have merged in many dialects but were historically /e/ and /eː/, with /ɛ/ also occuring, especially before ⟨**r**⟩ in Scotland. In Ulster it is usually /ɛː/. Conseqently the distinction between the vowels in spelling had broken down where ⟨**a-e**⟩ and ⟨**ae**⟩ final were common for vowel 4 and ⟨**ai**⟩, ⟨**ay**⟩ final, for vowel 8, the latter increasingly used to represent the former, though before the nasals /m/ and /n/ the traditional ⟨**a-e**⟩ spelling survived in words such as *ane*, *ance*, *bane*, *hame*, *lame*, *nane*, and *stane* etc. (Murison 1977: 28-29), also occurring in words such as *face*, *gate*, *hale* and *Pace* etc. In Northern Scots vowel 4 before /n/ is realized /i/, traditionally represented by the cluster ⟨**ane**⟩ (Grant and Dixon 1921: 44).

O.E. ā, which becomes [e] in the other dialects, is diphthongised in this [Southern Scots]. Murray writes the diphthong *i'* representing [ɪə]. The first element is h.fr. half tense and slightly lowered, the second being very weak and often elided in rapid speech—e.g. *blate (modest), baith, braid, claes, drove* (v.), *grope, load* (n.) in *leead treis (shelmonts* or *frame laid on a cart), loaf, rope, soap.*[77] These words might be written *beeath, breead, cleeaz,* etc. [...]

　　O.E. ă in open position also developed into this diphthong—e.g. *made, spade, sale, tale, bake, cake, rake* (n.), *make, shake, lamiter (lame man), name, shame, tame.*[78] This sound was common in Teviotdale c.1870 (see D.S.C.S., pp. 105, 144), and can still be heard from middle-aged and old people in Langholm and Canobie and e.Dmf., but in other districts it is obsolescent or obsolete, as in Jedburgh, where it has been replaced by [è]. (SND I: xxix §97.1–2)

[In Southern Scots] When the word began with a vowel or *h* the stress fell on the second element of the diphthong and a *y* [j] sound was produced instead of *i* [ɪ], as in *yae, yin, ‡yick, ‡yicker, yill, yince, yits, hyim, hyirsch, hyil,*[79] for *one* (adj.), *one* (pron.), *oak, acre, ale, once,*

76　Headword forms in the SND.
77　blɪət, bɪəθ, brɪəd, klɪəz, etc. [Original footnote]
78　mɪəd, sprɪəd, sɪəl (but sail is seːl), etc. [Original footnote]
79　jeː, jɪn, jɪk, jɪkər, jɪl, jɪns, jɪts, hjɪm, hjɪrʃ, hjɪl. [Original footnote]

oats, home, hoarse, whole. Teviotdale has *yen, yek,* etc., in the above. (SND I: xxix §97.4)

In the central dialects at the present day there is a clear distinction between the vowels of *sale, tale, stane, late* &c., and *sail, tail, stain, wait.* The former is a close *e*-sound, tending towards *ee* (as in Eng. *See*), which I have not been able to find in any other language. The latter is an open vowel similar to that in Eng. *fair.* Although dialect speakers unconsciously make the distinction, it is not audible to every observer. The late Sir James Wilson, who made a special study of several Scottish dialects, once asked me, 'Do you make any difference between the vowel of the demonstrative *thae* (those) and the pronoun *they*?' 'Certainly', I said, 'they are quite distinct.' 'So my brother says,' he replied, 'but I can't hear the difference'; nor did he attempt to distinguish them in his various books. The distinction is also ignored in Grant and Main Dixon's 'Manual of Modern Scots'. In Wright's 'English Dialect Grammar' it is recognized (§9), but the close vowel is incorrectly equated with the French *é* in *été,* and in the pronouncing index there is much confusion between the two sounds.

The distinction also holds in such forms as *sae* (so) and *say, gae* (go) and *gay, strae* (straw) and *stray.* Before *k,* however, the open vowel appears where the close sound would be normal, as in *bake, cake,* &c., and in the past tense of strong verbs of the *ride* class e.g. *rade, drave, rase,* while other words of similar form, as *lade* (mill-stream), *lave* (remainder) have the close vowel. The interchangeable spelling in older Scottish makes it impossible to trace the exact history of the two sounds in the various dialects. (Craigie 1969b: 4)[80]

The sequence /er/ from this or any other source undergoes Pre-Rhotic Vowel Lowering to /ɛr/ in Ulster Scots and Glaswegian, and sporadically elsewhere; the /r/ is /ɹ/ in the Irish case and a pharyngealised vowel in the Scottish one, either one of which could conceivably foster lowering. (Johnston 1997b: 458)

[...] *Wame* undergoes Post-Velar Dissimilation quite regularly, with little lexical conditioning, resulting in transfer to BITE. In Mid-Northern dialects, and especially in Mid-Northern A, other consonants besides a preceding /w/ can trigger the change,

80   The forms *lade* and *lave* may be forms of *lead* 'to conduct, guide, etc.' and *leave* merged from vowel 3. The form *drave* may be merged from vowel 7.

including a dark /l/, so that *clothes* is [kɫëɪz~kɫəɪz~kɫʌɪz]. (Johnston
1997b: 461)

[...] *bairn* has [ɛːə], which matches MATE + /r/, while *start* varies
with the same vowel in Down, but /ɜɹ/ in Antrim [...] (Johnston
1997b: 487)

[...] [e] in Antrim [...] in Down [e(ː)] is found everywhere but
before /r/ and finally where [...] /ɛː/ appears [...] this, of course,
is also an extended Pre-Rhotic Lowering Rule [...] (Johnston
1997b: 462)

6.4.1 *Scots Style Sheet* recommendation
The *Scots Style Sheet* does not distinguish the vowels, suggesting ⟨**ae**⟩ and
⟨**ay**⟩, apparently word-finally otherwise ⟨**ai**⟩ and ⟨**a-e**⟩, apparently following traditional practice, giving examples such as *ae, ane* 'one', *ay* 'yes', *aye*
'always', *blae* 'blue-grey', *fray, frae* 'from', *hain* 'store', *cairt* 'cart', *maister*
'master', *bane* 'bone', and *hame* 'home'.

6.4.2 Purves' recommendation
Purves (1979) does not distinguish the vowels suggesting ⟨**ae**⟩, ⟨**ay**⟩, ⟨**ai**⟩,
and ⟨**a-e**⟩ mentioning that ⟨**ai**⟩ is not used terminally,[81] giving examples
such as *ay* 'yes' and *aye* 'always', *fray, say, blae, brae* 'hillside', *wae* 'woe', *graen*
'groan', *maen* 'moan', *braid* 'broad', *haill* 'whole', *nairrae* 'narrow', *alane*
'alone', *bane* 'bone' *hame* 'home', *stane* 'stone', and *wame* 'belly'. Purves also
suggested ⟨**e**⟩ for the realization /ɛ(ː)/ in some dialects in words such as
gether 'gather', *herm* 'harm', *hert* 'heart', *Merch* 'March', and *trekkil* 'treacle'.

6.4.3 McClure's recommendation
McClure (1980) distinguished vowels 4 and 8, suggesting ⟨**ae**⟩ and ⟨**ai**⟩
respectively, commenting that vowel 8 may merge with vowel 4.

6.4.4 *Scots Language Society* recommendation
The *Scots Language Society* suggested ⟨**ae**⟩, ⟨**ai**⟩, or ⟨**a-e**⟩ giving examples
such as *maen* 'moan', *baith* 'both', *dwaible* 'pliant', *hain* 'store', *sair* 'sore', *bane*
'bane', *hame* 'home', *vase* and *ay* 'yes', *aye* 'always', and *brae* 'hillside'.

6.4.5 *Aiberdeen Univairsitie Scots Leid Quorum* recommendation
The *Aiberdeen Univairsitie Scots Leid Quorum* did not distinguish the vowels,
suggesting following the traditional spellings ⟨**ai**⟩, ⟨**a-e**⟩ initially and

81   Except in *thai* 'they' apparently culled from Middle Scots.

internally and ⟨ae⟩, ⟨ay⟩ finally giving such examples as *faither* 'father' *sair* 'sore', *sklate* 'slate', *say*, and *sae* 'so' etc. Allan (1995) commented on the 'disagreement' of the vowel value in Central dialects, citing the examples *hairt* 'heart' and *aiss* 'ash(es)', using ⟨**ai**⟩ as the default.[82]

6.4.6 *SLD* recommendation

SLD did not distinguish the vowels, suggesting ⟨**ae**⟩ word-finally, and otherwise ⟨**ai**⟩ or ⟨**a-e**⟩ in examples such as *brae* 'hillside', *thae* 'those', *sair* 'sore' and *hame* 'home'. Macleod (1996) included such forms as *been* 'bone' and *steen* 'stone' for the North-eastern realizations in the cluster traditionally written ⟨**ane**⟩, something apparently justified on the basis that ⟨**-a-**⟩ would not do for both sounds in Central *stane* and North-eastern *steen* (Macleod 2000: 66), although such a realization is predicable, only occurring in the cluster ⟨**ane**⟩. Such predictable North-eastern realizations were also added as variants in the headword list based upon the contents of the *Essential Scots Dictionary* providing examples such as *aince/eence*[83] 'once' but *ane/een*[84] 'one', *alane/aleen* 'alone', *anely*[85] 'only' but not *eenly*, *anerly* 'only' but no *eenerly*.[86] Interestingly the "eye dialect" *agane* [87] 'again' [əˈgen, əˈgɛn, əˈgɪn Sc.; əˈgɪən s.Sc.] (SND I: 27 s.v. "AGAIN") was provided.

6.4.7 Robinson's recommendation

Robinson's (1997) suggestions were based or correspondences to Standard English suggesting ⟨**ai**⟩, ⟨**ae**⟩, and ⟨**a-e**⟩ in words such as *airm* 'arm', *cairt* 'cart', *pairt* 'part', *shairp* 'sharp', *fae* 'foe', *sae* 'so', *tae* 'toe', *ane* 'one',[88] *bane* 'bane', *hame* 'hame', and *stane* 'stone'.

6.4.8 *Scots Spelling Comatee* recommendation

The *Scots Spelling Comatee* did not distinguish the vowels, recommending ⟨**ai**⟩ initially and medially and mainly ⟨**ae**⟩ finally, giving examples such as *ain* (ones 'own', *airt* 'direction', *hain* 'store', *pairt* 'part', *brae* 'hillside', *strae* 'straw', and *thae* 'those'.

---

82 SND has headword *hert* [hɛrt, hert] and *ass* with, among others, possible [es, ɛs].
83 *Aince* was the headword along with other phonetic spellings such as *yince* and *wance*.
84 *Ane* was the headword form, along with other phonetic spellings such as *yin* and *wan*.
85 This may simply be a modern writer's calque on English 'only'. The only occurrences in the SND are in the 2005 supplement, the traditional form being *anerly*.
86 https://web.archive.org/web/20061015063701/http://www.scotsdictionaries.org.uk /HeadWordList/A.html, accessed 2021-10-30. The 2004 ESD gives the headwords *aince*, *yince*, *wance*; *alane*, *aleen* (p. 2); *ane*, *yin*, *een* (p. 3); *anely*, *eenly*, *anerly*, and *eenerly* are not given, but both *again*, *agane* are (p. 2).
87 The spelling *agane* may suggest a Northern realization [əˈgin] cf. *ane*, *bane* and *stane* etc.
88 Robinson also suggested *yin*.

6.4.9 Discussion of vowels 4 and 8

Traditionally ⟨a-e⟩, ⟨ai⟩, ⟨ae⟩, and ⟨ay⟩ were variously used for those vowels.

3. [e] Same sound as in the Scottish educated pronunciation of *fate*, Fr. *fé*. This sound occurs when *a* is followed by a consonant + a vowel, generally *e*. Ex. *bane* (bone), *pape* (pip), *sape* (soap), *gane* (gone), *rade* (rode), *rape* (rope), *wale* (choose). (SND I: 1 s.v. "A")

2. It is joined with *i* or *y*, the latter being used generally in final position, to denote [e], [e¹], [è]. Ex. *rair* (roar), *airmy*, *laits* (morals), *gait* (a goat), *quait* (quiet), *flay* (frighten). (SND I: 1 s.v. "A")
5. It is joined with *e* to indicate [e], [e¹], [è] and [ɛ], long or short. Ex. *tae* (toe), *maet* (meet),[89] *blae*, *brae*, *haet* (whit). (SND I: 1 s.v. "A")

3. *e* is found in various vowel digraphs: (1) *ae*: (i) [e: Gen.Sc., but e¹: em.Sc.(a)], representing usually O.E. and O.N. *ā* in final syllables, e.g. *blae*, *frae*, *strae*, *faem*; (SND V: 192 s.v. "E")

Traditional writing did not seem to use ⟨a-e⟩ for vowel 4 and ⟨ai⟩ initially and medially for vowel 8 as systematically as the examples given in Aitken (1984: 95) imply: *ake* 'oak', *ate* 'oat', *bate* 'boat', *hale* 'whole', *hame* 'home', *late*, *mare* 'more', *pale*, *sape* 'soap', *stane* 'stone' and *bait*, *braid* 'broad', *hail*, *pail*, *pair*. Although *ake* and *ate* appeared as alternative forms in the SND,[90] the most common in citations were forms with ⟨ai⟩. The other's headword forms reflected Aitken, except *bait* 'boat', *mair* 'more', and *saip* 'soap', with ⟨ai⟩ and both *hale* or *hail* 'whole' apparently equally common. It is likely that the prevalent traditional forms simply reflected the Middle Scots convention rather than a modification of standard English along the lines of replacing ⟨o-e⟩ with ⟨a-e⟩ in words such as *ane* 'one', *bane* 'bone', *hale* (whole), *hame* 'home', *lane* 'lone', *stane* 'stone'[91] or ⟨ai⟩ in words such as *braid*, *mair* and *saip*.[92] One or the other of those vowels has also been allocated by some in Latinate words such as *aixercise* 'exercise', *maimber* 'member', *maimorie* 'memory' and *praiciuss* 'precious', although that is in fact vowel 16. Both ⟨ae⟩ and ⟨ay⟩ usually occurred finally in words such as *brae* 'hillside', *flae* 'flea', *frae* 'from', *gae* 'go', *sae* 'so', *day*, *lay*, and *say*, with the established

---

89   Typo in the SND for "meat".
90   Along with *yik* and *yit*, representing Southern Scots realizations.
91   All of which are headwords in DOST for vowel 4. (See Aitken 2002: lvi)
92   Both ⟨ai⟩ and ⟨a-e⟩ forms occur in DOST. The latter reflecting the merger of vowel 8 with vowel 4.

exception of *claes* 'clothes',[93] their application, apparently ⟨ae⟩ for an underlying vowel 4 and ⟨ay⟩ for vowel 8.

As the initial and medial use of ⟨a-e⟩ for vowel 4 and ⟨ai⟩ for vowel 8 along with the word-final use of ⟨ae⟩ for vowel 4 and ⟨ay⟩ for vowel 8 is unambiguous, even in the cluster ⟨ane⟩,[94] which can then unambiguously also represent the Northern realization /in/. The initial /jɪ/ in Southern dialects, being environmentally conditioned, is predictably mastered by native speakers who have it. That would be in keeping with traditional practice, though the choice of grapheme may depend on a judicious study of prevailing forms and application of the tendencies suggested above. The SND certainly provides a guide here, and if a form exists which has been regularly used and conforms to the chosen "rules", its acceptance as the "norm" cannot be dismissed lightly.

6.5 VOWELS 5 AND 18

Vowels 5 and 18, usually /oː/ and /o/~/ɔ/, although vowel 5 often merges with vowel 18 in Central and Southern dialects and vowel 18 often merges with vowel 5 in other dialects.

> In Scots, especially mid and south Scots (whence most of the Ulster Scots) *ŭ* is normally tense *o* and can be written *oa* [...] G. B. Adams records the Scots tense *o* for Antrim, but (from the point of view of Scots usage) inconsistently. Thus he gives *froth* [froːθ], *lost* [loːst] but *frost* [frɔst]. If the [ɔ] forms are not intrusions from a non-Scots dialect then they illustrate the type of variable quantity discussed above. (Braidwood 1964: 64)

> Scots *oa* in words such as *froath* (= froth). This was not traditionally shown in any special way in Scots, and only appears sporadically in writing. (Macafee 1996: xxi)

> The North Mid group goes further and turns long mid vowels to diphthongs after /w/ [...] (Johnston 1997a: 59)

> Merger with COT is more or less complete in vernacular Scots, except in Argyll, Bute and adjacent parts of north Ayrshire, extreme south Ayrshire, Wigtownshire and Ulster on one side, and central Perthshire, north central Fife and parts of Berwickshire on the other. (Johnston 1997b: 480)

---

93 All examples occurring as headword forms in the SND.

94 This may take precedence over morphemic spellings in, for example, *gae* 'go' < *gane* 'gone', which in central and southern dialects is [geːn] and in northern dialects [giːn].

In the south-west, in Galloway and Ulster, there is a trend towards lower and lower isolative forms as one moves away from the Central Belt, and thus, a decreased likelihood of the COT/COAT merger [...] In the rest of Gallovidian, and in most Antrim dialects, Mid [ɔ(ː)] is the rule, without merger except before /x/ and final /r/, as in Caithness. In County Down, [ɒ(ː)] is the majority form except pre-rhotically, and unrounded low [ä(ː)-ä̈(ː)] becomes regular, not somewhat lexically conditioned as in the rest of Scotland, around labials. The forms approach the usual Hiberno-English [ɑ(ː)] [...] as one goes southwards. There is something of a tendency to have raising to /o/ before /g n ŋ/, and for [ɔː] to appear as the reflex for both COT and COAT before /k x/ in Gallovidian and Ulster Scots. (Johnston 1997b: 483)

6.5.1 *Scots Style Sheet* recommendation

The *Scots Style Sheet* did not mention those vowels, the assumption being that traditional practice should be followed, usually ⟨**oa**⟩ or ⟨**o-e**⟩ for vowel 5 and ⟨**o**⟩ for vowel 18.

6.5.2 Purves' recommendation

Purves (1979) seemed to assume that the two vowels were the same, suggesting ⟨**o**⟩ and ⟨**o-e**⟩ but commented; "the digraph, 'oa' is sometimes used to represent this sound, but it is seldom found in specifically Scottish words" (p. 68), adding that it should be kept in words shared with English. Purves gave examples such as *ablo* 'below', *corbie* 'raven', *thon* 'that', *bole* 'hatch', *brose* 'gruel', *poke* 'bag', *troke* 'trade' and *boat, foal,* and *loanin* 'lane'.

6.5.3 McClure's recommendation

McClure (1980) differentiated the vowels, suggesting ⟨**oa**⟩ for vowel 5, and commented that "this is a decidedly un-Scots spelling; but there is no obvious alternative" and ⟨**o**⟩ for vowel 18, commenting on its merger with vowel 5 in some dialects.

6.5.4 *Scots Language Society* recommendation

The *Scots Language Society* did not mention these vowels, the assumption being that traditional practice should be followed, usually ⟨**oa**⟩ or ⟨**o-e**⟩ for vowel 5 and ⟨**o**⟩ for vowel 18.

6.5.5 *Aiberdeen Univairsitie Scots Leid Quorum* recommendation

The *Aiberdeen Univairsitie Scots Leid Quorum* was seemingly aware of mergers, suggesting the traditional practice, using ⟨o⟩ for vowel 5 and ⟨o-e⟩, and, less often, ⟨oa⟩, for vowel 18.

6.5.6 *SLD* recommendation

SLD did not differentiate those vowels, simply suggesting ⟨o⟩, ⟨oa⟩, and ⟨o-e⟩ in words such as *oan* 'on', *goat* 'got', and *thole* 'endure'.[95] (Macleod 2000: 66) admitted the possibility of ⟨o⟩ being capable of representing both /ɔ/ and /o/ in *on* or *holiday*.[96] In the headword list based upon the contents of the *Essential Scots Dictionary* forms such as *ablow* and *alow* 'below', *afore* 'before', *athort* 'across', and *awbody* 'everybody' occurred.[97]

6.5.7 Robinson's recommendation

Robinson (1997) simply suggested ⟨oa⟩ where Standard English has ⟨o⟩ but also used ⟨o⟩ and ⟨o-e⟩.

6.5.8 *Scots Spelling Comatee* recommendation

The *Scots Spelling Comatee* seemed to recommend following traditional practice and were aware of mergers, recommended against ⟨oa⟩ spellings in words such as *on* and *stop*.

6.5.9 Discussion of vowels 5 and 18

The traditional graphemes seemed to be ⟨oa⟩, ⟨o-e⟩[98] for vowel 5 and ⟨o⟩[99] for vowel 18. As the merger of those vowels is not universal, treating them as separate vowels in a normative orthography would be advisable. The traditional graphemes are certainly unambiguous, though the choice of grapheme may depend on a judicious study of prevailing forms and application of the tendencies suggested above. The SND certainly provides a guide here, and if a form exists which has been regularly used and conforms to the chosen "rules", its acceptance as the "norm" cannot be dismissed lightly.

---

95 The form *boak* 'retch' was included, representing a vocalization of vowel 13 before /k/.

96 SND gives the Scots form *haliday* ['helɪde], /o/ or /ɔ/ simply being the Scottish English realizations.

97 https://web.archive.org/web/20061015063701/http://www.scotsdictionaries.org.uk /HeadWordList/A.html, accessed 2021-10-30. In the 2004 ESD *alow* and *awbody* are not given; the latter is given as *a'bodie* s.v. *a'*, *all*, *aw*, *aa*, *aal* (p. 1).

98 In older Scots the usual spelling was ⟨o⟩ with length indicated by ⟨e⟩ after a consonant e.g. *cole* 'coal'. (Aitken 2002: lvi)

99 Older Scots ⟨o⟩. (Aitken 2002: lviii)

3. *o* appears also in various digraphs: (1) *oa*, [for vowel 18 realised /o/] e.g. in the phonetic spellings *boax, coarn, Goad, joab, noat* [...] (SND VI: 455 s.v. "O"]

The modernism ⟨**oa**⟩ used to represent an /o/ realization of vowel vowel 18 is arguably eye dialect, and the traditional graphemes would be realized as /o/ or /ɔ/ unconsciously by native speakers. If the intention is to elicit a Scots-sounding pronunciation from a non-Scots-speaking reader, it is likely to fail, RP *goat* [gəʊt] being somewhat different from Scots *got* [got]. The use of final ⟨**-ow**⟩ for /oː/ may indicate an /ʌu/ realization, forms such as *ablo* and *alo* 'below' being less ambiguous.

6.6 VOWEL 6

Vowel 6 is generally /u(ː)/. In Southern Scots and Ulster dialects influenced by it, where word-final, it is usually diphthongized to /ʌu/.

In the dialect of the Sth. counties, **u** in final position has been diphthongized, producing **ʌu**. (Grant and Dixon 1921: 49)

6.6.1 *Scots Style Sheet* recommendation

The *Scots Style Sheet* suggested mainly ⟨**ou**⟩ in words such as *doun* 'down', *dour, drouth* 'thirst', *hou* 'how', *mouth, nou* 'now', *out, sou* 'sow', *south*, and *toun* 'town' but also suggested ⟨**oo**⟩ in *smool* 'slink' and for historic vowel 7 in *smooth* and *snoove* 'twist'.

6.6.2 Purves' recommendation

Purves (1979) suggested ⟨**ou**⟩, rejecting ⟨**oo**⟩,[100] which he considered borrowed from English, giving examples such as *allou* 'allow', *cou* 'cow', *douce* 'gentle', *goun* 'gown', *mou* 'mouth', *nou* 'now', *ploum* 'plum', *shouther* 'shoulder', *sou* 'sow', *soum* 'swim', and *toun* 'town'. Purves also suggests that in *smouthe* 'smooth' and ⟨**u-e**⟩ in *dule* 'grief', *bure* 'bore', *hure* 'whore', and *swure* 'swore', all from historic vowel 7.

6.6.3 McClure's recommendation

McClure (1980) suggested ⟨**ou**⟩, rejecting the Anglicism ⟨**oo**⟩ as unetymological, being used in English to represent the modern realization of Old English /oː/ (vowel 7).

---

100 But considered it necessary in *woo* 'wool', usually [uː], and to differentiate his homophones *croun* 'crown' and *croon* 'sing', the latter with vowel 7.

6.6.4 *Scots Language Society* recommendation

The *Scots Language Society* suggested ⟨ou⟩ in words such as *cou* 'cow', *fou* 'full', *soum* 'swim', *doun* 'down', *stour* 'dust', and *flouer* 'flower' but commented that there may be a case for ⟨oo⟩ in *about* and *out* in order "to avoid confusion with the English pronunciation", the ⟨ss⟩ rendering that unnecessary in words such as *crouss* 'cheerful', *houss* 'house', and *mouss* 'mouse'. In a few words such as *dule* 'grief', *bure* 'bore', *hure* 'whore', and *wure* 'wore' ⟨u-e⟩ was suggested, all from historic vowel 7.

6.6.5 *Aiberdeen Univairsitie Scots Leid Quorum* recommendation

Aiberdeen Univairsitie Scots Leid Quorum suggested ⟨ou⟩ in preference to ⟨oo⟩ which it suggested be abandoned. Examples given were *cou* 'cow', *dou* 'dove', *doun* 'down', *dour, fou* 'full', *founer* 'founder', *houss* 'house', *our, out, stoun* 'stun', *toun* 'town'. A few exceptions were words such as *true, grue* 'shudder', and *awfu* 'awful'. In a few "classical" words such as *depute* 'deputy' and *chuse*[101] 'choose' but also *hure* 'whore', *muve* 'move', *pruve* 'prove', and *wure* 'wore' ⟨u-e⟩ was suggested, the latter from from historic vowel 7. Allan (1995) reiterated those suggestions, adding exceptions such as *cruel, fuel, jewel* and *room*, also mentioning the Southern Scots word-final diphthongization in words such as *you*.

6.6.6 *SLD* recommendation

SLD suggested ⟨ou⟩ and ⟨oo⟩, giving the examples *coo* 'cow', *drouth* 'thirst', and *toun* 'town', recommending ⟨oo⟩ in words such as *hoose* 'house' and *moose* 'mouse' where ⟨ou⟩ could "suggest an English pronunciation".[102] Macleod and Cairns (1993: vii) suggested ⟨oo⟩ in examples such as *aboot* 'about', *doon* 'down', *droon* 'drown', *hoose* 'house', *oot* 'out', *coo* 'cow', and *flooer* 'flower' giving exceptions in ⟨ou⟩ where a pronunciation with vowel 13 also occurs, in for example *roup* 'cry', and where "one spelling is established", in for example *souch* 'sigh' and *roup*[103] 'auction'. Macleod (1996) did not apply ⟨ou⟩ or ⟨ou⟩ consistently, having, for example, *doon* 'down' and *toon* 'town' but *tousle* 'rumple', *dour*, and *coor* 'cower', though she later commented that there would be no harm in a more systematic use of ⟨ou⟩ in words such as *broun* 'brown', *doun* 'down', and *toun* 'town' where it is unlikely to be given a Standard English pronunciation, preferring ⟨oo⟩ in *cooncil* 'council', *hoose* and *moose* (Macleod 2000: 66).

---

101 Occurs variously as [tʃɔɪs, tʃɔɪz, tʃiːz, tʃɑɪz].
102 See https://web.archive.org/web/20061015063228if_/http://www.scotsdictionaries .org.uk/ScotsSpellingGrammar.htm, accessed 2021-10-30.
103 [rʌup; Sh., Ork. rup; Rnf., †Ayr., Wgt., Dmf. roːp] (SND VII: 488 s.v. "ROUP")

6.6.7 Robinson's recommendation

Robinson (1997) suggested ⟨oo⟩, corresponding to Standard English ⟨ou⟩ an ⟨ow⟩, in words such as *coo* 'cow', *cooncil* 'council', *doot* 'doubt', *hoose* 'house', *moose* 'mouse', *noo* 'now', *oor* 'our', *oot* 'out', and *toon* 'toun'.

6.6.8 *Scots Spelling Comatee* recommendation

The Scots Spelling Comatee suggested ⟨ou⟩ in words such as *couthie* 'sociable', *dour* 'sullen', *stour* 'dust', *fouth* 'abundance', and *thoum* 'thumb' and in Standard English cognates with ⟨ow⟩, and ⟨ou⟩ where Standard English has ⟨ou⟩ pronounced [aʊ] as in *house, mouse*.

6.6.9 Discussion of vowel 6

The traditional grapheme was undoubtedly ⟨ou⟩,[104] a point clearly emphasized by Robert Louis. Stevenson:

> Yet the temptation is great to lend a little guidance to the bewildered Englishman. Some simple phonetic artifice might defend your verses from barbarous mishandling, and yet not injure any vested interest. So it seems at first; but there are rocks ahead. Thus, if I wish the diphthong *ou* to have its proper value, I may write *oor* instead of *our*; many have done so and lived, and the pillars of the universe remained unshaken. But if I did so, and came presently to *doun*, which is the classical Scots spelling of the English *down*, I should begin to feel uneasy; and if I went on a little farther, and came to a classical Scots word, like *stour* or *dour* or *clour*, I should know precisely where I was—that is to say, that I was out of sight of land on those high seas of spelling reform in which so many strong swimmers have toiled vainly. To some the situation is exhilarating; as for me, I give one bubbling cry and sink. The compromise at which I have arrived is indefensible, and I have no thought of trying to defend it. (Stevenson 1905: 152)

> The spelling *ow* also appears in such words as *bow, brown, drown, how, now*, etc., esp. in the 18th c., though [u] is intended, partly though influence of St. Eng., partly phs. as a survival from Mid.Sc. where *u* and *w* were not clearly distinguished in MSS. In the course of the 19th c. *oo* came to be used chiefly for this sound, as a borrowing from St. Eng. orthography, though found as early as the 17th c. in Sc. (SND VI: 455 s.v. "O")

---

104 In older Scots usually ⟨ou⟩, with the alternatives ⟨ov, ow⟩ the latter usually word final and shared with vowel 13. (Aitken 2002: lvii)

This spelling [⟨**ou**⟩] is gen. preferred in this dictionary, hence HOUR, HOUSE, LOUD, MOUSE, MOUTH, POUCH, SOUR [ur, hus, lud, mus, muθ, putʃ, sur], etc. (SND VI: 455 s.v. "O")

Nevertheless, the the 18th and 19th century writers clearly had no problem associating ⟨**ow**⟩ with that vowel, though modern readers are likely to associate that with vowel 13. Arguably, the use of ⟨**ou**⟩ in words such as *about, house* and *out* might prove equally ambiguous. Spellings such as *houss* 'house' and *mouss* 'mouse' may not have the desired result, being equally likely to be interpreted /ʌu/ by the uninitiated. Furthermore, their advocates never suggested *outt* 'out' by analogy. McClure's (1980: 28) argument that ⟨**oo**⟩ is an unetymological imported Anglicism which traditionally represented the modern Standard English outcome of Anglo–Saxon ⟨**ō**⟩[105] is undeniable but, to a modern reader, is unquestionably unambiguous in words such as *aboot, hoose,* and *oot*. Arguably ⟨**ou**⟩ would be the preferred grapheme in a regularized orthography, but the case for ⟨**oo**⟩ where Standard English cognates have ⟨**ou**⟩ is a strong one. The case for ⟨**oo**⟩ where Standard English cognates have ⟨**ow**⟩ is not so strong, though traditional practice would seem to be a random mixture of both ⟨**ou**⟩ and ⟨**oo**⟩, as the following headword forms in the SND suggest *broun* 'brown', *croun* 'crown', *flour* 'flower', *goun* 'gown' *pouther* 'powder', *shour* 'shower', *toul* 'towel', *tour* 'tower', *toun* 'town', and *coor* 'cower', *doon* 'down', *droon* 'drown', and *pooer* 'power', all which could unambiguously be regularized using ⟨**ou**⟩ to give *broun* 'brown', *croun* 'crown', *flouer* 'flower', *goun* 'gown' *pouther* 'powder', *shouer* 'shower', *touel* 'towel', *tour* 'tower', *toun* 'town', and *cour* 'cower', *doun* 'down', *droun* 'drown', and *pouer* 'power'. The grapheme ⟨**u-e**⟩ traditionally used in words such as *dule* 'sorrow' and *hure* 'whore' might arguably be kept where the realization is now generally /u/, although strictly speaking the underlying phoneme is vowel 7.

6.7 VOWEL 7

Vowel 7 has its origin in Old English /oː/, which became /ø/ and later also /y/. Old French ⟨**u(i)**⟩ also merged with the realizations of this vowel (Steiger 1913: 38). Forms such as /i/[106] and /e/[107] appeared around the 17th century and were brought to Ulster by incoming Scots from south-west Scotland. That was partially replaced by a subsequent development

---

105 This of course was also often used in traditional Scots writing for vowel 7, no doubt by analogy with English cognates.

106 This form still exists in Northern Scots. A further development, with the notable exception of Caithness, occurred whereby /wi/ occurs after /g/ and /k/. e.g. *cuit* [kwit] 'ankle', *guid* [gwid] 'good', *sc'uil* [skwil] 'school' etc.

107 Such forms are also found in Fife, East Perthshire, and Dundee.

originating in Lothian which spread westwards, whereby the original long vowel became /eː/ before /v/, /ð/, /r/, /z/, /ʒ/, ∅, and at the end of a word, otherwise short /ɪ/∼/ï/ in Ulster. That has also been spreading south towards the Borders and northwards through Fife and into Angus. In Central dialects, initially that may be preceded by /j/, for example, 'use' [jɪs] (n.) and [jeːz] (v). Before /k/ and /x/ that developed to /j(u)/ or /j(ʌ)/ although if an /r/ precedes the vowel, the realization is generally /u/ or /ʌ/.

> [...] **y** is an **ɪ** pronounced with lip-rounding [...] and is generally heard short and occurs before all consonants except **r** and *voiced fricatives*. In a few dialects this vowel is tense and very nearly equivalent to Fr. *u* in *mur*. (Grant and Dixon 1921: 45)

> [...] **ø** occurs in final position and before *voiced fricatives*, such as **z**, **v, ð** and **r**, and is normally long. (Grant and Dixon 1921: 46)

> The original vowel in most of the words containing **y** or **ø** appears to have been a long *o* in O.E. and Scan. And *u* in Fr. [...] This *o* (or *u*) became fronted and became **ø**. **ø** remained before *voiced fricatives* and **r** and in final position, but in other cases it was generally raised and shortened to **y**. In many districts of the Mid. Area, recent unrounding has taken place so that **y** becomes **ɪ** and **ø** becomes **e**. (Grant and Dixon 1921: 46)

> The word ABUNE illustrates the outcome of the Scots vowel traditionally spelled *ui* or *u*+consonant+*e*. the form *abin* is now usual in Scotland south of the River Tay, and is found in Ulster in south Antrim and east Down. The form *abane*, found in Scotland in the area between Stonehaven and the River Tay, is found in north Antrim and over into Co. Londonderry. The form *abeen*, which occurs in Ulster in Co. Donegal, west Down and the southern part of the Ards peninsula, is found in Scotland from Stonehaven northwards to Caithness, but also, and more relevantly, there are traces of this vowel in such words in Dumfriesshire, Kirkcudbrightshire, and Wigtownshire. These southwestern counties contributed many families to the population of Ulster. (Macafee 1996: xxx)

> The mn.Sc.(a) dialect agrees with sn.Sc. in having *ee* [i] in words like [...] *moon, spoon,* shoe, *moor* become *meen, speen, shee, meer; good,*

cool become *gweed, cweel*, this is the case generally when a back stop consonant preceded the vowel [...] (SND I: xxxiv §128)

[...] the mn.Sc.(b) area, including U.Bnff., Mry. and Nairn. It differs from Abd. Speech [...] *ford, moor, poor*, which have *oo* and *yoo* [uː, juː] instead of *ee* [...] (SND I: xxxvi §142)

When a back consonant (*g* or *k*) precedes the vowel, in Crm. and Avoch, no *w* is developed as in the N.E., hence for *good, school, cool, cuits* (*ankles*) we get *geed, skeel, keel, keets*, as we find also in Cai. See §35.2. When the vowel comes before *r*, or a guttural, the development is the same as in Mry. and Cai.—e.g. *fyoord, myoor, pyoor*, [...] for St.Eng. *ford, moor, poor* [...] (SND I: xxxvi §146)

When followed by a back consonant [x] or [k], a diphthong [iu, ju or jʌ] is most common, though some dialects have simple [u] or [ø]. (SND I: xix §35.6)

[...] but in Scots it generally becomes [y] or [i], except that before a back vowel it becomes [juː] and before *r* [ø]. The first two sounds are spelt *ui* or *u-e*, the last *eu*. (Tulloch 1980: 292)

6.7.1 *Scots Style Sheet* recommendation

The *Scots Style Sheet* suggested ⟨**ui**⟩ or ⟨**u-e**⟩ giving examples such as *puir* 'poor', *muir* 'moor', *fluir* 'floor', *guid* 'good', *tuim* 'empty', *spune* 'spoon', *shune* 'shoes', *sune* 'soon', *tune, use, mune* 'moon', and *abune* 'above' but included *wuid* 'wood', which has vowel 15. The *Style Sheet* clearly distinguished between that and the realization after /x/ and /k/, giving examples such as *beuk* 'book' *leugh*[108] 'laughed', *leuk* 'look', and *neuk* 'nook'.

6.7.2 Purves' recommendation

Purves (1979) suggested ⟨**ui**⟩[109] in words such as *bluid* 'blood', *guid* 'good', *uise* 'use' (v.) and *uiss* 'use' (n.) but also included examples such as *buik* 'book', *huik* 'hook', *luik* 'leuk', *tuik* 'took' but also *neuk* 'nook' and *teuch* 'tough', indicating that he did not systematically distinguish between the former and realizations before /k/ and /x/.

---

108 One assumes the ⟨**gh**⟩ is a typographical error, as it would contradict the *Style Sheet*'s recommendation for ⟨**ch**⟩.

109 This was also suggested in *fuisionless*, although a realization with /ø/ occurs, it is usually /uː/, *guislin* 'gosling' was also suggested but that has vowel 4 or 8.

6.7.3 McClure's recommendation

McClure (1980) suggested ⟨**ui**⟩ in words such as *guid* 'good', *muin* 'moon', *spuin* 'spoon' and ⟨**eu**⟩ in the "reflex of historical /oː + (velar)/" (p.28), giving examples such as *heuk* 'hook', *teuch* 'tough', and *eneuch* 'enough'.

6.7.4 *Scots Language Society* recommendation

The *Scots Language Society* suggested ⟨**ui**⟩ in words such as *guid* 'good' *ruif* 'roof', *uise* 'use' (v.), and *uiss* 'use' (n.) but also included the example *buik* 'book' and suggested ⟨**eu**⟩ in *neuk* 'nook', indicating no systematic distinguishing between the former and realizations before /k/ and /x/.

6.7.5 *Aiberdeen Univairsitie Scots Leid Quorum* recommendation

The *Aiberdeen Univairsitie Scots Leid Quorum* suggested ⟨**ui**⟩ in words such as *guid* 'good', *puir* 'poor', *truith* 'truth', and *fluir* 'floor' but also included *cuid* 'could', *shuid* 'should', *fuit* 'foot', and *wuid* 'wood', which clearly do not belong here,[110] and ⟨**u-e**⟩ was suggested in words such as *muve* 'move', *pruve* 'prove', and *chuse* 'choose'. Those were distinguished from the realizations after /k/ and /x/, suggesting ⟨**eu**⟩, with examples such as *heuk* 'hook', *leuk* 'look', *neuk* 'nook', and *teuch* 'tough'. Allan (1995) described the same in more detail.

6.7.6 *SLD* recommendation

SLD suggested ⟨**ui**⟩ and ⟨**u-e**⟩, giving examples such as *spuin* 'spoon' and *guse* 'goose' but also *buik* 'book' and *teuch* 'tough', not distinguishing between the former and realizations before /k/ and /x/. The form *shae* 'shoe'[111] was also suggested.[112] Macleod and Cairns (1993: x) and Macleod (1996: viii), commenting on vowel 7 that "in the Northern mainland dialects this sound does not occur; -ee- is used instead, as in **beet** for 'boot'." The author(s) apparently failed to realize that /i/ is the north-eastern realization of this phoneme. It could be equally argued that "this sound does not occur" in central dialects either since it has merged with vowels 4 or 15. Consequently spellings such as *yiss, eese* 'use' (n.), *yaise, yuise, eese* 'use' (v.), *uisless* 'useless', *yuisfae* 'useful', and *usual* were also included. In the headword list based upon the contents of the *Essential Scots Dictionary*, predictable north-eastern realizations were also provided as a variant in words such as

---

110 The realizations [kud, kʌd + ne.Sc. kwɪd] result from Anglo–Saxon long ⟨**ū**⟩ and the usual modern realizations of 'should' are [ʃud or ʃid]. Vowel 15 occurs in 'foot' and 'wood'.

111 This is a well established spelling in traditional writing.

112 See https://web.archive.org/web/20061015063228if_/http://www.scotsdictionaries .org.uk/ScotsSpellingGrammar.htm, accessed 2021-10-30.

abuin/abeen 'above', *abuise/abeese* 'abuse' (v.), *adae/adee* 'ado', *nuin/neen* 'noon', and, *affoord* 'afford', which also traditionally has vowel 7.[113]

6.7.7 Robinson's recommendation

Robinson (1997) essentially described this as equivalent to English ⟨**oo**⟩, suggesting ⟨**ui**⟩ and ⟨**u**⟩, but recognized that it covered a "great variety of pronunciations" (p.29), even mentioning *beuk* 'book' as a literary spelling, but was seemingly unaware as to the causes, failing to recognize the nature of many realizations, especially those before /k/ and /x/. Among spellings that Robinson suggested were *bluid* 'blood', *guid* 'good', *puir* 'poor' *buik* 'book', *luk* 'look', *stud* 'stood' and *tuk* 'took', but also *jist* 'just' and *boord* 'board', the latter representing a Mid Ulster English realization.

> The /ʉ/ in *board, door*, etc. is now a well-known rural stereotype that is specific to non-US [Ulster Scots] dialects in Ireland. It appears to be exclusively English in origin. There is no mention of this pronunciation in the descriptions of southern and central Scots (Wilson 1926, Wettstein 1942, Zai 1942), since ESc [Early Scots] /oː/ was fronted before /r/ as in other environments, showing up in modern Scots as /eː/, /øː/ or some similar front vowel. Gregg's phonological questionnaire, designed to establish the boundaries between US and MUE [Mid Ulster English], includes the items *floor, board, door, poor*, which regularly appear as /fleːr/ or /flëːr/ in CUS [Conservative Ulster Scots] areas but as /flʉːr/ or /floːr/ in MUE areas (1963: 35; 1972). [...] (Harris 1985: 158–9)[114]

6.7.8 *Scots Spelling Comatee* recommendation

The *Scots Spellin Comatee* described this vowel in some detail, clearly recognizing the various dialect realizations, including those before /k/ and /x/, and also pointing out that *fit* 'foot' and *wid* 'wood' had vowel 15. For the former ⟨**ui**⟩ was recommended and for the latter ⟨**eu**⟩, ⟨**u-e**⟩ being recommended in words such as *muve* 'move' and *pruve* 'prove'. Both *cuid* 'could' and *shuid* 'should' were included, although it was admitted that they did not strictly belong here,[115] apparently for want of a satisfactory solution.

---

113 https://web.archive.org/web/20061015063701/http://www.scotsdictionaries.org.uk/HeadWordList/A.html, accessed 2021-10-30. In the 2004 ESD the following forms are given: *abuin, aboon, abeen; abuise, abeese; adae, adee, ado; affuird* is given but not *affoord* (p. 1); *muin, meen, min, moon* is given (p. 121).

114 The Survey of English dialects records /uː/, /ʊə/, or some similar high round nucleus in *door*, (reference V.1.8) and *floor* (V.2.7) in parts of the north and southwest of England.

115 "In the sixteenth century, loss of the sound /l/ in *should* and *would* (due probably to their occurrence in positions of weak sentence stress) led to analogical extension of the retained symbol ⟨l⟩ to another modal verb *could*, earlier *coude*. All three verbs are inherited from

[…] **y** is commonly written (1) *ui*, (2) *u-e*, (3) *oo*. (Grant and Dixon 1921: 45)

[…] **ø** is written (1) *ui*, (2) *u+e*, (3) *oe*, (4) *o*, (5) *oo*. (Grant and Dixon 1921: 46)

[…] *ui*, (i) for [ø, y, later unrounded to ɪ], alternating with the earlier *u-e*, which is now usu. retained only before nasals, as in Brume, *dune* (DAE), Lume, Mune, Spune, Tume. Tune, etc., also Blude, Schule, and representing O.E. *ō*, O.N. *ó*, O.Fr. *u* […], as in Buit, *n*.¹, Cuil, Fuil, Guid, Huilie, Muir, Puir, Shuir, Tuil, Wuid. (SND IX: 467 s.v. "u")[116]

[…] This spelling [ui] has become a literary standard also in n.Sc. where the actual pronunciation is [i]. (SND IX: 467 s.v. "u")

[…] *eu*, (i) for [ju], as in Feu; alternating with [(j)ʌ] according to dialect, in words orig. with O. and Mid.Eng. *ǭ* before *ch* [x] or *k*, as Beuk, Deuk, Eneuch, Heuch, *leuch* (Lauch), Leuk, Pleuch, Teuch. (SND IX: 467 s.v. "u")

[…] *e* is found in various vowel digraphs: (1) *ae*: […] (ii) [e] representing an unrounding of [ø] from O.E. *ō* in final syllables, now prevalent in m.Sc., e.g. *dae*, *shae* […] (SND III: 192 s.v. "e")

This [⟨oo⟩] is a 16th c. adaptation of the Eng. spelling for the equivalent Eng. sound [u] developed from the same sources and given currency in the 18th c. esp. by Ramsay. (SND VI: 455 s.v. "o")

6.7.9 Discussion of vowel 7

As the various realizations of that vowel are predictable across dialects and by phonological environment, two unambiguous traditional graphemes readily offer themselves, ⟨**ui**⟩ and ⟨**eu**⟩, both used in Middle Scots as alternatives to ⟨**u-e**⟩.[117] The ⟨**eu**⟩ for the realizations before the back consonant /x/ or /k/, although strictly speaking ⟨**ui**⟩ is historically accurate, the differing realizations of vowel 7 before /x/ or /k/ are a strong

---

Old English but whereas ⟨l⟩ is historically correct in the first two (OE *sceolde*, *wolde*) it is inorganic in the last (OE *cuðe*)." (Scragg 1975: 58)

116 Also the SND headwords use (SND IX: 512–513) and eese (SND III: 213) for the North-East realizations of the noun and verb.

117 DOST records *bluid*, *guid*, *puir*, *beuk*, *leuch*, *leuk*, *neuk* and *teuch*.

justification for ⟨eu⟩. Word-final occurrence of that vowel poses a problem because ⟨ui⟩ was never traditionally used in that position.[118] When not using Standard English spellings, ⟨ae⟩, apparently representing a Central Scots realization, was employed, even by Northern writers. The use of ⟨ui⟩ in words such as *adui* 'ado', *dui* 'do', *shui* 'shoe', and *tui* 'to' would be likely to prove so unfamiliar that adhering to the traditional *dae, dae, shae* and *tae* is arguably the better option. Those few exceptions are arguably not beyond the scope of human ingenuity. The other graphemes ⟨u-e⟩, which occurred in Older Scots, and the 18th and 19th century use of ⟨oo⟩ are arguably ambiguous because the modern reader might associate those with vowel 6.

6.8 VOWEL 9

Vowel 9 is /oi/, /ɔi/, or /oe/ in most Scots dialects. This vowel was not mentioned by the *Scots Style Sheet*, Purves (1979), the *Scots Language Society*, the *Aiberdeen Univairsitie Scots Leid Quorum*, *SLD* and Robinson (1997), although McClure (1980) recommended ⟨oy⟩ in words such as *boy, joy,* and *toy,* and Allan (1995) suggested ⟨oi⟩ medially and ⟨oy⟩ finally, otherwise, the assumption being that traditional practice was to be followed.

> *o* is conjoined: (1) with *i* or *y* to form the diphthong [ɔi, oe] though this is rare in Sc. [...] (SND VI: 455 s.v. "O")

That vowel, not being common in Scots, poses little problem, the traditional ⟨oi⟩, initially and medially, and ⟨oy⟩ finally perhaps negate the need for further innovation.

6.9 VOWEL 12

Vowel 12 is /aː/, /ɑː/, or /ɔ(ː)/ in most Scots dialects, in Ulster /ɔː/, /ɑː/, or /ɑʷ/ in Antrim and Down, and usually /aː/ in Donegal. Older Scots ⟨-al(l)⟩ /al/ (vowel 12a) had on the whole merged with vowel 12 (except intervocallically) in the Middle Scots period.

> [...] It [o] is common in Mid Sc. In the North, in Galloway and in the Southern Counties it is of rare occurrence, being replaced by a broad **ɑ** sound. It varies over the country from **o** to **ɔ** and **o** on the one hand and to **ɑ** and **a** (in Celtic areas) on the other. (Grant 1921: 51)

> [...] **ɑ** is generally fully long when final, and before a voiced fricative and **r**. It is also long when it represents an older

---

118 Word final ⟨o⟩ was the usual spelling in Middle Scots. (Aitken 2002: lviii)

diphthong, arising generally from a lost consonant (**l**, **g**, **w**) [...]
(Grant 1921: 52)

When preceded by a back vowel, [l] is not lost but vocalised.
(Tulloch 1980: 187)

[...] indicating the variation from the cognate English by including
apostrophes. This is a bad method because it has bad side-effects.
Though an English reader may find this helpful, it supports the
prejudice that Scots is a corrupt dialect, a perversion of the true
English caused by the vulgar habit of dropping consonants.
(Tulloch 1980: 193)

[...] has a wide range of isolative realisations within Scotland,
ranging from high-mid [o(ː)], through low-mid [ɔ(ː)] [...], [ɑ(ː)] [...]
and [ɒ(ː)] [...] to [aː~æː] [...] This vowel may merge with CAT or
COT (and COAT), or contrast with one of these nuclei in terms of
length alone, as it does not always obey Aitken's Law. (Johnston
1997b: 488)

[...] *half* is transferred to CAT. Roughly the same forms are extant
in Ulster Scots, with the most common forms being Down [ö(ː)]
and Antrim [ɑ(ː)] [...] (Johnston 1997b: 490)

In most modern Scots dialects these items show up with /ɑː/ or
/ɔː/ (hence spellings such as *auld*, *cauld*) reflecting a development
from Esc /al/ [...] Some modern Scots dialects show a
development of the vowel in the COLD class that is similar to that
in southern types. In Galloway and parts of northeast Scotland,
for instance, we find /əʉ/ or /ʌu/ in this set, which indicates a
merger of Esc /ald/ with /ould/ (Milroy 1982b: 25). This is also
the pattern found in CUS [Conservative Ulster Scots] (Gregg
1959: 418) [...] (Harris 1985: 159)

[...] there is no convincing contemporary evidence for *ould* in earlier
periods when it is supposed to have been more widespread in
Lowland Scots, nor is it a necessary stage in the development of the
regular Modern Scots forms. Rather it is supposed that it was an
alternative development, later replaced. I tend to agree with
Johnston (1997b:489) that there must be *some* influence from dialects
of England, via Hiberno-English, even if only reinforcement, and

that we may even have to see the eastern and western developments as separate phenomena in Scotland, with occurrences in
Kintyre, South-West Scotland and Glasgow coming from, or at
least reinforced by contact with, Ulster. (Macafee 2001: 125)

Consider the reflex of velarised [ɫ] before [d] in Irish English: this
led to the diphthong [au], as in the words *old* [aul] and *bold* [baul]
with the common post-sonorant stop deletion. (Hickey 2004: 72)

Vowel 4 in final position after /w, hw/, e.g. twa 'two', wha 'who',
has been captured by Vowel 12 except in Southern and southern
East Central, where it develops normally to /e/ [...] (Macafee
2004: 67)

6.9.1 *Scots Style Sheet* recommendation

The *Scots Style Sheet* only mentioned replacing the eschewed apostrophe
that represented historic /l/ vocalization with ⟨aa⟩, giving such examples
as *caa* 'call', *baa* 'ball', *faa* 'fall', and *staa* 'stall' etc., the assumption being
otherwise to follow traditional practice, giving examples with word-final
⟨a⟩ and ⟨aw⟩ such as *ava* 'at all', *awa* 'away', *wha* 'who', *blaw* 'blow', *braw*
'splendid', and *snaw* 'snow'.

6.9.2 Purves' recommendation

Purves (1979) suggested ⟨a⟩, ⟨au⟩, and ⟨aw⟩, normally word-final, giving
such examples as *awa* 'away', *wha* 'who', *dad* 'lump', *dwam* 'daze', *whar*
'where', *auld* 'old', *bauld* 'bold', *fauss* 'false', *maun* 'must', *saut* 'salt', *whaup*
'curlew', *braw* 'splendid', *raw* 'row', *snaw* 'snow', and *thraw* 'throw'. Purves
suggested that ⟨aw⟩ should be used where ⟨a'⟩ traditionally represented
word-final historical /l/ vocalization in words such as *baw* 'ball', *caw* 'call',
and *waw* 'wall' etc., commenting that the use of ⟨aa⟩ for historic /l/
vocalization "amounts to [...] a disguised apostrophe and is therefore
undesirable in principle." (p.63), although ⟨aa⟩ was proposed for a few
words such as *aa* 'owning' and *haar* 'mist'.[119]

6.9.3 McClure's recommendation

McClure (1980) suggested ⟨aa⟩, admitting its unhistorical pedigree but
claiming that it is now widely accepted, arguing that ⟨aw⟩ was associated

119 The traditional spelling *awe*, related to *aucht*, would conform better to Purves's
suggestions. The only words systematically spelled ⟨aa⟩ in traditional writing known to
me are *haar* 'mist' and *haaf* 'open sea'; the latter from Shetland derives from Old Norse
(see Jakobsen 2021:286 s.v. *haf*).

with English [ɔ], and that its not always being the North-East realization
and ⟨**aa**⟩'s lack of association with any particular sound ([ɔ, ɒː, ɑː]),
rendered it more appropriate for a pan-dialectal spelling.

6.9.4 *Scots Language Society* recommendation

The *Scots Language Society* suggested ⟨**a**⟩, ⟨**au**⟩ and ⟨**aw**⟩, normally word-
final, giving examples such as *awa* 'away', *wha* 'who', *auld* 'old', *glaur* 'mud',
waur 'worse', *saut* 'salt', *aw* 'all' *braw* 'splendid', *faw* 'fall', and *snaw* 'snow'. It
was also suggested that *caa* 'call' be distinguished from *caw* 'drive'.[120]

6.9.5 *Aiberdeen Univairsitie Scots Leid Quorum* recommendation

The *Aiberdeen Univairsitie Scots Leid Quorum* suggested ⟨**au**⟩ medially and
⟨**aw**⟩ finally, giving examples such as *auld* 'old', *caur* 'car', *daur* 'dare', *saut*
'salt', *aw* 'all', *craw* 'crow', *daw* 'dawn', *faw* 'fall', *law* and *waw* 'wall' and the
'exceptions' *twa* 'two', *awa* 'away', and *na* 'no'. Allan (1995) expanded on
that, mentioning that it included the Northern and Southern realization
/aː/ and that ⟨**au**⟩ is usually medial and ⟨**aw**⟩ word-final, though it was
also suggested that *caa* 'call' be distinguished from *caw* 'drive'. Added to the
exceptions above were *haar* 'mist', *talk*, and *walk*.

6.9.6 *SLD* recommendation

SLD suggested ⟨**au**⟩, ⟨**aw**⟩, and ⟨**aa**⟩ giving the examples *glaur* 'mud',
braw 'splendid' and *faap*, assumed to be a Northern form of *whaup*
'curlew'.[121] Macleod and Cairns (1993: vii) suggested -*a(u)* in examples such
as *spra(u)chle* 'sprawl' and *tra(u)chle* 'to draw' in order "to cover regional
variation in this vowel [...]", adding that in "some North-Eastern words
however, -aa- is used", citing the example *aager* 'auger'. For historical /l/
vocalization, *SLD* suggested three forms, giving the examples *aw/aa* 'all',
ca/caa/caw 'call', and *fa/faw/faa* 'fall'.[122] Macleod and Cairns (1993: vii)
eschewed an apostrophe where "they represent 'missing' English letters"
suggesting -*a(w)*, in for example, *ba(w)* 'ball' and *ca(w)* 'call'. Macleod (1996:
v) suggested: "some words are given with more than one spelling [...] **ca**,
caw, **call** *v* 1 call [...]".[123] In the headword list based upon the contents of
the *Essential Scots Dictionary* for historical /l/ vocalization *a* and *aw* 'all' were
given but also *amaist* 'almost', *awbody/abody* 'everybody', *awreddy/areadies*

---

120 The two are in fact the same word, the meaning 'drive' originating in the 'call' to working
     animals to get them to do something.
121 See https://web.archive.org/web/20061015063228if_/http://www.scotsdictionaries
     .org.uk/ScotsSpellingGrammar.htm, accessed 2021-10-20.
122 See https://web.archive.org/web/20061015063228if_/http://www.scotsdictionaries
     .org.uk/ScotsSpellingGrammar.htm, accessed 2021-10-30.
123 Including the conspicuously Standard English form *call*.

'already', *awricht/aricht* 'all right', *awthegither/athegither* 'altogether', *aweys*[124] 'everywhere', and *awthing* 'everything'.[125] A variant for the predictable North-eastern realization in words such as *auld/aald* 'old' was also provided.

6.9.7 Robinson's recommendation

Robinson (1997) suggested ⟨**aa**⟩, corresponding to English ⟨-**all**⟩ and ⟨**al**⟩, as in 'walk', ⟨**au**⟩, corresponding to English ⟨**e**⟩, in 'where', suggesting *quhaur*,[126] and English ⟨**a**⟩ in words such as *baun* 'band', *haun* 'hand', *laun* 'land', *staun* 'stand', *saut* 'salt', also adding that the forms *bann*, *hann*, *lann*, *stann*, and *satt* are also 'found' for those examples. Added to that was ⟨**aw**⟩ and ⟨(**a**)**a**⟩, "corresponding to English ⟨**ow**⟩", in such words as s*naw/snaa* 'snow', *blaw/bla* 'blow', and ⟨**á**⟩ representing the long "a" in words such as *awá* 'away' and *twá* 'two', though he suggested that a "suitable convention" already existed, giving examples such as *aa/aw* 'all', *anaw/anaa*,[127] *caa/caw* 'call'. Robinson also suggested ⟨**ou**⟩ for the possible Ulster realizations in words such as *oul* 'old', *boul* 'bold', *foul* 'fold', *houl/howl* 'hold', and *toul* 'told'.

6.9.8 *Scots Spelling Comatee* recommendation

The *Scots Spellin Comatee* recommended ⟨**aw**⟩ and apparently ⟨**au**⟩ medially in words such as *faut* 'fault' and *haud* 'hold', giving examples such as *craw* 'crow', *draw*, and *shaw* 'copse' for the former, ⟨**aa**⟩ being reserved for historic /l/ vocalization in words such as *aa* 'all', *caa*[128] 'call', *faa* 'fall', and *haa* 'hall', arguing that ⟨**aa**⟩ was a useful key to historic /l/ vocalization for those "bound" to English.

6.9.9 Discussion of vowel 12

The traditional graphemes for vowel 12 were generally ⟨**au**⟩ initially and medially, and ⟨**aw**⟩ root-final, both inherited from Middle Scots.[129] The

---

124 This is an 'eye dialect' running together of two words *aw* and *weys* 'all ways'.

125 https://web.archive.org/web/20061015063701/http://www.scotsdictionaries.org.uk /HeadWordList/A.html, accessed 2021-10-30. In the 2004 ESD the following forms are given: *a'bodie*; *a ways*, *a'weys* (s.v. *a'*, *all*, *aw*, *aa*, *aal* p. 1) *amaist* (p. 2); *a'ready*, *areddies* (p. 3); *awthegither*, *athegither* (p. 4); *awricht*, *aricht*, *awthing* are not given, though s.v. English *everything* the form *a(w)thing(s)* is given (p. 269). For 'old' the headword is given as *auld*, *aul*, *ald*, *aal*, *owl(d)*, *old* (p. 3).

126 Robinson also suggested 'Ulster–Scots' ⟨**u**⟩ and ⟨**au**⟩, corresponding to English ⟨**e**⟩, giving the examples *whur* and *whaur*.

127 Since they are two distinct words, one would assume that they would be written separately as *and aw* 'and all'.

128 It was also suggested differentiating *caa* 'call' from *caw* 'drive', although the two are in fact the same word, the meaning 'drive' originating in the 'call' to working animals to get them to do something.

129 The usual Middle Scots spellings were ⟨au, av, aw⟩ with ⟨aw⟩ preferred word-finally. (Aitken 2002: lviii)

initial and medial vocalized outcome of Vowel 12a was often as above and root-final generally ⟨**a'**⟩, sometimes simply ⟨**a**⟩, as shown in the SND headwords *a'* 'all', *ba'* 'ball', *bauk* 'balk', *ca'* 'call', *cauk* 'chalk', *fa* 'fall', *fause* 'false', *ha* 'hall', *maut* 'malt', *saut* 'saut', and *wa* 'wall'. Final ⟨**a'**⟩ occurred in *awa* 'away', *wha* 'who', and *twa* 'two', with the realization /e/ in some Western and Southern varieties.[130]

> § 34. When O.E. *ā* was followed by *w*, *āw* becomes in Mod. Sc. either [ɑː] or [ǫː]. The spelling for either is *au* or, when final, *aw*, but for [ɑː] *aa* is found in some of the dialects. (SND I: xix)

> 2. *u* appears in various digraphs: (1) *au*, representing the sound [ǫː], in em. and wm. Sc. and gen. adopted as the standard spelling in other dialects also, where the vowel remains unrounded, exc. Sh. where the spelling *aa* is preferred. Hence CAULD, DRAUCHT, HAUCH, HAUD, LAUCH, MAUN, SAUT, WAUR. (SND IX: 467 s.v. "U")

> 2. [ɑː] Ex. (1) *twa*, *wha*; (2) *ba* (ball), *bla* (blow), *ca* (call), *wa* (wall). In (2) the consonant *l* or *w* has been vocalised and then absorbed by the preceding *a*, resulting in a long vowel sound the same as *a* in English *father*. The loss of *l* or *w* in these words is often marked by an apostrophe—e.g. *ba'*. (SND I: 1 s.v. "A")

> § 48 [...] (3) before Middle Sc. *ll* or *l* + *cons.* where *ll* and *l* were vocalised and absorbed by a—e.g. *ca'*, *caa* or *caw* from *call* [ɑː, ǫː]. (SND I: xxi)

> 4. It is joined with *w* to represent (1) [ɑː] (see II. 1) and (2) [ǫ] (See II. 3) generally in final position. Ex. *blaw*, *caw*, *maw*, *raw* (row of houses, etc.). (SND I: 1 s.v. "A")

The use of ⟨**au**⟩ initially and medially for vowel 12 in words such as *auld* 'old', *bauld* 'bold', *baum* 'balm', *cauld* 'cold', *chaumer* 'chamber', *daur* 'dare', *lauch* 'laugh', *maun* 'must', *sauf* 'safe', and *wauk* 'wake' is straightforward, as is using ⟨**aw**⟩ finally in words such as *claw*, *knaw* 'know', *law*, and *snaw* 'snow'.[131] However, using an apostrophe for a sound which the language lost hundreds of years ago seems pointless. Attempts to avoid the apostrophe for root-final /l/ vocalization by simply using ⟨a⟩ as in *ca* 'call' and *fa*

---

130 All headword forms in the SND.
131 All headword forms in the SND.

'fall' prove troublesome, with suffixed forms such as *caed* 'called', *cain* 'calling', *caer* 'caller', and *fain* 'falling' indicating an /e/ realization, usually forcing recourse to an apostrophe as in *ca'in* and *fa'in*. Similarly, "disguising" the apostrophe with a further ⟨a⟩ as in *caa* and *faa* produces unfamiliar suffixed forms such as *caain* and *faain*. The traditional grapheme ⟨aw⟩ avoids that, suggesting regularizing words such as *aw* 'all' , *caw* 'call', *cawed* 'called', *cawin* 'calling', *cawer* 'caller', *faw* 'fall', *fawen* 'fallen', *fawin* 'falling', and *haw* 'hall' etc. along the lines of *blaw* 'blow', *braw* 'splendid', *draw*, *gnaw*, *slaw* 'slow', and *snaw* 'snow' etc. However, in some dialects vowels 12 and 12a are still different albeit similar underlying phonemes. The most marked difference is shown in some North-East realizations of vowel 12 in words such as *blaw* [bljɑ:v], *gnaw* [gnjɑ:v], *taw* [tjɑ:v], and *snaw* [snjɑ:v] against /a:/ for word-final vowel 12a. No obvious apostrophe-free traditional graphemes offer themselves to differentiate vowels 12 and 12a, although using ⟨au⟩ initially and medially for both vowels 12 and 12a, and ⟨aw⟩ root-final for vowel 12, and ⟨aa⟩ for root-final vowel 12a has been suggested. The traditional grapheme ⟨au⟩ clearly offers itself for medial /l/ vocalization in words such as *fause* 'false', *haud* 'hold', and *saut* 'salt'.[132] In a few words such as *ava* 'at all', *awa* 'away', *twa* 'two', and *wha* 'who', final ⟨a⟩ traditionally occurred,[133] often with an apostrophe. Adhering to such familiar forms poses no problems to those familiar with traditional Scots and neither does the /e/ realization of the last three in some Western and Southern dialects.

Robinson's (1997) suggested use of ⟨a⟩ simply reflects a merger of vowel 17 with vowel 12, the realization in words like hand and man being the same in some Ulster varieties and Ulster English, although the Ulster writers cited above usually differentiated ⟨au⟩ (vowel 12) and ⟨a⟩ (vowel 17). The possible Ulster realization /əu/ before ⟨ld⟩ is predictable by its phonetic environment, rendering forms such as *oul* 'old', *boul* 'bold', *foul* 'fold', *houl/howl* 'hold', and *toul* 'told' redundant. Furthermore, the ⟨ou⟩ might be confused with vowel 6. Such realizations may simply indicate a shift towards Ulster English. The ⟨oul⟩ forms were not used by the Ulster writers analysed above, forms in ⟨au⟩ being universal. Even the Northern writers analysed above generally differentiated between ⟨au⟩ (vowel) 12 and ⟨a⟩ (vowel 17), although, for some of them at least, vowel 12 would be merged with vowel 17. The SND, for the letter A, commented that "for *a* in open syllables, in words of Latin or otherwise learned (e.g. Biblical) origin" were often spelt "*aa, au, aw*", citing 19th century examples such as *adjawcent, awtheist,*

---

132 The l-vocalization of Older Scots vowel 17 resulted in reverse spellings with silent *l* in other vowel 12 words e.g. *chalmer* 'chamber' and *Falkirk* (Aitken 2002: lviii).

133 DOST records *awa, twa, wha* (and *quha*).

inspiraution, paurent, saavor, Awbraham, Bawbel, Dauvit, and *Sawtan.*[134] Regularization based on ⟨**au**⟩ initially and medially,[135] and ⟨**aw**⟩ finally, along with the few exceptions mentioned with final ⟨**a**⟩, would be in keeping with traditional practice, though the choice of grapheme might depend on a judicious study of prevailing forms and application of the tendencies suggested above.

6.10 VOWEL 13

Vowel 13 is usually /ʌu/ but vocalization to /oː/ may occur, especially before /k/.

> [...] with forms of the type [ʌu] being the most common [...] with the intermediate [ɔu] found occasionally. (Johnston 1997b: 497)

> Most *howk* items are transferred to COAT, with the number of transfers greatest in the South-West [Central] and South Mid B [South-East Central] as well as in Argyll [...] The number of items tails off as one goes north and east [...] (Johnston 1997b: 498)

6.10.1 General recommendation

The *Scots Style Sheet* simply suggested ⟨**ow**⟩ and ⟨**owe**⟩, giving examples such as *gowpit* 'gawped', *growe* 'grow', *knowe* 'knoll', *powe* 'poll', *rowe* 'roll', *thow* 'thaw', and *yowl* 'howl'. Purves (1979) had much the same, giving examples such as *bowk* 'retch', *bowl*, *chowe* 'chew', *cowp* 'overturn', *dowp* 'end', *fowk* 'folk', *howf* 'den', *lowe* 'glow', *lowp* 'leap', *thowe* 'thaw', and *yowe* 'ewe', with McClure (1980) adding *gowd* 'gold' and *gowf* 'golf' as further examples. The Scots Language Society and the *Aiberdeen Univairsitie Scots Leid Quorum* followed suit, the latter commented that ⟨**ow**⟩ be used word-initially and ⟨**owe**⟩ word-finally.

6.10.2 *SLD* recommendation

SLD suggested ⟨**ow**⟩ and ⟨**owe**⟩ word-finally giving, examples such as *gowd* 'gold', *growe* 'grow', *lowe* 'glow', and *thowe* 'thaw' but also suggesting that ⟨**ou**⟩ be possible in *coup/cowp* 'overturn', *doup/dowp* 'end', *loup/lowp* 'leap', and *smout/smowt* 'smolt'[136] but recommending ⟨**ow**⟩ "for pronunciation".

---

134 SND X: 325 s.v. "A".

135 A few exceptions with medial ⟨**aw**⟩ such as *bawbee* 'a coin' and *bawsant* 'streaked' exist but are easily found in the SND.

136 See https://web.archive.org/web/20061015063228if_/http://www.scotsdictionaries .org.uk/ScotsSpellingGrammar.htm, accessed 2021-10-30. The examples *coup, dowp,* and *loup* have possible /u/ realizations (SND: [s.Arg.; kup, dup I.Sc. I.Sc., (sm.Sc. + lup]) though /ʌu/ is by far the most prevalent.

6.10.3 Robinson's recommendation

Robinson (1997) suggested ⟨**ow**⟩, corresponding to English ⟨**ol**⟩, in words such as *fowk* 'folk', *gowf* 'golf', and *knowe* 'knoll', but also had *alow* 'ablaze', *fowertie* 'fourty', *glowe* 'glow', *growe* 'grow', *lown* 'calm', *owre* 'over', *tow* 'rope', and *trow* 'believe'.

6.10.4 *Scots Spelling Comatee* recommendation

The *Scots Spelling Comatee* recommended ⟨**ow**⟩ word-internally and ⟨**owe**⟩ word-finally, giving examples such as *bowe* 'bow', *cowe* 'crop', *howe* 'hollow', *ower* 'over', and *nowt* 'cattle', and suggesting the possible exception *dow* 'be able'.

> The *ow* spelling is preferred in this dictionary to distinguish from [u] […] This phonetic value for *ow* became rare before 1750. (SND VI: 455 s.v. "O")

6.10.5 Discussion of vowel 13

Traditional practice would tend towards regularization, using ⟨**ow**⟩ and ⟨**owe**⟩ finally,[137] including historical /l/ vocalization in words such as *fowk* 'folk', *gowd* 'gold', *gowf* 'golf', *howe* 'hollow', *knowe* 'knoll', *powe* 'poll', *rowe* 'roll', and *smowt* 'smolt'.[138] The association with vowel 6 ⟨**ou**⟩ may be ambiguous owing to its association with vowel 12 but a case for its use as a variant form for words which have a /u/ realization may be made. Since vocalization to /o/ is predictable, usually conditioned by phonetic environment, such realizations will be produced unconsciously by native-speakers, who have them in words such as *bowk* 'retch' and *howk* 'dig'.

6.11 VOWEL 14

Vowel 14 is usually /ju/. In Northern dialects /jʌu/ may occur, especially word-finally.

> O.E. *ēaw* has [ʌu] in mn.Sc.—e.g. *dyow, fyow, hyow, nyow*, for *dew, few, hew, new*; so for the Rom. words *beauty, duty, mew, pewter* we find *byowty, dyowty, myow, pyowter*.[139] (Grant 1931: xxxiv)

6.11.1 *Scots Style Sheet* recommendation

The *Scots Style Sheet* did not mention that, the assumption being that traditional usage should be followed.

---

137 The usual Older Scots spellings were ⟨ow, ov, ou⟩ with ⟨ow⟩ preferred word-finally. (Aitken 2002: lviii)

138 DOST records *gowf, howe, knowe, pow*, and *rowe*.

139 djʌu, fjʌu, hjʌu, njʌu; 'bjʌutɪ, 'djʌutɪ, 'mjʌu, 'pjʌutɪr. [Original footnote]

6.11.2 Purves' recommendation

Purves (1979) also made no mention of that but used *new* and *news* in the sample texts after his suggestions, and *bewtifu* 'beautiful' in *A Scots Grammar* (1997), indicating regular use of ⟨**ew**⟩.

6.11.3 McClure's recommendation

McClure (1980) also made no mention that, the assumption being that traditional usage should be followed.

6.11.4 *Scots Language Society* recommendation

The *Scots Language Society* also made no mention that but included *newfangilt* 'newfangled' in the word lists published in *Lallans* 39-41 and 42, indicating that traditional usage should be followed.

6.11.5 *Aiberdeen Univairsitie Scots Leid Quorum* recommendation

The *Aiberdeen Univairsitie Scots Leid Quorum* did not mention vowel 14 either but Allan (1995) mentions it under /u/ (vowel 6), suggesting limiting ⟨**ew**⟩ to a few familiar words where the sound is "really" /ju/, giving the example *drew*. Allan also mentions ⟨**ue**⟩ in words such as *fuel*.

6.11.6 *SLD* recommendation

SLD suggests ⟨**eu**⟩ for /ju/, giving the example *teuch* 'tough',[140] which would indicate that the realization of vowel 7 before /k/ and /x/ is intended. Macleod (1996) includes *new*, and *few*, with *fyow* for Northern dialects, indicating that the spelling depends on the dialect being represented.

6.11.7 Robinson's recommendation

Robinson (1997) also made no mention that but used *new*, *Jews*, and *Judea* in the sample Bible texts after his suggestions, indicating that traditional usage should be followed.

6.11.8 *Scots Spelling Comatee* recommendation

The *Scots Spelling Comatee* also made no mention of that but the recommended spellings *few* and *new* indicate that traditional usage should be followed.

---

140 See https://web.archive.org/web/20061015063228if_/http://www.scotsdictionaries
    .org.uk/ScotsSpellingGrammar.htm, accessed 2021-10-30.

6.11.9 Discussion of vowel 14

The traditional practice would tend towards regularized use of ⟨ew⟩[141] as exemplified in the SND headwords *dew, few*, and *new* and variously as in Romance words such as *beauty, duty, fuel, pewter*, etc. As the traditional spellings are unambiguous and the realization /jʌu/ in Northern dialects predictable, those native speakers who have such a realization will produce it unconsciously, making further innovation redundant.

6.12 VOWEL 15

Vowel 15 varies between /ɪ/ and /ʌ/ in Scotland, although /ɛ/ may also occur and after /w/ and /ʍ/, the realization may be /ʌ/. In Ulster /ɪ/ (/ä/) or /ë/ also occur. The latter especially in Donegal. (Gregg 1972: 121)

> This appears to be the popular Anglo-Irish sound in *bull, foot, (fut), full, put* (between low-back advanced and low-mixed retracted [...] It is fronted in certain words: *pit* for *put* (esp. when emphatic), *fit* for *foot* (fut). (Traynor 1953: xxi)

> In acoustic effect it is midway between *pit* and *pet*. (Traynor 1953: xx)

> [...] the late Latin practice of using ⟨o⟩ for earlier ⟨u⟩ caused some falling together of the two graphemes in French and later in English. Thus ⟨o⟩ replaced ⟨u⟩ in a large number of words [...] The use of ⟨o⟩ was valuable in distinguishing the vowel from a neighbouring consonant, particularly ⟨v⟩ (identical with ⟨u⟩ at this time [...] and ⟨w⟩ written ⟨uu⟩, as the name of the letter suggests). The fact that the convention survives also in the neighbourhood of ⟨n⟩ and ⟨m⟩ has led many commentators to suggest that ⟨o⟩ was preferred to ⟨u⟩ to make reading easier, since the characters ⟨u n m⟩ all consisted in bookhand of a series of minims (or straight down-strokes), the series in ⟨un ini iui uu iw im⟩ etc. being in danger of being misdivided and causing confusion. (Scragg 1975: 43–44)[142]

> [...] before a nasal consonant Scots replaces [ʌ] with [i] giving *rin* 'run' [...] and *hinny* 'honey' [...] The same variation occurs before other consonants like [z] in *hizzy* 'hussy' [...] and *dizzen* 'dozen' [...] (Tulloch 1980: 185)

---

141 The usual Older Scots spellings were ⟨ew⟩, ⟨ev⟩, and ⟨eu⟩ (Aitken 2002: lviii).
142 For example *come, love, monk, some, son, tongue, worry* etc.

The Survey of English Dialects records *foot*, [...] and *look* [...] with /ʌ/ in parts of the south east Midlands and the West Country [...] (Harris 1985: 154)

The most common reflex overall, and one that is increasing in frequency, is [ë] [...], although [...] [ë~ɪ] [...] are far from rare. Less commonly, and more localisedly, even [...] [æ~ä] [...] may occur, as may [...] [ə~ɜ] [...], [ʌ] [...] or [ɟ~ÿ] [...] (Johnston 1997b: 468)

[...] while Ulster Scots has [ɜ] = *girl*, as in other districts with [ɪ] [...] (Johnston 1997b: 473)

6.12.1 *Scots Style Sheet* recommendation
The *Scots Style Sheet* did not mention that, the assumption being that traditional usage should be followed.

6.12.2 Purves' recommendation
Purves (1979) suggested ⟨i⟩ in words such as *blind*, *birl* 'rotate', *bliss* 'bless', *brig* 'bridge', *dirl* 'vibrate', *git* 'get', *glif* 'fright', *ilk* 'each', *ither* 'other', *kist* 'chest', *mither* 'mother', *rid* 'red', *sic* 'such', *skirl* 'scream', *whilk* 'which', and *yit* 'yet', preferring ⟨u⟩ in words such as *wul* 'will', *wurm* 'worm', *wurship* 'worship', and *wush* 'wish'.

6.12.3 McClure's recommendation
McClure (1980) also suggested ⟨i⟩, following traditional usage.

6.12.4 *Scots Language Society* recommendation
The *Scots Language Society* suggested ⟨i⟩ in words such as *brig* 'brig', *finnd* 'find', *kist* 'chest', and *shilpit* 'puny' but did suggest ⟨u⟩ in *wul* 'will'.

6.12.5 *Aiberdeen Univairsitie Scots Leid Quorum* recommendation
The *Aiberdeen Univairsitie Scots Leid Quorum* suggested ⟨i⟩, following established usage, and giving the example *hill*, but ⟨u⟩ after ⟨w⟩ and ⟨wh⟩, giving the examples *wund* 'wind' and *whustle* 'whistle'. Allan (1995) expanded on that, commenting that the vowel might also be realized /y/ and /ʌ/, but gave *wull* 'will', *whurl* 'whirl', and *wurd* 'word'.

6.12.6 *SLD* recommendation
SLD did not mention that but suggested *will* or *wull* as options.[143]

---

143 See https://web.archive.org/web/20061015063228if_/http://www.scotsdictionaries

6.12.7 Robinson's recommendation

Robinson (1997) suggested ⟨**i**⟩ for various correspondences with English ⟨**e**⟩ or ⟨**u**⟩, giving examples such as *iver* 'ever', *niver* 'never', *rin* 'run', *sic* 'such', and *simmer* 'summer', but also suggested ⟨**u**⟩, especially after ⟨**w**⟩ and ⟨**wh**⟩, in words such as *furst* 'first', *twust* 'twist', *whun* 'gorse', and *wutch* 'witch' and ⟨**ä**⟩, for what is apparently the realization /ɪ̞/ (/æ̈/) described by Gregg (1972: 121), in words such as *bäg* 'big' and *pän* 'pin' but not in *biggin* 'building' or *yin* 'one', which would indicate that his use of ⟨**ä**⟩ is generally (and inconsistently) limited to vocabulary shared with Standard English.

6.12.8 *Scots Spelling Comatee* recommendation

The *Scots Spelling Comatee* suggested ⟨**i**⟩ but did comment on possible realizations with /ʌ/ or /ë/.

6.12.9 Discussion of vowel 15

The traditional grapheme ⟨**i**⟩[144] clearly offers itself here. As the environments where /ʌ/ may occur are phonologically predictable i.e. after /w/ and /ʍ/, those native speakers who have such a realization will produce it unconsciously, as will those who have a realization other than /ɪ/. Robinson's (1997) suggested use of ⟨**ä**⟩ is both confusing and unnecessary, his own failure to apply it consistently proving the point. That is also conditioned by phonological environment and will be unconsciously realized /ɪ̞/ (/æ̈/) or /ë/ by native-speakers. Further innovation would be unnecessary in an orthography designed for native-speakers.

6.13 VOWEL 16

Vowel 16 is usually /ɛ/ but also /ɛː/, especially in Ulster.

> [...] is most commonly [ɛ(ː)] [...] Realisations range from [...] [æ(ː)] [...] to [e(ː)]. Both Ingliding [ɛə~eə] and Upgliding [ɛɪ~eɪ] are occasionally attested [...] (Johnston 1997b: 470)
> [...] Ulster Scots, koinéised as it is, has a split development, with [æ] before voiceless sounds or clusters containing them, and long [ɛˑ(ə)], reminiscent of Gallovidian, elsewhere [...] (Johnston 1997b: 472–473)

When the vowel is short, and the syllable is closed, it usually has the sound [ɛ], e.g. *fecht*, *seck*, with variants [æ], esp. in s.Sc., e.g. *bed*,

---

.org.uk/ScotsSpellingGrammar.htm, accessed 2021-10-30.

144 Also usual in Middle Scots, although the lower Scots (as compared to English accents) realization was occasionally shown by the use of ⟨e⟩. (Aitken 2002: lviii)

leg, [ẹ], in em.Sc.(a), e.g. *ken, gless, fell* [...], except before *r*, where it tends to [e] [.] (SND III: 192 s.v. "ᴇ")

6.13.1 General recommendation

The *Scots Style Sheet*, the *Aiberdeen Univairsitie Scots Leid Quorum* and *SLD* did not mention it, although Allan (1995) gave the examples *fell* 'fierce' and *gless* 'glass' and Robinson (1997) suggested ⟨e⟩ for correspondences to English ⟨a⟩ in words such as *eftèr* 'after'. The assumption otherwise being that traditional usage should be followed.

6.13.2 Purves' recommendation

Purves (1979) suggested ⟨e⟩ in such words as *ken* 'know', *neb* 'nose', *pech* 'pant', *gled* 'glad' etc. but also included some words which have an underlying vowel 4 or 8, such as *gether* 'gather', *herm* 'harm', *Merch* 'March', *perk* 'park', and *trekkil* 'treacle'.

6.13.3 McClure's and *Scots Language Society* recommendation

McClure (1980) suggested ⟨e⟩, as did the *Scots Language Society*, in words such as *ken* 'know', *gled* 'glad', *sneck* 'notch', and *yett* 'gate', but also included some words which have an underlying vowel 4 or 8, such as *ferm* 'farm', *herm* 'harm', and *hert* 'heart'.

6.13.4 *Scots Spelling Comatee* recommendation

The *Scots Spelling Comatee* suggested ⟨e⟩ but pointed out those words with underlying vowel 4 or 8 such as *cairie/kerrie* 'carry', *gaither/gether* 'gather' and *pairt/pert* 'part' but not *exercise, leg* or *term*.

6.13.5 Discussion of vowel 16

The traditional grapheme ⟨e⟩ clearly offers itself here, but should arguably not be used in those words which also have an underlying /e(ː)/ realization, although *ferm* 'farm', *herbour* 'harbour', *hert* 'heart', *mervel* 'marvel', and *sterve* 'starve' are well established spellings.[145] It is arguably easier to render ⟨ai⟩ or ⟨a-e⟩ /ɛ(ː)/ (as is the case with vowels 4 and 8 anyway) than ⟨e⟩ /e(ː)/. This is also the underlying phoneme in Latinate words such as exercise, member, memory and precious, often mistaken for vowel 4 or 8 and written ⟨ai⟩ in an over-enthusiastic attempt to differentiate the language from Standard English. Those native-speakers who have a realization tending towards /e(ː)/ will produce that unconsciously.

---

145 All headword forms in the SND.

6.14 VOWEL 17

Vowel 17 has merged with /a/, /ɑː/ (vowel 12) in some dialects. /ɔ/ may occur for /a/ in some varieties, especially before /n/ and /ŋ/.

The same *a/o* relationship between Scots and English occurs before [m], [p], [b] and [f] but for a quite different reason. Here Scots has unrounded to [ɑ] producing *aff* 'off' [...], *drap* 'drop' [...], *tap* 'top' [...] and *Tammy Norie* 'a puffin' [...] The [ɑ] sound further appears where English has [ei] in *tak* 'take' [...] and *mak* 'make' [...] (Tulloch 1980: 185)

In broad MUE vernacular /ɛ/ is also the usual development of ME /a/ before velars e.g. in *sack, bag, bang*. (Harris 1985: 44)

A following /ŋ/ [...] may retract the CAT realisation or raise it, depending on whether the assimilation is to the backness or height of the following velar [...] (Johnston 1997b: 484)

Mid Scots varieties are split between Front-CAT varieties with isolative [a(ː)~ä(ː)] like [...] Antrim South-west Mid, and Back-CAT ones [...] which have [ɑ(ː)~ä(ː)~ɒ(ː)]. [...] Merger with CAUGHT [...] is generally confined to those varieties adjoining the linguistic north or south. [...] Northern-style near-mergers, with the environment before /t k/ excepted, prevail in County Down [...] (Johnston 1997b: 486)

Southwest Mid varies a great deal, but generally Antrim dialects have isolative [a], and Down ones [ɑ]. There is a tendency to back and lengthen the CAT vowel before voiced sounds, nasals, /l r/ and, in Down, voiceless fricatives [...] Some very front reflexes of the [æ~ɛ] type can occur before velars, and in *bag* they are lengthened to [ɛː] in Down and South Antrim ([L.] Milroy, 1994:139). Diphthongs of the [æi~ai] type can occur in BAG also. (Johnston 1997b: 487)

[...] *half* is transferred to CAT. Roughly the same forms are extant in Ulster Scots, with the most common forms being Down [ö(ː)] and Antrim [ɑ(ː)] [...] (Johnston 1997b: 490)

6.14.1 *Scots Style Sheet* and recommendation
The Scots Style Sheet did not mention it, the assumption being that traditional usage ⟨a⟩ should be followed. Purves (1979) followed suit but included suggestions such as *drak* 'absorb',[146] *dad* 'lump', and *whar* 'where'[147] under vowel 12, although there is also *waddin* 'wedding'.

6.14.2 McClure's recommendation
McClure (1980) suggested following traditional usage.

6.14.3 *Scots Language Society* recommendation
The *Scots Language Society* did not mention it, the assumption being that traditional usage should be followed.

6.14.4 *Aiberdeen Univairsitie Scots Leid Quorum* recommendation
The *Aiberdeen Univairsitie Scots Leid Quorum* also suggested following traditional usage, giving the examples *cat* and *wash*. Allan (1995) expanded on that mentioning that /a/ prevails in West Central dialects but that the /ɑ/ realization is both etymologically and phonemically distinct from vowel 12.

6.14.5 *SLD* and Robinson's recommendation
SLD did not mention vowel 17, the assumption being that traditional usage ⟨a⟩ should be followed, indicated by suggestions such as *cantie* 'cheerful', *cannae* 'can't', and *cannie* 'careful'.[148] Similarly with Robinson (1997), indicated by suggestions such as *alang* 'along', *bak* 'back', *bad, fashed* 'bothered', *pad* 'path', *sab* 'sob', *tak* 'take', and *wast* 'west'.

6.14.6 *Scots Spelling Comatee* recommendation
The *Scots Spellin Comatee* followed suit, indicated by suggestions such as *cat, drap* 'drop', *habber* 'stammer', *knap* 'knock', *mak* 'make', *sclatch* 'bedaub', *shak* 'shake', and *tak* 'take'.

6.14.7 Discussion of vowel 17
The traditional grapheme ⟨a⟩[149] clearly offers itself here. Since the environments where /ɔ/ may occur are phonologically predictable (before /n/ and /ŋ/), and those native-speakers who have such a realization will produce it unconsciously. For mergers see vowel 12.

---

146 Also vowel 4 or 8 [drek, drɑ(ː)k] (SND III: 138 s.v. "DRAIK.").
147 Also vowel 4 or 8 [ʍaːr, ʍɒːr; em.Sc. (b) and s.Sc. have now usu. ʍeːr] (SND X: 121 s.v. "WHAR").
148 See https://web.archive.org/web/20061015063228if_/http://www.scotsdictionaries.org.uk/ScotsSpellingGrammar.htm, accessed 2021-10-30.
149 Also usual in Middle Scots. (Aitken 2002: lviii)

6.15 VOWEL 19

Vowel 19 is usually /ʌ/, but /æ/~/ä/ and /ë/ are also attested. (Johnston 1997b: 476)

6.15.1 *Scots Style Sheet* and Purves' recommendation

The *Scots Style Sheet* did not mention it, the assumption being that traditional usage ⟨u⟩ should be followed. Purves (1979) suggested ⟨u⟩, giving examples such as *bull*, *dubs* 'puddles', *grund* 'ground', *hurl* 'ride', *hunder* 'hundred', *lug* 'ear', *puddok* 'toad', *pull*, and *push*.

6.15.2 McClure's and *Scots Language Society* recommendation

McClure (1980) suggested ⟨u⟩. The *Scots Language Society* also did so, giving examples such as *bul* 'bull', *drumlie* 'turbid', *dubs* 'puddles' *ful* 'full', *hunder* 'hundred', and *lug* 'ear'.

6.15.3 *Aiberdeen Univairsitie Scots Leid Quorum* recommendation

The *Aiberdeen Univairsitie Scots Leid Quorum* indicated following traditional usage but preferred ⟨u⟩ for vowel 15 after ⟨w⟩ and ⟨wh⟩, while Allan (1995) simply added detail.

6.15.4 *SLD* recommendation

SLD did not mention it, the assumption being that traditional usage ⟨u⟩ should be followed, as indicated in examples such as *grutten* 'weeped', *hurlie* (a 'hand-cart', *pund* 'pound', and *scunnersome* 'objectionable'.[150]

6.15.5 Robinson's recommendation

Robinson (1997) did not mention it, the assumption being that traditional usage ⟨u⟩ should be followed, but often used that for vowel 15 after ⟨w⟩ and ⟨wh⟩.

6.15.6 *Scots Spelling Comatee* recommendation

The *Scots Spellin Comatee* suggested following traditional usage.

6.15.7 Discussion of vowel 19

The traditional grapheme ⟨u⟩[151] clearly offers itself here. For mergers see vowel 15.

---

150 See https://web.archive.org/web/20061015063228if_/http://www.scotsdictionaries .org.uk/ScotsSpellingGrammar.htm, accessed 2021-10-30.

151 Also usual in Middle Scots. In the vicinity of letters written with minimum strokes ⟨o⟩ was used for clarity rather than ⟨u⟩. (Aitken 2002: lviii) e.g. *come*, *some* and the prefix *on-* 'un-'.

7
MORPHEMES AND GRAMMAR

If the investigation of morphemic features is begun with the assumption of a direct relationship between spelling and sound, then problems appear immediately. (Venezky 1970: 41)

7.1 THE NEGATIVE PARTICLE -*NA*

The traditional negative particle ⟨**-na**⟩ was suggested by all except *SLD* (2002), which suggested the modernism ⟨**-nae**⟩, although Macleod (1996) and *SNDA* (1999: 4.7.2) included both ⟨**-nae**⟩ and ⟨**-na**⟩. *SNDA* (1999: 4.7.4) suggested the form *mauna* 'mustn't', with a single ⟨**n**⟩, as against *maunna* presumably in order to conform to double-consonant rules, but contradicted that with forms such as *aipple* 'apple' and *cairrie* 'carry' (3.2, 4.2.2). In the headword list based upon the contents of the *Essential Scots Dictionary*[152] apparently only ⟨**-nae**⟩ was chosen, as shown in examples such as *amnae* 'amn't' and *arnae* 'aren't'. Robinson (1997) also suggested ⟨**-nae**⟩.

> The unstressed, gen. enclitic form of No, not, chiefly used with aux.
> verbs, as *canna, dinna, haena, winna*, etc., (SND VI: 377 s.v. "NA *adv.*²")

The obvious choice for a normative orthography would be the traditional ⟨**-na**⟩ inherited from Middle Scots,[153] the modernism ⟨**-nae**⟩ over-emphasizing an /e/ realization.

7.2 THE PRESENT PARTICIPLE -*IN*

All suggested ⟨**-in**⟩ for the present participle and verbal noun except the *Scots Style Sheet* (1947) and Purves (1979), which suggested differentiating the present participle ⟨**-an**⟩ from the verbal noun ⟨**-in**⟩. Although differentia-

---

152 https://web.archive.org/web/20061015063701/http://www.scotsdictionaries.org.uk /HeadWordList/A.html, accessed 2021-10-30. In the 2004 ESD the headwords *amna, amnae; arna, arnae* are given (pp. 2–3); while the cross-reference *canna, cannae* points to *can*, in that entry the forms *cannae, canna* and *cudnae, cudna* are given in that order (p. 19).

153 The enclitic negative particle […] is *na* […] as in ModSc. (Aitken 2002: cxviii)

tion of the present participle and verbal noun may still occur in some peripheral dialects, it has generally not been indicated in writing since the Middle Scots period.

> Final *d* from the Sc. *pr.p.* ending *-and* is regularly dropped in all dials., e.g. *eatin, gaun, hingin, stannin.* (SND III: 1 s.v. "D")

> in the unaccented termination *-ing*, as in vbl.ns. and adjs. *comin, fleein, makin, rinnin,* etc.; *mornin, herrin, shillin,* [...] (SND IV: 217 s.v. "G")

Many would find it difficult to differentiate the present participle and verbal noun in practice and since those who have differentiated realizations would produce them unconsciously, its representation in writing is not necessary, leaving ⟨**-in**⟩ as the obvious choice in a normative orthography.

7.3 WEAK VERB PRETERITES IN *-IT, -T, -'T, -(E)D*, AND *-'D*

The historical development of the past tense of weak verbs is described as follows in the *Scottish National Dictionary*:

> Main verbs fall into two groups: 'weak' and 'strong'. The weak verbs form the preterite (the past tense form) and past participle by adding a suffix, in OE *-ed*; in ESc *-id/-yd*; later *-it/-yt* or, after vowels, *-d*. There is occasional confusion with the ending *-at(e)* from Romance sources, e.g. *imbarcat(t)* as a past tense or past participle of imbark (Meurman-Solin, 1993: 233).[154]

> **5**. *d* was unvoiced to *t* in the *pa.p.* of weak verbs, *-ed* becoming *-it*, early in the Mid.Sc. period and has remained so, e.g. *crabbit, happit, wannert, feart, dozent*, but prevails in nn.Sc., e.g. *chapped, cropped* (both dissyllables), *mashed, stuffed*.
> In s.Sc. and em.Sc. (a) after *l, r, m, n, ng*, or a vowel in a monosyllable, *d* is regularly restored, e.g. *telld, belangd, dee'd*, Eng. told, belonged, died, though *t* forms are also found.[155]

> **3**. Finally (1) for orig. *d*: (i) in the pa.t. and pa.p. of weak verbs where the ending forms a separate syllable. See P.L.D. § 63; in n., wm. and sm.Sc. also freq. after stems ending in *-l, -m, -n, -ng, -r*, and in monosyllabic vowel stems, though usage fluctuates.[156]

---

154 "History of Scots to 1700 §7.8.6 The past tense and past participle inflection of weak verbs", https://web.archive.org/web/20210507131058/https://dsl.ac.uk/about-scots /history-of-scots/grammar/, accessed 2021-10-30.

155 SND III: 1 s.v. "D".

156 SND IX: 177 s.v. "T".

§ 63. *t* replaces *d* in the pa.p. suffix *ed* and in ppl. adjs. This was the common usage in Middle Sc. Examples in Mod.Sc., *stoppit* or *stopt*, *jaggit* or *jaggt*, *rummlt*, for *stopped, jagged, rumbled*.[157]

7.3.1 *Scots Style Sheet* recommendation

The past participles ⟨-it⟩, ⟨-t⟩, or ⟨ed⟩ in weak verbs were discussed in the *Scots Style Sheet* (1947), which suggested "Past tense and past participles of weak verbs in -it, -t and -ed according to euphony [...]".

7.3.2 Purves' recommendation

Purves expanded on the Scots Style Sheet commentary slightly.

> It is now normal to also use '-t', '-d' and '-ed', according to euphony. Verbs ending in '-b', '-d', '-g', '-k', '-p' and '-t' add on '-it' [...] Verbs ending in '-il', '-en', '-er', '-ch', '-sh', '-ss' and 'f', usually add on '-t' [...] Otherwise the tendency is to employ '-ed' or '-d', the latter being often added when the infinitive already ends in silent '-e' [...] (Purves 1979: 64)

7.3.3 McClure's recommendation

McClure did not treat verbal accidence explicitly.

7.3.4 *Scots Language Society* recommendation

The *Scots Language Society* also expanded on the Scots Style Sheet commentary somewhat.

> Past tense and past participles of weak verbs ending in '-b', '-d', '-g', '-k', '-p' and '-t' add on '-it' [...]Verbs ending in '-il', '-en', '-er', '-ch', '-sh', '-ss' and 'f', usually add on '-t' [...] Otherwise '-ed' may be used [...] or '-d' when the infinitive already ends in silent '-e' [...] (SLS 1985)

7.3.5 *Aiberdeen Univairsitie Scots Leid Quorum* recommendation

The *Aiberdeen Universitie Scots Leid Quorum* (Lovie 1995) suggested the inflection ⟨-it⟩ after ⟨b⟩, ⟨d⟩, ⟨g⟩, ⟨k⟩, ⟨p⟩, and ⟨t⟩. The inflection ⟨-t⟩ was suggested after ⟨f⟩, ⟨s⟩, ⟨n⟩, ⟨l⟩, ⟨th⟩, ⟨ch⟩, ⟨sh⟩, ⟨ce⟩, and ⟨s⟩ /s/ and sometimes ⟨r⟩, and after silent ⟨e⟩, ⟨-'t⟩, and that final ⟨-le⟩ change to ⟨-ilt⟩. The inflection ⟨-ed⟩ was suggested after ⟨m⟩, ⟨ve⟩, ⟨w⟩, ⟨we⟩, ⟨x⟩, ⟨y⟩, ⟨z⟩, ⟨ou⟩, and ⟨se⟩ /z/, all verbs ending ⟨e⟩, except those previously mentioned and sometimes after ⟨r⟩, adding that after ⟨ee⟩, ⟨'d⟩ and that ⟨-ed⟩ displace a final ⟨e⟩.

---

157 SND I: xxii §63.

7.3.6 *SLD* recommendation

SLD was not so clear:

> Past tenses and past participles end with *-it* or *-t*, eg *leukit, gaithert*. Sometimes the English ending *-ed* or *-d*, is used, eg *leuked, gaithered*.
>
> For verbs ending with *-le*, eg *ettle, fankle, pauchle*, the past tense and participle often ends with *-elt*: *Yon cassette tape's no workin—the tape's aw fankelt*.
>
> Some verbs ending with *-ll*, eg *tell* and *dwall*, drop one of the 'l's to become *-elt* : *Ah telt ye*.
>
> For strong and irregular verbs, see list at end of GB [Grammar Broonie], eg *tint* (from *tyne*), *grat, grutten* (from *greet*) see Verb List.[158]
>
> Some irregular English verbs, like *keep* and *tell*, are *regular* in Scots: *Ah telt ye* (English 'told'); *Ah've keepit a seat for ye* (English 'kept'). (*SLD*)[159]

> Past tenses and past participles end with *-it* or *-t* [...] sometimes the English form, ending with *-ed* or *-d* is used [...] For verbs ending with *-le* [...] the past tense & participle often ends with *-elt* [...] Some verbs ending with *-ll* [.] drop one of the 'l's to become *-elt* [.] (*SNDA* 1999: 4.3.1, 4.3.2, 4.3.3)

> For many of the verbs you can also use the English form, if it fits your sentence better [...] Most Scots verbs however form the past tense and past participle by adding *-(**i**)t* [.] or *-(**e**)d* as in English [...]. (Macleod 1996: 369)

Rennie (1999: 21) mentioned an apostrophe in *dee'd* the past tense of *dee* 'die'. A more precise description was offered in Macleod and Cairns (1993: viii):

> for past tense, past participle:
> -it after -b, -d, -g, -k, -p, -t, as in *biggit, howkit*
> -t after -il, -en, -er, -ch, -tch, -sh, -ss, -f as in *laucht, fasht, fleetcht*
> -(e)d, as in *kaimed, hained, breenged, chowed*
> -elt for verbs ending in -le, as in *sprauchelt, trauchelt*.

---

158 https://web.archive.org/web/20061015063412/http://www.scotsdictionaries.org.uk /VerbList.htm, accessed 2021-10-30. This included the advice given in Macleod 1996 p.369.

159 https://web.archive.org/web/20070722185928/http://www.scotsdictionaries.org.uk /Scots/Grammar/Verbs.html, accessed 2021-10-30

7.3.7 Robinson's recommendation

Robinson (1997) suggested that verbs which end with a stressed vowel take a ⟨-**d**⟩ ending, verbs which end in a consonant take ⟨-**it**⟩, and verbs which end in a liquid or nasal consonant take ⟨-**t**⟩.

7.3.8 *Scots Spelling Comatee* recommendation

The *Scots Spellin Comatee* (2000) recommended ⟨-**it**⟩ after ⟨**b**⟩, ⟨**d**⟩, ⟨**g**⟩, ⟨**k**⟩, ⟨**p**⟩, and ⟨-**t**⟩, ⟨-**t**⟩ after ⟨**f**⟩, ⟨**ss**⟩, ⟨**en**⟩, ⟨**l**⟩, ⟨**sh**⟩, ⟨**tch**⟩, ⟨**ch**⟩, sometimes ⟨**r**⟩ and after an unstressed *"ee"* sound, ⟨**le**⟩ changes to ⟨-**elt**⟩, ⟨-**ed**⟩ after others including ⟨**se**⟩ /z/ and ⟨-'**d**⟩ after ⟨**ee**⟩. Unchanged past participles of Latinate verbs were also mentioned.

7.3.9 Discussion of weak verb preterites

Clearly the phonetic nature of the past tense morpheme is conditioned by phonetic environment:

> The verbal or adjectival termination *ed* becomes **ət** after **p, t, k, b, d, g**, except in Caithness dialect where it is **əd**. (Grant and Dixon 1921: 8)

> The connecting vowel is dropped when the verb ends in any consonant except **p, t, k, d, b, g**. After an accented vowel **d** (instead of **t**) is more common in the Mid and Sth. dialects as also after a liquid or nasal. (Grant and Dixon 1921: 113)

> The dental termination of the past participle, borrowed from French or Latin, does not take on final "-d" or "-ed" in Scottish. (Grant and Dixon 1921: 182)

> In unaccented syllables, the sound of *e* is reduced and can be represented in a broad transcription by [ə] but there is a tendency in Sc. to retain a slight trace of the original quality of the vowel somewhere in the range between [ɛ] and [ɪ] [...] As a result, *e* is occasionally written for the historical *i* in the ending *-it* of the *pa.t.* and *pa.p.* of weak verbs, e.g. *cracket*. (SND III: 192 s.v. "E")

> With dialect differences, the resulting preferences are therefore: [-ɪt] after stops [...] [-t] after non-stop consonants (voiceless fricatives in particular) and unstressed vowels [...] [-d] after voiced non-stop consonants and stressed vowels [...] and a few other Latin participles used without a Scots inflection [...] there are irregular weak verbs, mostly shared with English [...] but also

some independent items [...] Several verbs that are declined irregularly in English may be treated as regular verbs in Scots [...] A small number of verbs in the St E weak irregular paradigm may be strong verbs in Scots. (Görlach 2002: 96–97)

Those phonetic descriptions suggest ⟨-t⟩, ⟨-it⟩, and ⟨-(e)d⟩ or ⟨-'d⟩. Since the realization of the past-tense morpheme is conditioned by phonetic environment, an orthography-based description depends on the chosen graphemic representations of those environments noting that the original ⟨-it⟩ /ət/~/ɪt/, inherited from Middle Scots,[160] has be subject to an ongoing process of simplification to /t/ or voiced /(ə)d/.

7.3.9.1 Stems ending in voiced and voiceless stops: *-it, -t, -ed*

Where the realization is still /ət/~/ɪt/ after the stop consonants /b/, /d/, /g/, /k/, /p/, and /t/ usually represented by ⟨b⟩, ⟨d⟩, ⟨g⟩, ⟨ck⟩~⟨k⟩, ⟨p⟩, and ⟨t⟩ the spelling ⟨-it⟩ is an unambiguous solution for a normative orthography, where a final "silent" ⟨-e⟩ follows those it is dropped when forming the past tense, in words such as *rub > rubbit, gaird > gairdit* 'guard', *rag > raggit, swick > swickit* 'deceive', *keek > keekit* 'peep', *like > likit, drap > drappit* 'drop', *keep > keepit, hurt > hurtit*, and *licht > lichtit* 'light'. However, in some varieties of Scots the inflection has been reduced to /t/ after /k/ and /p/; in order to represent these, ⟨-t⟩ (or ⟨-'t⟩ after a final "silent" ⟨-e⟩) would give *keekt, like't*, and *drapt*. The forms *keekt* and *drapt* are also an unambiguous choice, however, in Standard English the spelling ⟨-(e)d⟩ can be used to represent the realization /t/ suggesting an alternative to forms such as **like't**, where **liked**, a tidier form avoiding the apostrophe, also presents itself as a sound choice in a normative orthography.

7.3.9.2 Stems ending in nasals: *-it, -t,* and *-ed*

The original ⟨-it⟩ may still occur after the fully voiced nasal stops /m/, /n/, and /ŋ/, usually represented by ⟨m⟩, ⟨n⟩, and ⟨ng⟩, in words such as *jam > jammit, corn > cornit*, and *fang > fangit* 'seize', where the preterite is disyllabic. Today, however, the suffix ⟨-t⟩ or ⟨-ed⟩ is often more likely, giving monosyllables which may have the preterite ending realized as either voiceless or voiced: *jamt~jammed* (alongside *jammit*), *cornt~corned* (alongside *cornit*), and *fangt~fanged* (alongside *fangit*). In many cases the original ⟨-it⟩ is no longer current and the choice is binary: *tuim > tuimt~tuimed* 'empty', *droun > drount~drouned* 'drown', *ken > kent~kenned* 'know', *mean > meant~meaned, soum > soumed* 'swim', and *stang > stangt~stanged* 'sting'. Thus there is a class of stems ending in nasals with three possible weak past tense endings, and

---

160 Middle Scots employed both ⟨-it⟩ and ⟨-yt⟩, and ⟨-d⟩ after vowels. (Aitken 2002: cxiii)

a class with only two, providing a sound choice for a normative orthography.

7.3.9.3 Stems ending in liquids: -t and -ed

After the voiced liquids /l/ and /r/, usually represented by ⟨ll⟩~⟨le⟩ and ⟨r⟩, the suffix ⟨-t⟩ is added; the "silent" ⟨-e⟩ in ⟨le⟩ could be followed by an apostrophe or be dropped giving ⟨lt⟩, unless a consonant it in which case it is changed to ⟨elt⟩. In some places the suffix remains voiced, and spellings in ⟨ed⟩ should be allowed to permit this realization: *bile* > *bile't*~*biled* or *byle* > *bylt*~*byled* 'boil',[161] *fill* > *fillt*~*filled*, *spile* > *spile't*~*spiled* or *spyle* > *spylt*~*spyled* 'spoil', *taigle* > *taigelt*~*taigled* 'hinder', *blether* > *blethert*~*blethered* 'gossip', and *fear* > *feart*~*feared* 'frighten'. A handful of words ending in ⟨ll⟩ have established spellings where the ⟨llt⟩ is simplified: *dwall* > *dwalt*~*dwalled*, *kill* > *kilt*~*killed*, *sell* > *selt*~*selled*, *spell* > *spelt*~*spelled*, *spill* > *spilt*~*spilled*, *tell* > *telt*~*telled*.

7.3.9.4 Stems ending in voiceless affricates and fricatives: -t

After /tʃ/, /f/, /s/, /θ/, /ʃ/, and /x/ represented by ⟨ch⟩, ⟨f⟩, ⟨s⟩~⟨se⟩, ⟨th⟩, ⟨sh⟩, and ⟨ch⟩, the past tense of weak verbs is usually formed with /t/ written ⟨-t⟩; where a final "silent" ⟨-e⟩ follows those it is dropped: *ratch* > *ratcht* 'scratch', *watch* > *watcht*, *fuff* > *fufft* 'puff', *bliss* > *blisst* 'bless', *miss* > *misst*, *souse* > *soust* 'strike', *traipse* > *traipst* 'tramp', *graith* > *graitht* 'equip', *mooth* > *mootht* 'mouth', *fash* > *fasht* 'fret', *vainish* > *vainisht* 'vanish', and *pech* > *pecht* 'pant'.

7.3.9.5 Stems ending in voiced affricates and fricatives: -(e)d

After /dʒ/, /ð/, /v/, /z/ usually represented by ⟨(d)ge⟩, ⟨the⟩, ⟨ve⟩, ⟨se⟩, ⟨ze⟩, and ⟨zz⟩ the past tense of weak verbs usually have a voiced realization; for these, ⟨-(e)d⟩ is an unambiguous choice for a normative orthography, in words such as *fidge* > *fidged* 'fidget', *peenge* > *peenged* 'whine', *kythe* > *kythed* 'reveal', *smuithe* > *smuithed* 'smooth', *impruive* > *impruived* 'improve', *scrieve* > *scrieved* 'glide along', *lowse* > *lowsed* 'loosen', *uise* > *uised* 'use', *heeze* > *heezed* 'lift', and *bizz* > *bizzed* 'buzz'.

7.3.9.6 Stems ending in stressed vowels: -it, -ed, and -'d

After stressed vowels the past-tense is usually a voiced /(ə)d/ suggesting again ⟨-(e)d⟩, where an apostrophe may be inserted (in a few words) to avoid homonyms or to represent an elided ⟨e⟩ in ⟨-ed⟩, in words such as *bou* > *boued* 'bow', *caw* > *cawed* 'call', *dee* > *dee'd* 'die', *lee* > *lee'd* 'fib', *pey* > *peyed* 'pay', *rowe* > *rowed* 'roll', *saw* > *sawed* 'saw wood', and *snaw* > *snawed*

---

161 See §6.2.11 for discussion of vowel 10.

'snow'. In some dialects, however, a voiceless realization may occur; here the apostrophe in ⟨-'t⟩ can serve to prevent confusion, giving *bou't, caw't, dee't, lee't, pey't, rowe't, saw't,* and *snaw't,* etc.

7.3.9.7 Stems ending in unstressed vowels: *-it, -d*

After unstressed vowels (as in disyllables, usually ⟨ae⟩, ⟨ie⟩, and ⟨y⟩), the past-tense may be either a voiceless /ət/~/ɪt/ or a voiced /əd/~/ɪd/, where either ⟨-it⟩ replaces the stem ending entirely, or ⟨-d⟩ is added, with ⟨y⟩ changing first to ⟨ie⟩: *follae > follit~follaed* 'follow', *jundie > jundit~jundied* 'jostle', and *mairy > mairit~mairied* 'marry', etc.

7.3.9.8 The past participle adjective in *-it*

The past participle adjective, however, may still be realized with /ət/~/ɪt/; in such cases ⟨-it⟩ is most appropriate: *beluvit* 'beloved', *blissit* 'blessed', *impruivit* 'improved', and *ratchit* 'scratched', etc.

7.3.10 Summary

Difficult as it is to explain the above in an easily digestible manner, native speakers should manage that instinctively "according to euphony" as the *Scots Style Sheet* (1947) suggested. Adding ⟨-it⟩ to *all* verbs, a practice often seen in contemporary writing, misrepresents the underlying phonology and may simply be the result of those unacquainted with spoken Scots lacking the necessary *phonemic awareness*. Such persons would clearly benefit from a regularized dictionary which included the past-tense inflections.

7.4 THE ADJECTIVAL SUFFIX *-OUS*

Only Purves (1979) commented on the adjectival suffix ⟨-ous⟩, suggesting ⟨-uss⟩, as in *byuss* 'extra-ordinary', *cantankeruss* 'quarrelsome', *mischieviuss* 'mischievous', *contermaciuss* 'obstinate', *praiciuss* 'precious', and *sairiuss* 'serious'. SND headwords include *byous* 'extraordinary', *carnaptious* 'irritable', *contermacious* 'obstinate', *fashious* 'annoying', *releegious* 'religious', *sairious* 'serious', *timeous* 'in good time', and *undeemous* 'enormous' suggesting the traditional spelling ⟨-ous⟩ should be retained in a normative orthography.

7.5 THE SUFFIX *-FU*

For the suffix ⟨-fu⟩ '-ful', Purves (1979) suggested ⟨-fu⟩. SNDA (1999: 2.3) suggests ⟨-fae⟩ but in the headword list based upon the contents of the *Essential Scots Dictionary awfy* 'awful' was given, along with the variants *affa* (Northern) and *aafil* (Orkney),[162] the etymological form *awfu* not being

---

162 If not an Orkney realization of Standard English it is the doublet *awful*; the form *aafu* is

mentioned.[163] Certainly the realizations of the vowel across dialects seem to mirror those of the negative particle ⟨-na⟩, perhaps by analogy. The forms ⟨-fa⟩, ⟨-fae⟩, ⟨-fy⟩ over-emphasize local realizations. The form ⟨-fu⟩ would be an etymologically sound choice for a normative orthography.

7.6 FINAL -*R* IN -*AR*, -*ER*, -*OUR*, -*URE*, AND -*ER*

A number of traditional etymological spellings now include a reduced vowel /ə/ before final /r/. Those include both ⟨-ar⟩ and ⟨-er⟩ for the agent suffix, ⟨-our⟩ in words such as *colour, honour,* and *odour,* ⟨-ure⟩ in words such as *pleasure, leisure, future,* and *picture,* and final ⟨-er⟩ in comparatives and words such as *beaver, faither* 'father', *maister* 'master', and *mutter.*

> In unaccented syllables, the sound of *e* is reduced and can be represented in a broad transcription by [ə] but there is a tendency in Sc. to retain a slight trace of the original quality of the vowel somewhere in the range between [ɛ] and [ɪ] [...] (SND III: 192 s.v. "E")

Few made any specific suggestion for dealing with those, the assumption being that traditional practice should be followed. For the agent suffix Purves (1979) seemed to prefer ⟨-ar⟩ but also used *customer* and *percentor* 'precentor'. Rennie (1999) mentions ⟨-ar⟩ as a Scots form in *makar* 'poet', *cottar* 'cottager', *soutar* 'shoemaker' but does not implicitly state that ⟨-er⟩ forms should not be used in others. The ⟨ar⟩ form was certainly used in Older Scots but may, in many words, seem unfamiliar to contemporary Scots speakers. Purves's (1979) use of ⟨-ir⟩ in words such as *beavir* 'beaver', *eftir* 'after', *evir* 'ever', and *nevir* 'never' may be influenced by the vowel quality ranging between [ɛ] and [ɪ], perhaps suggesting an /ɪr/ realization. It may equally be influenced by Middle Scots practice, the forms *bevir/bavir, eftir, evir/ewir,* and *nevir/nifir/nawir* all being cited in DOST.[164] Interestingly in the headword list based upon the contents of the *Essential Scots Dictionary* the form *eftir* 'after' was apparently the choice;[165] otherwise ⟨er⟩ was used in words such as *aither* 'either', *anither* 'another', and *awthegither* 'altogether'. A normative orthography would, perhaps, best be served by using the

also given in the Orkney Dictionary (1996: 1).

163 https://web.archive.org/web/20061015063701/http://www.scotsdictionaries.org.uk /HeadWordList/A.html, accessed 2021-10-30. In the 2004 ESD the headword *awfu, awfie, aafu* is given (p. 4)

164 *Dictionary of the Older Scottish Tongue* available at http://www.dsl.ac.uk

165 https://web.archive.org/web/20061015063701/http://www.scotsdictionaries.org.uk /HeadWordList/A.html, accessed 2021-10-30. In the 2004 ESD the headword *efter, aifter, after* is given (p. 43).

familiar ⟨er⟩, a judicious study of the literary record establishing where ⟨-ar⟩, ⟨-er⟩, and Latinate ⟨-or⟩ forms prevailed as an agent suffix. Only Purves (1979) suggested using ⟨-or⟩ where ⟨-our⟩ was traditionally used, in examples such as *honor* and *odor*. A native speaker is unlikely to realize ⟨-our⟩ as /uːr/ in unstressed position, rendering it an unambiguous choice for a normative orthography. The case for an alternative to ⟨-ure⟩ can be made, since the Standard English realizations of words such as *creature* [ˈkriːtʃə(r)], *lecture* [ˈlɛktʃə(r)] and *picture* [ˈpɪkʃə(r)] have /tʃə(r)/ or /ʃə(r)/ where Scots has /tər/ as in [ˈkretər], [ˈlɛktər], and [ˈpɪktər]. Regularization to *craitur*, *lectur* and *pictur* would, arguably, better indicate the Scots realization. In a normative orthography that same regularization could then be applied to words such as *leisur* [ˈliːʒər] and *pleisur* 'pleasure' [ˈpliːzər]~[ˈplezər]~[ˈpliːʒər], avoiding, for example, Purves's (1979) ad hoc *craeter* 'creature', *future*, *lectur* 'lecture', *leisure*, *picter* 'picture', and *pleisure* 'pleasure'.

7.6.1 Anglo-Norman-derived endings *-ar* and *-or*

Although not analysed in the sample the SND provides an interesting insight in to the traditional treatment of many French- or Latin-derived words with endings derived from the Anglo-French form *-arie* and *-orie* which take the form *-ary* and *-ory* in Standard English. In Scots the Continental French *-aire* and *-oire* were the source and those were regularized to *-ar* and *-or*. The SND giving examples such as *dictionar* 'dictionary', *missionar* 'missionary', *necessar* 'necessary', *notar* 'notary', *ordinar* 'ordinary', *secretar* 'secretary', *summar* 'summary', *interrogator* 'interrogatory', and *inventor* 'inventory' etc.[166]

7.7 THE CAUSATIVE SUFFIX *-FEE*

The final syllable in Romance words or those formed by analogy such as *argifee* 'argue', *glorifee* 'glorify', *pecifee* 'pacify', *qualifee* 'qualify', *saitisfee* 'satisfy', *sauntifee* 'sanctify', and *terrifee* 'terrify'.[167] The traditional realization was clearly /fi/, though the literary record also includes spellings such as ⟨-fie⟩ and ⟨-fy⟩. The ⟨y⟩ in the spelling ⟨-fy⟩ may perhaps have been interpreted as an /i/ realization of the word-final ⟨y⟩ described below. The continued influence of the southern standard also affected the realization in speech which often became /fəɪ/.

---

166 SND X: 536 (Supplement) s.v. "Y". Also at https://web.archive.org/web/20211030132649/https://dsl.ac.uk/entry/snd/snds4656 accessed 2021-10-30
167 All headword forms in the SND.

[…] in the pronunciation of older people (fi, fi), but with the more modernized (fei) or (fɐi); *terrify*, older (tær·əfi), newer (tær·ifɐi). (Murray 1873: 136)

Murray's description of the pronunciation with a diphthong may simply represent the usual Southern Scots realization of vowel 11, though the influence of the southern standard is equally likely for all dialects. In a normative orthography the spelling ⟨**-fee**⟩ would be less ambiguous, especially if the intention is to reinforce the traditional Scots realization.

7.8 THE ADJECTIVAL/DIMINUTIVE SUFFIXES -*Y* AND -*IE*

The adjectival and adverbial suffix was usually written as ⟨**-y**⟩ or ⟨**-ie**⟩, whereby ⟨**-ie**⟩ prevailed in words which appeared to be particularly Scots. The diminutive was usually always formed with ⟨**-ie**⟩.

Final *ie* or *y* has in most parts of m.Sc. [e], elsewhere some variation of *i* [ɪ, ḭ or i]. In n.Sc. and e.Per. final *ie* or *y* varies (1) according to the character of the preceding vowel, (2) according to the preceding consonant. In the first case if the stem vowel is *ee* [i] or *ey* [əi, ei] final *ie* or *y* tends to become *ee* [i]—e.g. *wheelie*, *weety* (*wet*), *wily*.[168] Secondly if the preceding consonant is a voiced plosive or fricative—e.g. *d* or *z*—the suffix is [i] as *body*, *bosie* (*bosom*).[169] (SND I: xvii §28.21)

The *Scots Style Sheet* (1947) and McClure (1980) made no mention of that but both Purves (1979) and The *Scots Language Society* suggested ⟨**-ie**⟩ across the board. The *Aiberdeen Universitie Scots Leid Quorum* (Lovie 1995) made no mention of it but Alan (1995: 94) followed Purves and the *Scots Language Society*. *SLD* simply mentions the following "The -*ie* ending (as opposed to -*y*) is commonly used at the end of diminutives, eg *lassie*, *bairnie*, and adjectives, eg *bonnie*, *cantie*. But note that -*y* is more common for adverbial endings, eg *bonnily*, *cantily*."[170] Macleod and Cairns (1993: vii) suggested using ⟨**-ie**⟩ rather that ⟨**-y**⟩ at the end of a word citing *bonnie* 'pretty' and *canny* 'careful'. In Rennie (1999: 7, 13) it is suggested when forming the present participle of verbs that ⟨**-ie**⟩ be changed to ⟨**-y**⟩, the author giving the examples *coorie* > *cooryin* 'crouch' and *cairrie* > *cairryin* 'carry', and when forming adverbs from adjectives to add ⟨**-lie**⟩ or ⟨**-ly**⟩ but to drop the ⟨**e**⟩

168 ˈʍili, ˈwiti, ˈwɔili. [Original footnote]
169 ˈbɔdi, ˈboːzi. [Original footnote]
170 https://web.archive.org/web/20070722185928/http://www.scotsdictionaries.org.uk /Scots/Grammar/Verbs.html, accessed 2021-10-30.

where it ends an adjective, the author giving the examples *bonnie* > *bonnily* 'pretty' and *braw* > *brawlie* 'splendid'. The *Scots Spelling Comatee* (2000) suggested using ⟨-ie⟩ for words unique to or characteristic of Scots, including diminutives, and ⟨y⟩ for shared vocabulary, including Latinate and Greek suffixes such as ⟨-ity⟩, ⟨-logy⟩, and ⟨-graphy⟩. Robinson (1997) also suggested ⟨-ie⟩ and ⟨-lie⟩ for diminutives, adjectives and adverbs.

The grapheme ⟨-ie⟩ presents an unambiguous traditional choice for diminutives in a normative orthography. In order to homogenize the appearance of adverbs and adjectives, but also many other words, the choice has to be either ⟨-(l)ie⟩ or ⟨-(l)y⟩. Mixing forms is clearly inconsistent and renders it difficult to explain where to apply one form or the other. Following Standard English practice by using ⟨-(l)y⟩ enables both Scots and shared vocabulary to mell together as a homogenous language, giving regular patterns such as *cairy* > *cairyin* 'carry', *bonny* > *bonnily* 'pretty', *braw* > *brawly* 'splendid', and *stour* > *stoury* 'dust' which blend in well with forms such as *body*, *funny*, *happy* and *ony* 'any', incidentally avoiding unfamiliar forms such as *funnie* 'funny', and *happie* 'happy'.

7.9 THE SUFFIX COGNATE WITH STANDARD ENGLISH *-OW*

Although not a morpheme, the pronunciations of the final unstressed vowel, usually written ⟨-ow⟩ in Standard English cognates, has a range of realizations similar to that of the negative particle traditionally written ⟨-na⟩.

> The ending *ow* tends to have a short *ay* [e] sound in most of the central dialects and in other districts an [ə] vowel as in *barrow*, *marrow*, etc., ['bare] as against ['barə]. (SND I: xvii §28.21)

The various realizations, depending on word, stress and dialect /ə/, /e/, /ɪ/, /i/, occasionally /o/, and /u/ in a few words, have had various representations in the traditional literature, for example the numerous forms used in the Scots cognate of "window": ⟨-a⟩, ⟨-ae⟩, ⟨-aw⟩, ⟨-ey⟩, ⟨-ie⟩, ⟨-o⟩, ⟨-ow⟩, ⟨-y⟩ (SND X: 195 s.v. "WINDOW"). Similarly in the Scots cognates of words such as "arrow", "barrow", "fellow", "marrow", "meadow", "narrow", "shadow", "sorrow", "swallow", "wallow", "widow", "winnow", and "yellow". Where ⟨-ow⟩[171] was not used, the most frequent written representations seemed to be ⟨-a⟩ or ⟨-ae⟩ where ⟨-a⟩ probably represented /ə/ and ⟨-ae⟩ /e/, /ɪ/, or /i/. For a normative orthography ⟨-ow⟩ would likely indicate the diphthong /ʌu/ or simply be interpreted

---

171 This was often used in Scots words with a similar phonology such as ['sɔibə, 'sɔibi] 'sybow' where *sybae* would perhaps be a better orthographic representation of its realization.

/ɔ:/ as in Standard English, both unlikely realizations in Scots. The parallels with the negative particle offer both ⟨-**a**⟩ and ⟨-**ae**⟩ the latter perhaps better able to subsume the realizations /ə/, /e/, /ɪ/, and /i/ giving such spellings as *arrae, barrae, fallae, marrae, meidae, nairae, shaidae, sorrae, swallae, wallae, weedae, windae, winnae,* and *yellae* for the Standard English cognates above.

7.10 GRAMMAR

Most 18th and 19th century writing in Scots usually followed the grammatical conventions of Standard English of its time. For example, the use of the Northern Subject Rule was conspicuous by its absence and the use of *wha* 'who', as a relative pronoun, conspicuous by its presence. One aspect of language planning mentioned by Haugen (1961: 68) was, besides a normative orthography, a codified grammar. With regards to Scots, the question arises as to whether the grammar of the spoken dialects is to be its foundation or that of Standard English, the written variety, or "language of the book", with which most Scots-speakers are familiar.

> I think there is nothing to complain of or apologise for, unless it be that the editors of the Scottish newspapers have not always been careful to discern between the vernacular and the vulgar, and have frequently allowed a thin veneer of Scottish spelling to pass muster as a genuine representation of the popular speech. (Craigie 1924: 9)

> Even prose writing, though more hopeful [than metrical writing], does not go very far, either, along pure dialect lines. Most Scottish writing in what is variously called Braid Scots, Lowland Scotch, Lallans or just Scots is therefore composed in some sort of a standard language rather than in dialect; or if a dialect we must call it, then it is a literary dialect created by men of the pen. (Mackie 1952: 123-4)

> The use of 'wha' as a relative pronoun, non-existent in natural speech (in which it is simply an interrogative), is also recognised by all Scots speakers as 'Scots of the book'. It is a hallmark of literary Scots—a mark of the literary devil catching out the writer who pretends to be giving us 'dialect.' (Mackie 1952: 129)

> Scots is rich in idiom. [...] It is this richness of the language our poets and prose-writers ought to seek to recapture and convey. So

much Scottish writing seems to have been written in English and converted into Scots, a pointless procedure. (Mackie 1961: 30)

Where the subject was *not* a personal pronoun or the pronoun was separated by intervening words from the verb, the rule was that all persons ended in -*s* in the singular and plural alike. So when the Ettrick Shepherd sings how nice it is to meet a bonnie lassie 'when the kye comes hame', his Scots is as unexceptional as his sentiments [...] (Murison 1977: 44)

As usual Scott does not maintain consistency. [...] The Scottish use, in certain circumstances, of -*s* inflections of the verb [...] mostly gives way to the Standard English restriction of -*s* to the third person singular. (Tulloch 1980: 267)

In addition, the present century has seen the conscious creation of a 'mainstream' variety of Scots—a standard literary variety, [...] referred to as 'synthetic Scots', now generally goes under the name Lallans (= 'Lowlands'. [...] In its grammar and spelling, it shows the marked influence of Standard English, more so that other Scots dialects. (Crystal 1995: 333)

The influence of St E is therefore likely to be stronger on written texts than on speech. Consequently, writing in Scots is a conscious process, influenced (to varying degrees) by St E [...] (Görlach 2002: 38)

It is striking that a policy document *about* Scots should be written *in* Scots (even if some of the grammatical elements in the 'Scots' represented suggest a translation from English). (Millar 2006: 76)

8

CONCLUSION

If written Scots is to have a more prominent place in public life, especially in the realms of "official", expository, or transactional writing, communicative efficiency will, arguably, be greatly facilitated by the use of a "standard" or perhaps less pedantically—a *regularized* orthography, although, in the words of M. A. K. Halliday, "we tend to take it for granted that spelling should be totally uniform; but there is no compelling reason why it should be, provided the principles are clear".[172] A standard certainly need not imply an across-the-board application of the principle of a single spelling for each word. Where a particular dialect form or pronunciation cannot be relatively instinctively or easily predicted from the application of the graphemic representation chosen, a few dialect variants can easily be accommodated. Most well-read persons will soon become familiar with such forms, much as is the case with such variation in, for example, British and American English. Such forms will simply indicate the provenance of the writer and not readily hinder intelligibility.

In the introduction to the 1985 edition of the *Concise Scots Dictionary* it describes the language of contemporary Lowland Scotland as "fluid" with "a wide and almost infinitely variable range of speech-styles, ranging from the full Scots of some fisher-folk and farming people in the North-East through various intermediate 'mixtures of Scots and English', to a variety of Standard English spoken in a Scottish accent."[173]

The preceding analysis draws on the "full Scots" mentioned above with its "linguistic distinctiveness" and "remarkable literature", among other features, described in introduction to the 1985 edition of the *Concise Scots Dictionary* as the "attributes of a language rather than a dialect",[174] whereas the "various intermediate mixtures of Scots and English" are described as the country's everyday vernacular, but now no more than that."[175] That

---

172 Halliday 1985: 29.
173 Scottish National Dictionary Associaton Ltd 1985: xii-a.
174 Scottish National Dictionary Associaton Ltd 1985: xiii-b.
175 Scottish National Dictionary Associaton Ltd 1985: xii-b.

would indicate that the Scots Language is the speech-style at the "full Scots" end of the continuum described above. After all, is it logical that Scots can be a mixture of Scots and something else? Apparently not, the 2003 *Edinburgh Companion to Scots* tells us that "over much of the lowlands, Scots is now at an advanced stage of language death."[176]

The 2017 edition of the *Concise Scots Dictionary* describes the same continuum from "broad Scots" to "a variety of Standard English spoken in a Scottish accent." However, the "various intermediate mixtures of Scots and English" are no longer dismissed as no more than the country's everyday vernacular, indicating that the continuum in its entirety has now become the Scots language. Sometimes simply referred to as 'Scottish Language' i.e. (the English) language as spoken by Scottish people.

> Due in no small part to its geographical spread, Scots varies in its spoken form, ranging from the 'broad' usage of some fishing and farming communities, through various intermediate mixtures of Scots and English, to a variety of Standard English spoken in a Scots accent (i.e. Standard Scottish English, or SSE).[177]

> Scots covers everything from dialects which the English – or even other Scots – wouldn't understand, to the way we're speaking just now, which is English with a Scottish accent." (Iseabail Macleod, *The Scots Magazine*, Dec. 1997, electronic edition)[178]

> It is important to stress too that Scots should be seen not as a single entity, but one which ranges from a very 'broad' regional and social type (like, say, the rural speech of Aberdeenshire or the Working Class usage of Glasgow) to a form which has similarities to Standard English. In other words, the linguistic manifestations of Scots should be seen as a type of scale or cline, encompassing a very broad range of usage and formal characteristics. (Jones 2002: 5)

> Even at the level of casual observation it is clear that, while there indeed seems to be a 'posh', prestigious form of Modern Scots, it is in several important ways different from its Standard English, Received Pronunciation counterpart. [...] This formal, upper-class

---

176 Macafee 2003:51.
177 https://web.archive.org/web/20211026163048/https://dsl.ac.uk/about-scots/what-is-scots/ accessed 2021-10-30.
178 Cited in Dossena 2005: 15.

version of Scots is often referred to as **Scottish Standard English**. (Jones 2002: 24)

The historical reality is of course that Scottish Standard English is not Scots, although to varying degrees influenced by it, but the result of previous and current generations of Scots adopting southern Standard English.

> However, the situation is similar linguistically to one of dialect contact (Trudgill 1986) in that the indigenous language of the Lowlands (Scots) was a closely related variety. The resulting shift produced complex structural compromises, especially in phonology, which have not always been well understood. In particular the apparent 'mergers' of LOT/THOUGHT and FOOT/GOOSE (Wells 1982: §5.2.3) are not processes of sound change at all, but lexical transfers (see Macafee 2002). Many of the characteristic outcomes of dialect contact described by Trudgill (1986, 1999) and by Britain and Trudgill (1999) are or were present. There are copious examples in Jones (1995) and elsewhere of interdialectal forms, hypercorrections and spelling pronunciations, but unfortunately, he systematically misinterprets them as sound changes in eighteenth-century Scots. (Macafee 2004: 60–61)

Similarly, Standard English can be seen as providing the means for official, expository, or transactional writing where a situation of diglossia is assumed to be the norm.

> **Diglossia** is a sociolinguistic situation in which two very different varieties of a language are both used in a society, but in different situations. Typically, one is used in more formal or literary situations such as formal writing, university lectures, and news broadcasts, and is learned and encouraged in school. The other is used in conversation, informal television situations, folk literature, etc., and is preferred at home. (Rogers 2005: 17)

That is to a large extent characteristic of the position of the "establishment", even among those apparently well-disposed towards Scots.[179] Learning and Teaching Scotland does not see any necessity for a "standard Scots" and is quite content to approach the issue by simply expecting pupils

---

179 For further discussion see *Lounge Linguists and Literati* (Tait 2002) available at https://web.archive.org/web/20070315084337/http://myweb.tiscali.co.uk/wirhoose/but/wan/girn.htm, accessed 2021-10-30.

to, for example, "Write a poem in Scots. (It is important not to be worried about spelling in this—write as you hear the sounds in your head.)"[180] Of course the phonetic "write as you hear the sounds in your head" pre-supposes some knowledge of sound-to-letter correspondences, which are of course provided by Standard English, a language that the same organiza-tion intends children to be "writing fluently and legibly with accurate spelling and punctuation".[181]

> **A first word of warning**—ignore matters of spelling in the early stages of writing Scots. [...] At least initially, accept any form of phonetic spelling that pupils arrive at as long as you (and they!) can understand it. (Robertson 1996: 21)

> The great majority of teachers with whom I spoke were interested in teaching about the local vernacular and encouraging its use in certain spheres. The only sour note was when I introduced the idea of a spelling norm for Scots: many of the teachers felt that this would be an authoritarian imposition upon a creative act (which tells us something of how they viewed the vernacular's position in communication). Many also believed strongly that the teaching of another system to children who struggled with English spelling would be counter-productive for the teaching of English. (Millar 2005: 196)

> With creative artists, this tendency shows itself in what literary critics term 'phonetic spelling'. [...] Its main failing is that its supposedly phonetic status is based upon an adherence to the conventions (or at least tendencies) of English spelling [...] (Millar 2005: 191)

Such a position clearly sees writing in what is now considered Scots as reserved for the informal, obviating the necessity of a regularized norm. Ultimately such an approach treats the varieties of Scots as dialects of English, where the standard from which they deviate is Standard English. Such a position would exclude Scots from inclusion in European Charter for Regional or Minority Languages as that "does not include either dialects

---

180 See https://web.archive.org/web/20060819115622/http://www.ltscotland.org.uk/5to14/specialfocus/scots/ideas/index.asp, accessed 2021-10-30.
181 https://web.archive.org/web/20060822154746/http://www.ltscotland.org.uk/5to14/htmlunrevisedguidelines/Pages/englang/main/elng1003.htm, accessed 2021-10-30.

of the official language(s) of the State or the languages of migrants".[182] That, dialects of English approach, perhaps offers an explanation for the reluctance of *SLD* to regularize the headword forms in the likes of the *Scots School Dictionary* (now *The Essential Scots Dictionary*). Here numerous spellings for the same underlying phonemes are variably applied along with numerous spellings for predictable dialect realizations. One explanation for the choices made was that the most common form was selected as the headword. The most common form, would of course, vary according to the corpus consulted, depending on where and when individual items in it were written—rendering the outcome potentially arbitrary and contradictory. For example, in the list based upon the contents of the *Essential Scots Dictionary*, *aucht* 'eight' is given as the headword form, but the most common form is now in fact *echt* or *aicht*.[183]

> [...] [eçt, ɛçt, eˡçt] [...] O.Sc. has *eght*, from 1516. This form, from Mid.Eng. *e* forms, has supplanted the native Aucht, which is now *obsol.* [...] (SND III: 201 s.v. "ECHT")

The decisions behind the SNDA's choice of phonetic transcriptions for the *Concise Scots Dictionary* were of a more systematic nature.

> One difference between *SND* and *CSD* is here that *SND* pretends to what I suspect is an illusory or spurious precision in its account of the local distribution of fairly minutely differentiated forms. But the more important difference of course is that the *CSD*'s transcription system employs the theory of structural dialectology, which was only beginning to develop when Grant was compiling his volumes, though it is now, I daresay, generally accepted and used by dialectologists.[184]
>
> According to this theory, in the version of it used by CSD, the Scottish dialects share a common system of phonemes—a diasystem—but each individual dialect has its own local realizations of each common phoneme. So the phoneme we symbolize as /ɑ/ is realised as an open unrounded sound, nearly always long, in all of its phonetic environments, in most Southern and Northern dialects as [aː] or [ɑː], but in most Central Scots

182 Part I – General provisions, Article 1 – Definitions, a.

183 https://web.archive.org/web/20061015063701/http://www.scotsdictionaries.org.uk/HeadWordList/A.html, accessed 2021-10-30. In the 2004 ESD the headword *aucht*, *aicht, echt, eight* is given (p. 3).

184 K.M. Petyt, *The Study of Dialect: An Introduction to Dialectology* (London 1980), especially chap. 5, "Structural Dialectology." [Original footnote]

dialects as an open to half-open lip-rounded sound /ǫː/, e.g. in the word for *fall*, Northern and Southern [faː] or [fɑː], Central [fǫː]. Similarly, the phoneme /ɛ/ is realized as (more or less) [e] in some Northern dialects, [ɛ] or [ɛː] in some Central dialects, [æ] in Southeastern and Southern dialects: e.g., in the word for *bed*, [bed], [bɛd], [bæd], and so on. Thus, once the common phoneme is stated, it is possible for the speaker of any particular local dialect to interpret it according to his own local rules of realization. (Aitken 1985: 144–145)

One assumes that the lexicographers at *SLD* were aware of the possibility that once such phonemes had been identified, the most common and regular graphemic representations of them could be taken as a basis for the spelling headword form—whereby "it is possible for the speaker of any particular local dialect to interpret it according to his own local rules of realization"—especially if it occurred reasonably often in the literary record, much as many of the examples quoted in the analysis above. That being particularly pertinent when one objective is to help those learning Scots.

There is one category of user for whom this may be particularly helpful, and that is the growing number, mostly of Scots Standard English speakers, who try to write or speak Scots. (Robinson 1986: 27)

If Scots is to be taken out of the playground, pub and *kailyaird*, and if it is generally accepted that a regularized orthography is a prerequisite, an essential assumption is that its application would be learnt or taught systematically as a linguistic system, i.e. language, in which the orthography is Scots and the graphemes have Scots realizations, and not, what is often the case, assumed Standard English sound-to-letter realizations.

The existence of an orthography for non-standard dialects can often make matters more complex for their 'survival', since speakers very often do not recognise the proposed spelling system as a type of the dialect they themselves speak on a daily basis. (Jones 2002: 6)

Without a foundation of strong public support, it is unreasonable to expect that any artificially codified variety of Scots can have a significant role in schooling. (Bailey 1987: 138)

It is certainly true to say that Scots orthography had never been completely independent or uninfluenced by practices further south. Written Scots has and had always been influenced by contemporary written Standard English, and there never was a "golden age" where Scots had a totally autonomous orthography with fully standardized spellings.

> DOST illustrates again and again that every conceivable spelling of a given word will turn up somewhere. (Macafee 1987: 4)

Of course the above quote implies a more chaotic situation than actually existed. Contemporary practice is often fairly regular, varying less than across time, perhaps owing to the ongoing adoption of southern practices.

> Scots already has already been partially standardised, at different periods in its history. (McClure 1980a: 20)

The closer inspection above clearly shows that many, if not all, well-read 18th and 19th century writers were aware of the concept of a "standard" or "pan-dialectal" Scots and the orthographic practices of which it was comprised. As shown above, many of those graphemes were inherited from the Middle Scots period, and as such predate the introduction of southern Standard English to Scotland. They are not, as is often assumed, Standard English that has been altered to show how the perceived Standard English letter-to-sound correspondences match a particular Scots dialect. Those graphemes are traditional and independent Scots ones that give Scots some of its "languageness". Nevertheless, since the "official" adoption of the southern written norm after the Union, 18th and 19th century Scots orthographic practices were influenced by those of written Standard English. The examples 18th and 19th century written Scots consulted employed particular graphemes, if not always consistently, representing particular phonemes—even across dialects where the realizations were often substantially, but predictably, different. Those can be identified by their continued recurrence in the literary record.

The analysis above clearly shows that the widely used and identifiable traditional Scots graphemes employed in the 18th and 19th, were used to represent varying dialect realizations. When applied consistently, or at least as consistently as possible, the graphemes indentified and chosen, arguably provide the basis for a regularized Scots orthography—stemming from tradition and not the idiosyncrasies of individual "language planners" or those harking after the apparent "golden age" before political union with

England. The, increasing widespread practice of writing particular dialects of Scots using Standard English letter-to-sound correspondes phonetically is, in effect, dialect writing, as the frame of reference is Standard English, not Scots itself. The choice is between writing Scots as an *Ausbausprache*, i.e. as a language that can be used for formal transactional communication— or as a local dialect of English. Both approaches are equally valid. However, one cannot claim that Scots is a language in its own right, and at the same time write Scots phonetically to show how a particular dialect deviates from the *Dachsprache*, Standard English.

9
EXAMPLES FOR COMPARISON: ROBERT BURNS

In order to illustrate the various proposed orthographies, Robert Burns's only surviving piece of Scots prose has been chosen. This was a letter to "Mr. William Nicol, Master of the High School, Edinburgh". At least two versions of the letter seem to be in existence, one in the collection by J. Logie Robertson[185] published in 1887, the other in the collection by J. De Lancey Ferguson[186] and first published by the Clarendon Press Oxford, in 1931. The Ferguson version has been used here. In it a footnote comments "Cromek 1808. Here collated with the original MS. In the Cowie collection, Glasgow. The first two paragraphs are transcribed, with a number of variations, in the Glenriddell MS."

Apart from differing use of punctuation, such as capitalization, commas, dashes and hyphens, the notable differences between the version below and that used by Robertson are as follows. In line 4 Robertson has *miles'* and *ridin'* with apostrophes, the former a genitive, the latter to indicate "elision" of ⟨**g**⟩. In line 5 Robertson has *ye* for *you*. In line 6 Robertson has *land lowper-like*. In line 9 Robertson has *very deil* for *vera devil*. In line 13 Robertson has *stomack* for *stomach*, incidentally providing a spelling more representative of the pronunciation. In line 15 Robertson has *ring-banes* for *ringbanes*. In line 16 Robertson has *aye* for *ay*. In line 18 Robertson has *ridin'* with an apostrophe, and *fifty miles* for the Scots *fifty mile*, and *deil-stickit* for *deil-sticket*. In line 19 Robertson has *on her tail* for *in her tail*. In line 23 Robertson has *bonnie* for *bonie*. In line 26 Robertson has *had* for *has*. In line 27 Robertson has *presbyteries* for *Presbytries*. The sentence beginning *They play'd…* ending in *…castock* was not included by Robertson. In line 31 Robertson has *ye* for *you*, *mysel* for *myself*. In line 32 Robertson has *fou* instead of *bitchified*.

185 Robertson, James Logie (1887) *The Letters of Robert Burns*, London: Scott. Pp. 58–60.
186 De Lancy Ferguson (1931) *The Letters of Robert Burns*, Oxford: Clarendon Press. 1971, reprint, Michigan: Scholarly Press Inc. Pp. 94–95.

9.1 ROBERT BURNS

Carlisle 1st June 1787—or
I believe the 39th o' May rather
Kind, honest-hearted Willie,

I'm sitten down here, after seven and forty miles ridin, e'en as forjesket and forniaw'd[187] as a forfoughten cock, to gie you some notion o' 5 my landlowper-like stravaguin sin the sorrowfu' hour that I sheuk hands and parted wi' auld Reekie.—

My auld, ga'd Gleyde o' a meere has huchyall'd up hill and down brae, in Scotland and England, as teugh and birnie as a vera devil wi' me.—It's true, she's as poor's a Sang-maker and as hard's a kirk, and tipper-taipers 10 when she taks the gate first like a Lady's gentlewoman in a minuwae,[188] or a hen on a het girdle, but she's a yauld, poutherie Girran for a' that; and has a stomach like Willie Stalker's meere that wad hae disgeested tumbler-wheels, for she'll whip me aff her five stimparts o' the best aits at a down-sittin and ne'er fash her thumb.—When ance her ring-banes and 15 spavies, her crucks and cramps, are fairly soupl'd, she beets to, beets to, and aye the hindmost hour the tightest.—I could wager her price to a thretty pennies that, for twa or three wooks ridin at fifty mile a day, the deil-stickit a five gallopers acqueesh Clyde and Whithorn could cast saut in her tail.—   20

I hae dander'd owre a' the kintra frae Dumbar to Selcraig, and hae forgather'd wi' mony a guid fallow, and mony a weel-far'd hizzie.—I met wi' twa dink quines in particlar, ane o' them a sonsie, fine, fodgel lass, baith braw and bonie; the tither was a clean-shankit, straught, tight, weel-far'd winch, as blythe's a lintwhite on a flowerie thorn, and as sweet and modest's 25 a new blawn plumrose[189] in a hazle shaw.—They were baith bred to mainers by the beuk, and onie ane o' them has as muckle smeddum and rumblegumtion as the half o' some Presbytries that you and I baith ken.— They play'd me sik a deevil o' a shavie that I daur say if my harigals were turn'd out, ye wad see twa nicks i' the heart o' me like the mark o' a kail- 30 whittle in a castock.—

I was gaun to write you a lang pystle,[190] but, Gude forgie me, I gat myself sae notouriously bitchify'd the day after kail-time that I can hardly stoiter but and ben.—

---

187 *For + gnaw + ed.*
188 Phonetic spelling of the French 'menuet' *minuet.* Perhaps a more opaque spelling.
189 Dissimilated variant of *primrose.*
190 Aphetic form of *epistle.*

35 My best respecks to the guidwife and a' our common friens, especiall
M^(r.) and M^(rs.) Cruikshank, and the honest Guidman o' Jock's Lodge.

I'll be in Dumfries the morn gif the beast be to the fore and the branks
bide hale.——

Gude be wi' you, Willie! Amen——

40 Rob^(t). Burns.

9.2 *THE SCOTS STYLE SHEET* 1947

Spellings are based on the modest recommendations set out in the *Style Sheet.*[191]

Carlisle, *June* 1 1787—or
I believe the 39th o May raither
Kynd, honest-hertit Willie,
I'm sitten doun here, efter sevin and fowertie miles ridin, e'en as forjeskit and forgnawed as a forfochten cock, to gie you some notion o 5 my landlowper-like stravaguin sin the sorrowfu hour that I sheuk hands and pairtit wi auld Reekie.

My auld, gaa'd gleyde o a meir has hochled up hill and doun brae, in Scotland and England, as teuch and birnie as a vera deevil wi me. It's true, she's as puir's a sang-maker and as hard's a kirk, and tipper-taipers 10 when she taks the gate, first like a lady's gentlewoman in a minuet, or a hen on a het girdle; but she's a yauld, poutherie girran for aa that, and has a stomack lyke Willie Stalker's meir that wad hae disgeestit tumbler-wheels, for she'll whip me aff her five stimparts o the best aits at a doun-sittin and ne'er fash her thoum. When ance her ringbanes and 15 spavies, her creucks and cramps, are fairlie soupelt, she beits to, beits to, and aye the hindmaist hour the tichtest. I could wager her price to a threttie pennies, that for twa or three wouks ridin at fiftie mile a day, the deilstickit a five gallopers aqueesh Clyde and Whithorn could cast saut in her tail.   20

I hae dandered owre aa the kintra frae Dunbar to Selcraig, and hae forgaithered wi mony a guid fallow, and mony a weel-faured hizzie. I met wi twa dink quines in particlar, ane o them a sonsie, fine, fodgel lass, baith braw and bonnie; the tither was a clean-shankit, straucht, ticht, weel-faured winch, as blythe's a lintwhite on a flouerie thorn, and as sweet and modest's 25 a new blawn plumrose in a hazle shaw. They were baith bred to mainers by the beuk, and onie ane o them has as muckle smeddum and rumblegumtion as the half o some presbyteries that you and I baith ken. They played me sic a deevil o a shavie that I daur say if my harigals were turnt out, ye wad see twa nicks in the hert o me like the mark o a kail- 30 whittle in a castock.

I was gaun to write you a lang epistle, but, Guid forgie me, I gat mysel sae notouriously bitchified the day efter kail-time that I can hardlie stoiter but and ben.

---

191 Mackie, Albert (1955) "The spelling of Scots", *Lines Review* 9, 29–31. Includes the Scots Style Sheet.

35   My best respecks to the guidwife and aa our common friends,[192] especiall
Mr. and Mrs. Cruikshank, and the honest guidman o Jock's Lodge.

I'll be in Dumfries the morn gif the beast be to the fore, and the branks
bide hale.

Guid be wi you, Willie! Amen!

40   ROB^T. BURNS.

---

192 "The practice of dropping the terminal 'd' is to be discouraged in writing."

9.3 DAVID PURVES

David Purves's spellings were taken from Purves's publications.[193] Where a word could not be found, spellings were decided by analogy with attested examples.

Carlisle 1st *June* 1787—ir

A believe the 39^t o' Mey raither

Kynd, honest-hertit Wullie,

A'm sutten doun here, eftir seiven an fowertie myles rydin, e'en as forjaskit an forgnawed as a forfochen cok, ti gie you sum notion o 5 ma landlowper-lyke stravaigin sen the sorrafu hour that A sheuk haunds an pairtit wi auld Reikie.

Ma auld, gawed gleyde o a meir hes hochilt up hill an doun brae, i Scotland an England, as teuch an birnie as a verra deivil wi me. It's true, she's as puir's a sang-makkar an as hard's a kirk, an tippertaipers 10 whan she taks the gait, first lyke a leddie's gentilwumman i a minuet, ir a hen on a het girdil; but she's a yauld, poutherie girran for aw that, an hes a stammik lyke Wullie Stalker's meir that wad hae disgeistit tummler-wheels, for she'll whup me af hir five stimparts o the best aits at a doun-sittin an ne'ir fash hir thoum. Whan aince her ringbanes an 15 spavies, hir cruiks an cramps, ar fairlie soupilt, she beits ti, beits ti, an aye the hindmaist hour the tichtest. A coud wager hir pryce ti a threttie pennies, that for twa ir thrie weeks rydin at fiftie myle a day, the deil-stikkit a five gallopers acqueish Clyde an Whithorn coud cast saut in hir tail.   20

A hae dandert owre aw the kintra frae Dunbar ti Selcraig, an hae forgethert wi monie a guid fallae, an monie a weill-faurt hizzie. A met wi twa dink quynes in pairteiklar, ane o thaim a sonsie, fyne, fodgil lass, baith braw an bonnie; the tither wes a claen-shankit, strecht, ticht, weill-faurt winch, as blyth's a lintwhyte on a flouerie thorn, an as sweet an modest's 25 a new blawn plumrose i a hazil shaw. Thai war baith bred ti mainners by the buik, an onie ane o thaim hes as mukkil smeddum an rummilgumtion as the hauf o sum presbyteries that you an A baith ken. Thai played me sic a deivil o a shavie that A daur say if ma harigals war turnt out, ye wad see twa nikks i the hert o me lyke the merk o a kail- 30 whuttle in a castok.

---

193 Purves, David (1975) "The spelling of Scots", *Lallans* 4, 26–27.
     Purves, David (1979) "A Scots orthography", *Scottish Literary Journal Supplement* 9, 62–76.
     Purves, David (1997) *A Scots Grammar*, Edinburgh: The Saltire Society.

A wes gaun ti wryte you a lang epistil, but, Guid forgie me, A gat masell sae notoriusslie bitchified the day eftir kail-tyme that A can hardlie stoiter but an ben.

35 Ma best respeks ti the guidwyfe an aw our common freins, espaiciall Mr. an Mrs. Cruikshank, an the honest guidman o Jok's Ludge.

A'll be in Dumfries the morn gif the baest be ti the fore, an the branks byde haill.

Guid be wi you, Wullie! Amen!

40 ROB^T. BURNS.

9.4 J. DERRICK MCCLURE

McClure's short paper[194] dealt only with vowels and was more of a *Gedankenspiel* than a set of suggestions likely to receive acceptance. I have left consonants much as they were. The transcription may not accurately reflect McClure's intentions.

Carliyl 1ˢᵗ *June* 1787—or
A beleiv the 39ᵗʰ o Miy raither
Kiyn, hoanest-haertit Willie.

A'm sitten doun heir, efter seiven an fowertei miyls riydin, eien as forjeskit an forngnaad as a forfochten cock, tui gei you sum notion o ma lanlowper-liyk stravaigin sin the sorraefou hour that A sheuk haans an pairtit wi aald Reikie. 5

Ma aald, gaad gliyd o a meir haes huchelt up hill an doun brae, in Scotlan an Inglan, as teuch an birnei as a verra deivil wi mei. It's trou, shei's as puir's a sang-maker an as haard's a kirk, an tippertaipers whan shei taks the gaet, first liyk a leddei's gentlewumman in a minouwae, or 10 a hen on a het girdle; but shei's a yaald, poutherei girran for aa that, an haes a stumack liyk Willei Staaker's meir that wad hae disgeistit tummler-wheils, for shei'll whip mei aff hir fiyv stimparts o the best aits at a doun-sittin an ne'er fash hir thoum. Whan aens hir ringbaens an spaiveis, hir creuks an cramps, ar fairlei souplt, shei beits tui, beits tui, 15 an ey the hinmaist hour the tichtest. A coud waiger hir priys tui a threttei penneis, that for twaa or threi wouks riydin at fiftei miyl a dae, the deil-stickit a fiyv gallopers acqueish Cliyd and Whithoarn coud cast saat in hir tail. 20

A hae daandert owre aa the kintra frae Dunbaar tui Selcraig, an hae forgaithert wi monei a guid fallae, an monei a weil-faart hizzie. A met wi twaa dink quiyns in parteiclar, aen o thaim a sonsei, fiyn, fodgel lass, baith braa an bonnei; the tither wis a claen-shankit, straacht, ticht, weil-faart winch, as bliyth's a lintwhiyt on a flouerei thoarn, an as sweit an moadest's 25 a new blaan plumroas in a hizzle shaa. Thae war baith bred tui mainers bey the beuk, an onei aen o thaim haes as muckle smeddum an rummlegumtion as the haaf o some presbitereis that you an A baith ken. Thae pliyd mei sic a deivil o a shaivei that A daar say if ma harigals ar turnt out, ye wad sei twaa nicks in the haert o mei liyk the merk o a kail- 30 whittle in a castock.

---

194 McClure, J. Derrick (1980) "The Spelling of Scots: A Phoneme–Based System" *Scottish Literary Journal* 12, 25–29.

A wis gaan tui wriyt you a lang epistle, but, Guid forgei mei, A gat masel sae notoriuslei bitchifeid the dae efter kail-tiym that A can haarlei stoyter but an ben.

35   Ma best respecks tui the guidwiyf an aa our coamon freins, especial Mr. an Mrs. Cruikshank, an the hoanest guidman o Joak's Ludge.

A'll bei in Dumfreis the morn gif the baest bei tui the foar, an the branks biyd hael.

Guid bei wi you, Willie! Amen!

40   Robᴛ. Burns.

9.5 *THE SCOTS LANGUAGE SOCIETY*

The recommendations[195] of the Scots Language Society were clearly influenced by Purves, discussed above. He was the editor of *Lallans* when the *Wurd Leit for Skreivars in Scots* was published. Spellings were based on the *Recommendations* or taken from the *Wurd Leit*, and where a word could not be found, spellings were decided by analogy with attested examples.

Carlisle 1ˢᵗ *June* 1787—or
A believe the 39ᵗʰ o Mey raither
Kynd, honest-hertit Wullie,

A'm sutten doun here, eftir seivin an fowertie myles rydin, e'en as forjaskit an forgnawed as a forfochen cock, ti gie you sum notion o 5 ma landlowper-lyke stravaigin sen the sorrafu oor that A sheuk haunds an pairtit wi auld Reikie.

Ma auld, gawed gleyde o a meir haes hochilt up hill an doun brae, i Scotland an England, as teuch an birnie as a verra deivil[196] wi me. It's true, she's as puir's a sang-makkar an as hard's a kirk, an tippertaipers 10 whan she taks the gait, first lyke a leddie's gentilwumman i a minuet, ir a hen on a het girdil; but she's a yauld, poutherie Girran for aw that, an haes a stammik lyke Wullie Stalker's meir that wad hae disgeistit tummler-wheels, for she'll whup me af hir five stimparts o the best aits at a doun-sittin an ne'er fash hir thoum. Whan aince her ringbanes an 15 spavies, hir cruiks an cramps, ir fairlie soupilt, she beits ti, beits ti, an aye the hindmaist oor the tichtest. A coud weiger hir price ti a threttie pennies, that for twa ir thrie weeks rydin at fiftie myle a day, the deil-stikkit a five gallopers acqueish Clyde an Whithorn coud cast saut in hir tail. 20

A hae dandert owre aw the kintrie frae Dunbar ti Selcraig, an hae forgethert wi monie a guid fallae, an monie a weill-faurt hizzie. A met wi twa dink quynes in pairteiklar, ane o thaim a sonsie, fyne, fodgil lass, baith braw an bonnie; the tither wes a claen-shankit, strecht, ticht, weill-faurt winch, as blyth's a lintwhyte on a flouerie thorn, an as sweet an modest's 25 a new blawn plumrose in a hazil shaw. Thai war baith bred ti mainners bi the buik, an onie ane o thaim haes as mukkil smeddum an rummilgumtion as the hauf o sum presbyteries that you an A baith ken. Thai played me sic a deivil o a shavie that A daur say if ma harigals war

---

195 Scots Language Society [David Purves] (1985) "Spelling recommendations", *Lallans* 24, 18–19.
    Scots Language Society [David Purves] (1992, 1993, 1994) "Wurd Leit for Skreivars in Scots" in *Lallans* 39, 40, 41 and 43.

196 By analogy with *deidil* 'diddle'.

30 turnt out, ye wad see twa nikks in the hert o me lyke the merk o a kail-
whuttil in a castok.

A wes gaun ti wryte you a lang epistle, but, Guid forgie me, A gat masel
sae notoriusslie bitchified the-day eftir kail-tyme that A can hardlie
stotter but an ben.

35 Ma best respeks ti the guidwyfe an aw our common freins, espaicial
Mr. an Mrs. Cruikshank, an the honest guidman o Jock's Ludge.

A'll be in Dumfries the morn gif the baist be ti the fore, an the branks
byde haill.

Guid be wi you, Wullie! Amen!

40 Rob^T. Burns.

9.6 ANGUS STIRLING

Stirling's proposals[197] failed to distinguish some underlying phonemes and it was often unclear how and where his suggested graphemes were to be applied. The transcription may not accurately reflect Stirling's intentions.

Carliil 1ˢᵗ *Jön* 1787—or
Ii believ the 39ᵗʰ o Mii räther
Kiinn, onist-härtit Wullie,

Ii'm sitten dun hier, eftir sieven ann fowertie miils riidin, ie'en as forjeskit ann forgnad as a forfochten cokk, tä gie yu summ noschun o 5 mii lannlowper-liik stravägin sinn the sorrafu ur thatt Ii schiuk hanns ann pärtit wi ald Riekie.

Mii ald, gad gliid o a mier häs hochilt upp hill ann dun brä, in Scotlann ann Inglann, as tiuch ann birnie as a verra dievil wi mie. It's tru, schie's as pör's a sang-makker ann as hard's a kirk, ann tipper-täpers 10 whann schie takks the gät, first liik a leddie's gentilwumman in a minuä, or a henn on a hett girdil; butt schie's a yald, putherie girran for a thatt, ann häs a stumakk liike Wullie Staker's mier thatt wudd hä disgiestit tummler-whiels, for schie'll whup mie aff hir fiiv stimparts o the best äts at a dun-sittin ann ne'er fasch hir thum. Whann äns hir ringbäns ann 15 spävies, hir criuks an cramps, ar färlie supelt, schie biets tä, biets tä, ann ey the hinnmäst ur the tichtist. Ii cud wäjir hir priis tä a threttie pennies, thatt for twa or thrie wuks riidin att fiftie miil a dey, the diel-stikkit a fiiv gallopers akwiesch Kliid ann Whithorn cud kast sat inn hir täl.   20

Ii hä dannerd ower a the kintra frä Dunbar tä Selkräg, ann hä forgäthert wi monnie a göd falla, ann monnie a wielfard hissie. Ii mett wi twa dink quiins inn parteiklar, äne o thäm a sonsie, fiin, fojel lass, bäth bra ann bonnie; the tither wus a clän-shankit, stracht, ticht, wiel-fard winsch, as bliith's a lintwhiit on a fluerie thorn, ann as swiet ann modist's 25 a niw blan plummros inn a hissil scha. Thä wurr bäth bredd tä mäners bii the biuk, ann onnie än o thäm häs as mukkil smeddum ann rummilgumschun as the haf o summ presbiteries thatt yu ann Ii bäth kenn. Thä pläd mei sikk a dievil o a shävie thatt Ii dar sä iff mii harigals wurr turnt ut, yie wudd sie twa nikks inn the härt o mie liik the merk o a käl- 30 whuttil in a castokk.

Ii wus gan tä wriit yu a lang pistil, butt, Göd forgie mie, Ii gatt miisell sä notoriuslie bitchified the dey efter käl-tiim thatt Ii kann hardlie stoiter butt ann benn.

---

197 Stirling, A. (1994) "On a standardised spelling for Scots", *Scottish Language* 13, 88–93.

35 Mii best respeks tä the gödwiif ann a ur common friens, espeschul
Mr. ann Mrs. Criukshank, ann the onist gödmann o Jokk's Luj.

   Ii'll bie inn Dumfries the morn giff the bäst bie tä the for, ann the branks
biid häl.

   Göd bie wi yu, Wullie! Amen!

40 ROB^T. BURNS.

9.7 *THE AIBERDEEN UNIVAIRSITIE SCOTS LEID QUORUM*

The AUSLQ *Innin*[198] was clearly influenced by Allan.[199] Alan (1995) was written in Scots following his own recommendations. Spellings are from that and the *Innin*. Where the words could not be found, spellings were decided by analogy with attested examples.

Carlisle 1st *Juin* 1787—or
A believe the 39nt o Mey raither
Kynd, honest-hairtit Wullie,

A'm sitten doun here, efter seiven an fortie myles rydin, e'en as forjaskit an forgnawed as a forfochten cock, ti gie you sum notion o 5 ma lanlowper-lyke stravaigin sin the sorraefu our that A sheuk hauns an pairtit wi auld Reikie.

Ma auld, gawed gleyde o a meir haes hochilt up hill an doun brae, i Scotlan an Englan, as teuch an birnie as a verra deivil wi me. It's true, she's as puir's a sang-makker an as hard's a kirk, an tippertaipers 10 whan she taks the gate, first like a leddie's gentlewumman in a minuet, or a hen on a het girdle; but she's a yauld, poutherie girran fur aw that, an haes a stomack like Willie Stalker's meir at[200] wad hae disgeistit tummler-wheels, fur she'll whup me aff hir five stimparts o the best aits at a doun-sittin an ne'er fash hir thoum. Whan aince hir ringbanes an 15 spavies, hir creuks an cramps, ar fairlie soupilt, she beits ti, beits ti, an aye the hinmaist our the tichtest. A cuid wager hir price ti a threttie[201] pennies, that fur twa or three weiks rydin at fiftie myle a day, the deil-stickit a five gallopers aqueish Clyde an Whithorn cuid cast saut i hir tail.   20

A hae daunert ower aw the kintra frae Dunbar ti Selcraig, an hae forgaithert wi monie a guid fallae, an monie a weil-faured hizzie. A met wi twa dink quynes i parteiclar, ane o thaim a sonsie, fyne, fodgel lass, baith braw an bonnie; the tither wes a claen-shankit, strecht, ticht, weil-faured winch, as blythe's a lintwhyte on a flouerie thorn, an as sweet an modest's 25 a new blawn plumrose in a hizzle shaw. Thay war baith bred ti mainers by the beuk, an onie ane o thaim has as muckle smeddum an rummle-gumtion as the hauf o sum presbyteries at you an A baith ken. Thay played me sic a deivil o a shavie that A daur say if ma harigals war

---

198 Lovie, Rod et al. (1995) *Innin ti the Scots Leid/An Introduction to the Scots Language*, Aiberdeen Univairsitie Scots Leid Quorum.

199 Allan, Alasdair (1995) "Scots spellin – ettlin efter the quantum lowp", *English World-Wide* 16:1, 61–103.

200 The demonstrative *that* is differentiated from the relative *at*.

201 Lovie et al. have *thertie*.

30 turnt out, ye wad see twa nicks i the hairt o me lyke the merk o a kail-
whuttle i a castock.

A wes gaun ti wryte you a lang epistle, but, Guid forgie me, A gat masel
sae notoriouslie bitchifee'd[202] the day efter kail-tyme that A can hardlie
stoiter but an ben.

35　Ma best respects ti the guidwyfe an aw our common friens, especial
Mr. and Mrs. Cruikshank, an the honest guidman o Jock's Ludge.

A'll be i Dumfries the morn gif the baest be ti the fore, an the branks
byde hail.

Guid be wi you, Wullie! Amen!

40　Robᵀ. Burns.

202　By analogy with *juistifee* 'justify'.

9.8 THE *SNDA* (LATER *SLD,* NOW *DSL*)[203]

Spellings are based on the first suggestion in the English-to-Scots section of *The Essential Scots Dictionary*[204] unless it was marked as a specific dialect form. Spellings for words not found were decided by analogy with attested examples.

Carlisle 1ˢᵗ *June* 1787—or
A believe the 39ᵗʰ o Mey raither
Kind, honest-hertit[205] Wullie,

A'm[206] sitten[207] doon here, efter[208] seeven an fowertie miles ridin, e'en as forjaskit an forgnawed as a forfochen cock, tae gie you some notion o 5 ma[209] lanlowper-lik,[210, 211] stravaigin sin the sorrafu oor at A shuk hans[212] an pairtit wi aul[213] Reekie.

Ma aul, ga'd[214] gleyde o a mear his[215] hochelt up hull an doon brae, i Scoatlan[216] an Englan, as teuch an birnie as a verra deevil wi me. It's true, shae's as puir's a sang-makar an as hard's a kirk, an tippertaipers 10 whan[217] shae taks the gate, first like a leddy's gentlewumman i a minuet, or a hen on a het girdle; bit shae's a yauld, pootherie girran fur aw[218] at, an his a stamack like Wullie Stalker's mear at wid[219] hae[220] disgeestit tummler-wheels, fur shae'll whup me aff[221] hir[222] five stimparts o the best aits[223] at a

---

203 The Scottish National Dictionary Association, Scottish Language Dictionaries Limited, and Dictionaries of the Scots Language

204 Macleod, Iseabail and Cairns, Pauline eds. (2004), *The Essential Scots Dictionary*, Edinburgh: Edinburgh University Press.

205 Also *hairt.*

206 Also *Ah'm.*

207 Also *sutten.*

208 Also *aifter.*

209 Also *mi*; the form *my* in the compound *mysel* was also suggested.

210 Also *laun(d).*

211 The "translation" *lik(e)* was suggested for 'likely'.

212 For the sake of regularity, *han* was chosen over *haun(d)*, although *han* was given as the second option, cf. *laun(d)* above.

213 The suggestion was *aul(d)* and *ald*, but that may have been an alternative form of Northern *aal.*

214 That choice was by analogy with the suggested *ba(w)*, *ga* being chosen as the first option. The form *ga'd*, with an apostrophe, was chosen for clarity over the possible *gad* or *gaed.*

215 Also *hes.*

216 *Scoats* was suggested for 'Scots'; *Scoatlan* was coined by analogy. For *lan* see above.

217 Also *whun.*

218 Also *aa* and *aal* cf. *ga* above.

219 Also *wud.*

220 Also *ha.*

221 Also *oaf.*

222 Also *hur*, and *her* in the compound *hersel.*

223 Also *yits.*

15 doon-sittin an ne'er fash hir thoum. Whan aince hir ringbanes an spavies, hir cruiks an cramps, ur fairly soopelt, shae beets tae, beets tae, an aye the hinmaist[224] oor the tichtest. A cud wager hir price tae a threttie pennies, at fur twa[225] or three[226] weeks ridin at fuftie mile a day, the deil-stickit a five gallopers aqueesh Clyde an Whithorn cud cast saut
20 i hir tail.

A hae dandered ower aw the kountra[227] frae[228] Dunbar tae Selcraig, an hae forgaithered wi monie a guid falla, an monie a weel-faured hizzie. A met wi twa dink quines[229] i parteeclar,[230] ane o thaim a sonsie, fine, fodgel lass, baith braw an bonnie; the tither wis a clean-shankit, stracht,[231] ticht, weelfaured
25 winch, as blithe's a lintwhite on a flooerie thorn, an as sweet an modest's a new blawn plumrose i a hissle shaw. They wur[232] baith bred tae mainners be the buik,[233] an onie ane o thaim his as muckle smeddum an rummle-gumtion as the hauf[234] o some presbyteries at you an A baith ken. They played me sic a deevil o a shavie at A daur say if ma harigals wur
30 turnt oot, ye wid see twa nicks i the hert o me lik the merk o a kail-whittle i a castock.

A wis gaunae write you a lang epistle, bit, Guid forgie me, A gat masel sae notoriously bitchifee'd[235] the day efter kail-time at A can hardly stoiter but an ben.
35 Ma best respecks tae the guid wife an aw oor common freens,[236] especiall Mr. an Mrs. Cruikshank, an the honest guidman o Jock's Ludge.

A'll be i Dumfries the morn gif the baist[237] be tae the fore, an the branks bide hail.

Guid be wi you, Wullie! Amen!
40 ROBᵀ. BURNS.

---

224 Also *hindmaist*.
225 Also *twae*.
226 For 'three', *chree* was suggested alongside the Southern Scots form threy. *Chree* is also assumed to be a Southern Scots form, but that was not clear.
227 Also *kintra*.
228 The first option was *fae*, though in this context *frae* is intended.
229 *Quine* was given as a North-East word for 'girl'.
230 The suggestion was *parteec(u)lar* but *particular* was suggested for 'particularly'.
231 The suggestion was *stra(u)cht*.
232 Also *war*.
233 Also *b(y)euk*.
234 Note that *half* was suggested in the compound *halflins* marked as a North-East word.
235 By analogy with *saitisfee* 'satisfy'.
236 The suggestion was *freen(d)*.
237 Also *beas*.

9.9 GEORGE PHILP

Philp gave a short description of his suggestions in his introduction to Graham's novel.[238] The publication also included a glossary. Where words could not be found, spellings wre decided by analogy with attested examples.

Carlisle 1st *Juin* 1787—or
I believe the 39*th* o Mey raither
Kind, honest-hertit Wullie,

I'm sitten doun here, efter seiven and fowerty miles ridin, e'en as forjeskit and forgnawed as a forfochten cock, to gíe you some notion o 5 my landlowper-lyke stravaigin sin the sorrafou hour at I sheuk hands and pairtit wi auld Reekie.

My auld, gaad gleyde o a meir has hochlt up hill and doun brae, in Scotland and England, as teuch and birny as a very deevil wi me. It's true, she's as puir's a sang-maker and as hard's a kirk, and tipper-taipers 10 when she taks the gate, first like a leddy's gentlewumman in a minuet, or a hen on a het girdle; but she's a yauld, pouthery girran for aa that, and has a stomack like Wullie Stalker's meir that wad hae disgeestit tummler-wheels, for she'll whup me aff her five stimparts o the best aits at a doun-sittin and ne'er fash her thoum. When yince her ringbanes and 15 spavies, her cruiks and cramps, are fairly souplt, she beits to, beits to, and aye the hinmaist hour the tichtest. I could wager her price to a thretty pennies, that for twa or three weeks ridin at fifty mile a day, the deil-stickit a five gallopers acqueesh Clyde and Whithorn could cast saut in her tail.   20

I hae daunert ower aa the kintra frae Dunbar to Selcraig, and hae forgethert wi mony a guid fella, and mony a weill-faurt hizzie. I met wi twa dink quines in partíclar, yin o them a sonsy, fine, fodgel lass, baith braw and bonny; the tither wis a claen-shankit, straucht, ticht, weill-faurt winch, as blythe's a lintwhite on a flouery thorn, and as sweet and modest's 25 a new blawn plumrose in a hazle shaw. They were baith bred to mainners by the beuk, and ony yin o them has as muckle smeddum and rummlegumtion as the hauf o some presbyteries at you and I baith ken. They played me sic a deevil o a shavie that I daur say if my harigals were turned out, ye wad see twa nicks in the hert o me lyke the mark o a kail- 30 whuttle in a castock.

I wis gaun to write you a lang epistle, but, Guid forgíe me, I gat mysel sae notoriously bitchified the day efter kail-time that I can haurly stotter but and ben.

---

238   Graham, William (1997) *Scorn, My Inheritance*, Glasgow, Scotsoun.

35   My best respecks to the guidwife and aa our common fríens, espaicial
  Mr. and Mrs. Cruikshank, and the honest guidman o Jock's Ludge.
     I'll be in Dumfries the morn gif the baest be to the fore, and the branks
  bide hale.
     Guid be wi you, Wullie! Amen!
40   Robᵀ. Burns.

9.10 PHILIP ROBINSON

Spellings were selected from Robinson's *Grammar*.[239] It also included a glossary. Where a word could not be found, analogy was attempted.

Carlisle 1st *Júin* 1787—or
A believe the 39^t o Mie rether
Kynn, hònest-hairtit Wullie,
A'm sutten doon heir, eftèr seiven an fawrtie miles ridin, e'en as forjeskit an forgnaad[240] as a forfochten cok,[241] tae gie you some notion o 5 ma lannlouper[242]-like stravaigin sin thà sorrafu hòor at A sheuk hauns an pairtit wi oul Reekie.

Ma oul, gaa'd gleyde o a meer haes hochlit up hill an doon brae, in Scotlann an Englann, as teuch an birnie as a vera deivil[243] wi me. It's trùe, scho's as puir's a sang-makker an as haird's a kirk,[244] an tipper-taipers 10 quhan scho taks thà gate, fàrss like a lady's gentlewuman in a minuet, or a hen on a het girdle; bot scho's a youl, poothèrie girran fur aa at, an haes a stomack like Wullie Stalker's mair at wud hae disgístit tummler-wheels, fur scho'll whup me aff her five stimparts o tha[245] bess aits at a doon-sittin an ne'er fash her thoom. Quhan yince her rängbanes an 15 spavies, her cruks[246] an cramps, ir fairlie sooplit, scho beets tae, beets tae, an aye the hinmaist hòor thà tichtest. A cud wager her price tae a thretie pennies, at fur twa ir thrie waeks ridin at fiftie mile a day, tha deil-stickit a five gallopers aqueesht Clyde an Whithorn cud cast saut in her tail. 20

A hae dandhèrt owre aa tha kintra frae Dunbar tae Selcraig, an hae forgaitherit[247] wi monie a guid fella, an monie a weel-fart[248] hizzie. A met wi twa dänk quines in partìclar, yin o thàim a sonsie, fine, fodgel lass, baith braa an bonnie; tha tither wuz a clain-shankit, stracht, ticht, weel-fart wunch, as blythe's a lintwhite on a flooerie thoarn,[249] an as sweet an modest's 25

---

239 Robinson, Philip (1997) *Ulster–Scots. A Grammar of the Traditional Written and Spoken Language*, The Ullans Press.
240 By analogy with *blaa* 'blow'.
241 By analogy with *bak* 'back'.
242 By analogy with *coup* 'overturn'.
243 By analogy with *seiven* 'seven'.
244 In Robinson's system one would expect *kärk* but his use of *ä* is generally (and inconsistently) limited to vocabulary shared with English.
245 Robinson's examples (1997: 64-5) would seem to indicate that the form *thà* occurs only after a consonant.
246 By analogy with *luk* 'look'.
247 Robinson used *gaitherit* (1997: 208) but on p.119 indicates that the verb conjugation would be gaithert cf. *dandhèrt*.
248 By analogy with *dar* 'dare'.
249 By analogy with *coarn* 'corn'.

a new blaan plumrose in a hazle shaa. The wur baith bred tae mainners[250] bae tha buik, an onie yin o thàim haes as muckle smeddum an rummle-gumtion as thà haaf o some presbätèries at you an A baith ken. The played me sic a deivil o a shavie at A dar say if ma harigals wur

30 turnt oot, ye wud see twa nicks in the hairt o me like the mairk o a kail-whuttle in a castok.

A wuz gonnae write you a lang epissle, bot, Guid forgie me, A gat masel sae notorioslie bitchified[251] theday eftèr kail-tim at A can harly stoiter but an ben.

35 Ma bess respects tae tha guidwife an aa oor common freens, especial Mr. an Mrs. Cruikshank, an thà hònest guidman o Jock's Ludge.

A'll be in Dumfries the moarn gif thà beess be tae tha fore, an thà branks bide hale.

Guid be wi you, Wullie! Amen!

40 Robᵀ. Burns

---

250 Doubled consonants after vowel digraphs by analogy with *feuggie* 'left-handed', *chaummer* 'chamber' and *haillie* 'holy'.

251 How Robinson would have dealt with the adjectival suffix could not be ascertained.

9.11 *THE SCOTS SPELLIN COMATEE*

Spellings are from the recommendations[252] in the Spellin Comatee's Report. The report was written in Scots, presumably following the recommendation of the comatee itself. Where a word could not be found, spellings were decided by analogy with attested examples.

Carlisle 1st *Juin* 1787—or
I believe the 39t o Mey raither
Kind, honest-hertit Willie,
I'm[253] sitten doun here, efter seeven an fowerty miles ridin, e'en as forjaskit an forgnawed as a forfochten[254] cock, ti gie you some notion o 5 ma landlowper-like straivagin sin the sorraefu hour[255] at[256] I sheuk haunds an pairtit wi auld Reekie.

Ma auld, gaad gleyde o a meir haes hochelt up hill an doun brae, in Scotland an England, as teuch an birnie as a verra deevil[257] wi me. It's true, she's as puir's a sang-makar an as hard's a kirk, an tippertaipers 10 whan she taks the gate, first like a leddy's gentlewumman in a minuet, or a hen on a het girdle; but she's a yauld, poutherie girran for aa at, an haes a stomack like Willie Stalker's meir at wad hae disgeistit tummler-wheels, for she'll whip me aff her five stimparts o the best aits at a doun-sittin an ne'er fash her thoum. Whan aince her ringbanes an 15 spavies, her creuks an cramps, ar fairly soupelt, she beits ti, beits ti, an aye the hindmaist hour the tichtest. I cuid wager her price ti a thretty pennies, at for twa or three wouks ridin at fifty mile a day, the deil-stickit a five gallopers acqueesh Clyde an Whithorn cuid cast saut in her tail.   20

I hae daundert ower aa the kintra frae Dunbar ti Selcraig, an hae forgaithert wi monie a guid fallae, an monie a weel-faurt hizzie. I met wi twa dink quines in parteicular, ane o thaim a sonsie, fine, fodgel lass, baith braw an bonnie; the tither wis a claen[258]-shankit, straucht, ticht, weel-faurt winch, as blythe's a lintwhite on a flouerie thorn, an as sweet an modest's 25

---

252 The Scots Spellin Comatee (2000) *Report an Recommends o the Scots Spellin Comatee* in *Lallans* issue 56. Also available at https://web.archive.org/web/20211030125719/https://evertype.com/scots/ScotsSpellinCom.pdf and at https://web.archive.org/web/20060620105026/http://www.zyworld.com/tallini/tribalisation/ScotsSpellinCom.doc accessed 2021-10-30.

253 The form *A* was also suggested.

254 It is assumed that the Comatee were aware of *for+focht+en* thus the full form has been used and not the common elided form *forfochen*.

255 It was unclear whether or not to use *hoor* or *oor*.

256 The form *that* was also suggested.

257 Spelt by analogy with *seeven* 'seven'.

258 Spelt by analogy with *baest* 'beast'.

a new blawn plumrose in a hissle shaw. Thay war baith bred ti mainers by[259] the beuk, an onie ane o thaim haes as muckle smeddum an rummlegumtion as the hauf o some presbyteries at you an I baith ken. Thay played me sic a deevil o a shavie at I daur say if ma harigals war
30 turnt oot, ye wad see twa nicks in the hert o me like the merk o a kail-whittle in a castock.

I wis gaun ti write ye a lang epistle, but, Guide forgie me, I gat masel sae notoriously bitchifee'd the day efter kail-time at can hardly stoiter but an ben.
35 My best respects ti the guidwife an aa oor common freins, especial Mr. an Mrs. Cruikshank, an the honest guidman o Jock's Ludge.

I'll be in Dumfries the morn gif the baest be ti the fore, an the branks bide hail.

Guid be wi you, Willie! Amen!
40 Robᵀ. Burns.

---

259 The form *bi* was also suggested.

9.12 ANDY EAGLE

Scots was often, and still is, written conform to Standard English grammar, and Burns was no exception. For Scots grammar forms based on Wilson (1923)[260] see the notes following the text.

Carlisle 1ˢᵗ *Juin* 1787—or
I believe the 39ᵗ o Mey raither
Kind, honest-hertit Willie,
I'm sitten doun here, efter seiven and fowerty miles' ridin, e'en as forjaskit and forgnawed as a forfochten cock, tae gie ye some notion o 5 ma laund-lowper-like stravagin sin the sorraefu oor that I sheuk haunds and pairtit wi auld Reekie.

Ma auld, gawed glyde o a meir haes hochelt up hill and doun brae, in Scotland and England, as teuch and birny as a verra deevil wi me. It's true, she's as puir's a sang-makker and as haurd's a kirk, and tipper-taepers 10 whan she taks the gate, first like a leddy's gentlewumman in a minuet, or a hen on a het girdle; but she's a yauld, pouthery garron for aw that, and haes a stamack like Willie Stalker's meir that wad hae disgeestit tummler-wheels, for she'll whip me aff her five stimparts o the best aits at a doun-sittin and ne'er fash her thoum. Whan ance her ringbanes and 15 spavies, her creuks and cramps, are fairly soupelt, she beets tae, beets tae, and aye the hindmaist oor the tichtest. I coud wager her price tae a thritty pennies, that for twa or three wouks ridin at fifty mile a day, the deil stickit a five gallopers aqueesh Clyde and Whithorn coud cast saut in her tail. 20

I hae daundert ower aw the kintra frae Dunbaur tae Selcraig, and hae forgaithert wi mony a guid fallae, and mony a weel-faured hizzie. I met wi twa dink queans in parteecular, ane o thaim a sonsy, fine, fodgle lass, baith braw and bonny; the tither wis a clean-shankit, straucht, ticht, weel-faured winch, as blithe's a lintwhite on a flouery thorn, and as sweet and modest's 25 a new blawn plumrose in a hazle shaw. Thay war baith bred tae mainers by the beuk, and ony ane o thaim haes as muckle smeddum and rummle-gumption as the hauf o some presbyteries that you and I baith ken. Thay played me sic a deevil o a shavie that I daur say if ma harigalds war turnt oot, ye wad see twa nicks in the hert o me like the merk o a kail- 30 whittle in a castock.

I wis gaun tae write ye a lang epistle, but, Guid forgie me, I gat masel sae notoriously bitchifee'd the day efter kail-time that I can haurdly stoiter but and ben.

---

260 *The Dialect of Robert Burns as Spoken in Central Ayrshire*, Oxford University Press.

35   Ma best respects tae the guidwife and aw oor common freends, especial
Mr. and Mrs. Cruikshank, and the honest guidman o Jock's Ludge.
    I'll be in Dumfries the morn gif the beast be tae the fore, and the branks
bide hale.
    Guid be wi you, Willie! Amen!
40   ROBᵀ. BURNS.

Line 4: "[...] nouns denoting number, money, time, weight, length, area or distance make no change for the plural after a numeral." p. 47, perhaps *fowerty mile's ridin*.

Line 5: "before an infinitive, **fur tay** is often used [...]" p. 67, *perhaps for tae gie*.

Line 16: [...] after any subject except a single pronoun [...] the plural present of [be] is the same as the third person singular [...]" p. 73, perhaps *is fair soupelt*. "[Ayrshire] rarely adds **lie** (ly) to an adjective to make it an adverb [...]" p. 63, perhaps *fair soupelt*.

Line 18: "[...] nouns denoting number, money, time, weight, length, area or distance make no change for the plural after a numeral." p. 47; however, *pennies* is the collective plural (SND: PENNY).

Line 28: "When two pronouns of different persons come together [...] in A[yrshire] the first person is generally put first." p. 56, perhaps *that me and you*. "[...] the ending **z** or **s** [...] is [...] often used in all persons of the plural unless the verb follows after a single pronoun [...]" p. 70, perhaps *that me and you baith kens*.

Line 29: "[...] the ending **z** or **s** [...] is [...] often used in all persons of the plural unless the verb follows after a single pronoun [...]" p. 70, perhaps *if ma harigalds wis*.

Line 33: "[Ayrshire] rarely adds **lie** (ly) to an adjective to make it an adverb [...]" p. 63, perhaps *notorious bitchifee'd*.

Line 38: "[...] the ending **z** or **s** [...] is [...] often used in all persons of the plural unless the verb follows after a single pronoun [...]" p. 70, Burns's use of the present subjunctive here, shown by the use of *be*, makes *bides hail* unlikely.

9.13 PHONETIC TRANSCRIPTION

This is a broad phonetic transcription of Robert Burns's letter as it may have been pronounced by Burns (based on Wilson (1923)).[261] It transcribes words in full and makes no allowance for connected speech such as assimilation and elision. Capital letters (not usual in the IPA) have been added here to facilitate comparison with the other texts.

Kɑːrˈləil fʌrst Dʒɪn[262] ˈsiːvntɪn ˈextɪ ˈsiːvn ɔr
ɑ bəˈliːv ðə ˈθrɪtɪ nəint ə Məi ˈreːðər
Kəin, ˈOnəst ˈHɛrtɪt ˈWʌlɪ,

ɑm ˈsɪtən dun hiːr,[263] ˈɛftər ˈsiːvn ən ˈfɔːrtɪ məilz ˈrəidɪn, iːn ɑz[264] fərˈdʒɛskɪt ən fərˈnjoːd ɑz ə fərˈfoxən kok, teː giː jiː sʌm ˈnoʃən ə   5
ma lɔːnˈlʌupərˈləik straˈvegɪn sɪn ðə ˈsoːrɑfɑ uːr ðət[265] ɑ ʃʌk hɒnz ən ˈpeːrtɪt wɪ o̩ːl ˈRiki.

Ma[266] o̩ːl, go̩ːd gləid oː ə miːr hɪz ˈhʌxʲəlt ʌp hʌl ən dun breː, ɪn[267] ˈSkotlən ən ˈIŋlo̩ːn, ɑz tjʌx ən ˈbɪrnɪ ɑs ə ˈvɛrɑ ˈdiːvəl wɪ miː. ɪts truː, shiːz ɑz peːrz ə ˈSɑŋˈmɑkər ən ɑz hɑrdz ɑ kɪrk, ən ˈtɪpərˈtepərz   10
ᴍɑn ʃiː tɑks ðə get, fʌrst ləik[268] ə ˈLɛdiːz ˈdʒɛntəlˈwʌmən ɪn ə ˈmɪnuʷeː, ɔr ə hɛn on ə hɛt ˈgɪrdəl; bʌt ʃiːz ə jo̩ːl, ˈpuːðəre ˈɡɛrən fər o̩ː ðɑt, ən hɪz ə ˈstɑmək ləik ˈWʌli ˈSto̩ːkərz miːr ðɑt[269] wʌd heː dɪsˈdʒɪstɪt ˈtʌmlər-ˈᴍilz, fər ʃiːl ᴍʌp miː ɑf hər[270] fɑːv ˈstɪmpərts oː ðə bɛst ets ɑt ə dun ˈsɪtɪn ən niːr faʃ hər θum. ᴍɑn jɪns hər rɪŋˈbenz ən   15
ˈspeːviːz, hər krʌks ən krɑmps, ɑːr ˈfeːrle ˈsupəlt, ʃiː bɪts teː, bɪts teː, ən əi ðə ˈhɪnməst uːr ðə ˈtɪçəst. ɑ kud ˈwɑdʒər hər prəis teː ə ˈðrɪtɪ ˈpeniːz, ðɑt fər twoː oːr ðriː wuks ˈrəidɪn ɑt ˈfɛftɪ məil ə deː, ðə dil stɪkɪt ə fɑːv ˈgaləpərz əˈkwiʃ Kləid ən ˈMʌthoːrn kud kɑst so̩ːt ɪn hər tel.   20

ɑ heː ˈdo̩ːnərt ʌur o̩ː ðə ˈkɪntrɑ freː Dʌnˈbo̩ːr[271] teː Sɛlˈkreg, ən heː fərˈgeðərt wɪ ˈᴍʌne ə gɪd ˈfɑlɑ, ən ˈᴍʌne ə wɪl fo̩ːrt ˈhɪzɪ. ɑ mɛt wɪ twoː dɪŋk kwinz ɪn pərˈtiklər, jɪn ə ðəm[272] ə ˈsonse, fəin, ˈfodʒəl lɑs, beθ bro̩ː ən ˈbone; ðə ˈtɪðər wʌz ə klin ˈʃaŋkɪt, stro̩ːxt, tɪçt, wɪl fo̩ːrt

---

261 *The Dialect of Robert Burns as Spoken in Central Ayrshire*, Oxford University Press.
262 Assimilation would produce [fʌrs dʒɪn].
263 Reduction to [iːr] may occur in colloquial speech.
264 Reduction to [əz] may occur in colloquial speech.
265 The stressed form is [ðɑt].
266 In colloquial speech before a vowel, reduction to [m] may occur.
267 Reduction to [ɪ] in unstressed positions before consonants may occur in colloquial speech.
268 Assimilation would produce [fʌrs ləik].
269 The relative pronoun is usually reduced to [ət] or [ðət] in colloquial speech.
270 Probably reduced to [ər] in colloquial speech.
271 As Burns wrote *Dumbar* that may be [dʌmˈbo̩ːr] cf. Dumbarton.
272 The stressed form is [ðem].

25 wʌnʃ, ɑz blɑːʳθz ə ˈlɪntʍəit on ə ˈfluːri θoːrn, ən ɑz swit ən ˈmodɪsts
ə njuː blo̩ːn ˈplʌmˌroːz ɪn ə ˈhezəl ʃo̩ː. Ðeː wʌr beθ brɛd teː[273]
ˈmenərz bɪ ðə bjʌk, ən ˈone jɪn oː ðem hɪz ɑz ˈmʌkəl ˈsmɛdəm ən
ˈrʌməlˈgʌmʃən ɑz ðə ho̩ːf ə sʌm ˈprɛsbɪtris ðɑt juː ən ɑ beθ kɛn.
Ðeː pleːd miː sɪk ə ˈdiːvəl oː ə ˈʃeːvi ðɑt ɑ do̩ːr seː ɪf ma ˈhɑːrɪˌgəlz wʌr
30 tʌrnt ut, jiː wʌd siː two̩ː nɪks ɪn ðə hɛrt oː miː ləik ðə mɑːrk oː ə kel-
ˈʍʌtəl ɪn ə ˈkʌstək.

ɑ wʌz go̩ːn teː[274] rəit yiː ə lo̩ːŋ əˈpɪsəl, bʌt, ɡɪd fərˈgiː miː, ɑ gat maˈsɛl
seː nəˈtoːrɪəs ˈbɪtʃɪfiːd ðə deː ˈɛftər kelˈtəim ðɑt ɑ kan ˈho̩ːrle
ˈsto̩ɪtər bʌt ən bɛn.

35 Ma bɛst rəˈspeks[275] teː ðə ˈɡɪdˌwəif ən o̩ː uːr ˈkomən frinz, əˈspiʃəl
ˈMɪstər ən ˈMɛstrəs Krʌkˈʃaŋk, ən ðə ˈɔnəst ɡɪdˈmɑn[276] oː Dʒoks Ludʒ.

ɑl biː ɪn Dʌmˈfris ðə mo̩ːrn ɡɪf ðə bist biː[277] teː ðə fo̩ːr, ən ðə braŋks
bəid hel.

ɡɪd biː wɪ juː,[278] ˈWʌlɪ! ɑːˈmɛn.
40 ˈRobərt Bʌrnz

Key to the IPA capital letters used above

ɑɑ Bb Dd Ðð ɡɡ Hh Ɪɪ Kk Ll Mm Oo Rr Ss Ww ʍʍ

---

273 Likely reduced to [tə] in colloquial speech.
274 Assimilation would produce [ɡo̩ːneː].
275 Assimilation would produce [bɛs rəˈspeks].
276 Assimilation would produce [ˈɔnəs ɡɪdˈmɑn].
277 Assimilation would produce [bis biː].
278 In colloquial speech [jiː] would be more probable. The nominative and objective is [jiː], unstressed [jɪ]. The accusative and dative is [juː].

9.14 SUMMARY FOR COMPARISON

9.14.1 Robert Burns

I met wi' twa dink quines in particlar, ane o' them a sonsie, fine, fodgel lass, baith braw and bonie; the tither was a clean-shankit, straught, tight, weel-far'd winch, as blythe's a lintwhite on a flowerie thorn, and as sweet and modest's a new blawn plumrose in a hazle shaw.

9.14.2 *The Scots Style Sheet* 1947

I met wi twa dink quines in particlar, ane o them a sonsie, fine, fodgel lass, baith braw and bonnie; the tither was a clean-shankit, straucht, ticht, weel-faured winch, as blythe's a lintwhite on a flouerie thorn, and as sweet and modest's a new blawn plumrose in a hazle shaw.

9.14.3 David Purves

A met wi twa dink quynes in pairteiklar, ane o thaim a sonsie, fyne, fodgil lass, baith braw an bonnie; the tither wes a claen-shankit, strecht, ticht, weill-faurt winch, as blyth's a lintwhyte on a flouerie thorn, an as sweet an modest's a new blawn plumrose i a hazil shaw.

9.14.4 J. Derrick McClure

A met wi twaa dink quiyns in parteiclar, aen o thaim a sonsei, fiyn, fodgel lass, baith braa an bonnei; the tither wis a claen-shankit, straacht, ticht, weil-faart winch, as bliyth's a lintwhiyt on a flouerei thoarn, an as sweit an moadest's a new blaan plumroas in a hizzle shaa.

9.14.5 *The Scots Language Society*

A met wi twa dink quynes in pairteiklar, ane o thaim a sonsie, fyne, fodgil lass, baith braw an bonnie; the tither wes a claen-shankit, strecht, ticht, weill-faurt winch, as blyth's a lintwhyte on a flouerie thorn, an as sweet an modest's a new blawn plumrose in a hazil shaw.

9.14.6 Angus Stirling

Ii mett wi twa dink quiins inn parteiklar, äne o thäm a sonsie, fiin, fojel lass, bäth bra ann bonnie; the tither wus a clän-shankit, stracht, ticht, wiel-fard winsch, as bliith's a lintwhiit on a fluerie thorn, ann as swiet ann modist's a niw blan plummros inn a hissil scha.

9.14.7 *The Aiberdeen Univairsitie Scots Leid Quorum*

A met wi twa dink quynes i parteiclar, ane o thaim a sonsie, fyne, fodgel lass, baith braw an bonnie; the tither wes a claen-shankit, strecht, ticht, weil-faured winch, as blythe's a lintwhyte on a flouerie thorn, an as sweet an modest's a new blawn plumrose in a hizzle shaw.

9.14.8 The *SNDA* (later *SLD*, now *DSL*)

A met wi twa dink quines i parteeclar, ane o thaim a sonsie, fine, fodgel lass, baith braw an bonnie; the tither wis a clean-shankit, stracht, ticht, weelfaured winch, as blithe's a lintwhite on a flooerie thorn, an as sweet an modest's a new blawn plumrose i a hissle shaw

9.14.9 George Philp

I met wi twa dink quines in partíclar, yin o them a sonsy, fine, fodgel lass, baith braw and bonny; the tither wis a claen-shankit, straucht, ticht, weill-faurt winch, as blythe's a lintwhite on a flouery thorn, and as sweet and modest's a new blawn plumrose in a hazle shaw.

9.14.10 Philip Robinson

A met wi twa dänk quines in partìclar, yin o thàim a sonsie, fine, fodgel lass, baith braa an bonnie; tha tither wuz a clain-shankit, stracht, ticht, weel-fart wunch, as blythe's a lintwhite on a flooerie thoarn, an as sweet an modest's a new blaan plumrose in a hazle shaa.

9.14.11 *The Scots Spellin Comatee*

I met wi twa dink quines in parteicular, ane o thaim a sonsie, fine, fodgel lass, baith braw an bonnie; the tither wis a claen-shankit, straucht, ticht, weel-faurt winch, as blythe's a lintwhite on a flouerie thorn, an as sweet an modest's a new blawn plumrose in a hissle shaw.

9.14.12 Andy Eagle

I met wi twa dink queans in parteecular, ane o thaim a sonsy, fine, fodgle lass, baith braw and bonny; the tither wis a clean-shankit, straucht, ticht, weel-faured winch, as blithe's a lintwhite on a flouery thorn, and as sweet and modest's a new blawn plumrose in a hazle shaw.

9.14.13 Phonetic transcription

ɑ mɛt wɪ twǫː dɪŋk kwinz ɪn pərˈtiklər, jɪn ə ðəm[279] ə ˈsonse, fəin, ˈfodʒəl lɑs, beθ brǫː ən ˈbone; ðə ˈtɪðər wʌz ə klin ˈʃaŋkɪt, strǫːxt, tɪçt, wil fǫːrt wʌnʃ, az blɑːrθz ə ˈlɪntʍəit on ə ˈfluːri θoːrn, ən ɑz swit ən ˈmodɪsts ə njuː blǫːn ˈplʌmˌroːz ɪn ə ˈhezəl ʃǫː.

---

279 The stressed form is [ðem].

10
AFTERWORD:
TRANSLATING WONDERLAND

As I mentioned in the Foreword, to date Lewis Carroll's classic *Alice's Adventures in Wonderland* has been translated into nine dialects of Scots, with two in preparation. These were written *as* dialect pieces, and were intended to take advantage of dialect accidence, syntax, and vocabulary. Naturally since a tendency to "spell as you speak" has been encouraged and promoted for some time, these translations differ orthographically as well as linguistically.

In the Foreword I suggested that orthographic distinctions mask the unity of the language and can pose a barrier to easy comprehension. It is easy for speakers from Central Scotland who say [ʍɪt] and [ʍəit] to listen to speakers of North-East Scots and understand them when they say [fɪt] and [fəit], but when reading, the spellings *fit* and *fite* can cause a reader to stumble while *whit* and *white* do not. Indeed, speakers of North-East Scots learn to spell Standard English *what* and *white* even where they may pronounce both with an initial [f].

I mentioned that in Standard English *brother* may be pronounced with a [ð] or a [v] or a [d] depending on dialect, but the spellings *bruvver* and *brudder* have no general currency outside "dialect writing". Now, dialect writing has its place, and can be a pleasure in Scots as it can be in English. Robert Louis Stevenson used it in *Treasure Island*, Bram Stoker used it in *Dracula*, and Emily Brontë used it in *Wuthering Heights*. But current practice fractures Scots into many varieties, which works to the detriment of the language, and often leads to "eye dialect" spellings which lead to further trouble.

In this section a short passage of about 450 words has been taken, from Chapter IV, "The Rabbit Sends in a Little Bill". The translator's original text is presented on the left-hand page, and the same text edited more in line with the regularized spellings upon which Andy's research has converged is given on the right.

No disrespect is intended to the original translators. They wrote as they wrote, and I was glad to publish them. For his part, Andy was at first reluctant to transcribe the texts into a regularized pan-dialect orthography based on the traditional literary conventions, because most of the texts were deliberate attempts to produce phonetically accurate dialect where the writer provides the pronunciation. In contrast, the piece by Burns was written using the literary conventions of his time where the reader provides the pronunciation—Burns was not attempting to produce phonetically accurate Ayrshire dialect. The intent here, however, is to show that their creativity as translators is in no way diminished with a unified, inclusive orthography. Indeed, such an orthography can allow each translator's text to be appreciated more easily, to every reader's pleasure.

In the transcriptions forms such as *aal, Ahlice, all, call, away, awey, awy, bright, caal, daughter* and *dowter, do, ever, fifth, goat* 'got', *high, hom* 'home', *how* (except in Southern Scots where it likely represents the local realization of Scots *hou*), *humbly, I, join, loud, might, my, off, own, oyster, right, sharp, sigh, soon, straight, use, venture, well,* and *when* have been left as they are or modified to conform to Standard English conventions as it is assumed that the intended pronunciation is much the same as the local Standard English one. Forms such as *look, shook,* and *took* have been assumed to have a Scots pronunciation with /u/ that is then represented by ⟨eu⟩.

In the normalized versions in this chapter, the traditional and etymological Scots spellings *I* and *and* have been preferred to the spellings *A* and *an*, both of which are spellings for forms of the indefinite article. Although the SND has an entry for the first person singular pronoun under *A*,[280] it also has an entry for the same under *I*.[281] The SND also says that "*And* is often written, but seldom so pronounced [ɑn, ən, n]"[282]—but the same can be said for the pronunciation of the conjunction in Standard English, at least in unstressed forms.

Words with vowels 1 and 10 ending in ⟨-nd⟩ and ⟨-nt⟩ are written ⟨-ind⟩ and ⟨-ynt⟩ respectively. Both ⟨i⟩ and ⟨y⟩ are attested in these environments but it is likely that *mint* [mɪnt] 'mint' alongside *mynt* [məɪnt] 'attempt, intention' makes a helpful distinction. Similarly it is preferable to distinguish *vice* [vʌɪs] 'wicked behaviour; substitute' and *vyce* [vʌɪs] 'voice'. This is a

---

280 SND I: 1 s.v. "A, AH, AW, AA. A', I". This gives the pronunciation [ɑː], [ɑɪ] (both emphatic) and [ə] (unstressed).

281 SND V: 246 s.v. "I". This notes the additional spelling *a* (etc.) as well as Dundonian *eh, ey*; it gives the pronunciation [ae] (stressed) alongside the unstressed pronunciations [ɑ], [ə], [ʌ], and south Angus [e].

282 SND 1: 56 s.v. "AN(D), AN' [with apostrophe]". This notes the additional spelling *a* (etc.) as well as Dundonian *eh, ey*; it gives the pronunciation [ae] (stressed) alongside the unstressed pronunciations [ɑ], [ə], [ʌ], and south Angus [e].

good example of how old spellings (deriving from Middle Scots variants) can be made to serve to distinguish words within Scots. See discussion above at §6.2.9 and §6.2.11.

Michael Everson

10.1 STANDARD ENGLISH (LEWIS CARROLL)

"Mine is a long and a sad tale!" said the Mouse, turning to Alice, and sighing.

"It *is* a long tail, certainly," said Alice, looking down with wonder at the Mouse's tail; "but why do you call it sad?" And she kept on puzzling about it while the Mouse was speaking, so that her idea of the tale was something like this:— [...]

"You are not attending!" said the Mouse to Alice, severely. "What are you thinking of?"

"I beg your pardon," said Alice very humbly: "you had got to the fifth bend, I think?"

"I had *not!*" cried the Mouse, sharply and very angrily.

"A knot!" said Alice, always ready to make herself useful, and looking anxiously about her. "Oh, do let me help to undo it!"

"I shall do nothing of the sort," said the Mouse, getting up and walking away. "You insult me by talking such nonsense!"

"I didn't mean it!" pleaded poor Alice. "But you're so easily offended, you know!"

The Mouse only growled in reply.

"Please come back, and finish your story!" Alice called after it. And the others all joined in chorus "Yes, please do!" But the Mouse only shook its head impatiently, and walked a little quicker.

"What a pity it wouldn't stay!" sighed the Lory, as soon as it was quite out of sight. And an old Crab took the opportunity of saying to her daughter "Ah, my dear! Let this be a lesson to you never to lose *your* temper!"

"Hold your tongue, Ma!" said the young Crab, a little snappishly. "You're enough to try the patience of an oyster!"

"I wish I had our Dinah here, I know I do!" said Alice aloud, addressing nobody in particular. "*She'd* soon fetch it back!"

"And who is Dinah, if I might venture to ask the question?" said the Lory.

Alice replied eagerly, for she was always ready to talk about her pet: "Dinah's our cat. And she's such a capital one for catching mice, you ca'n't think! And oh, I wish you could see her after the birds! Why, she'll eat a little bird as soon as look at it!"

This speech caused a remarkable sensation among the party. Some of the birds hurried off at once: one old Magpie began wrapping itself up very carefully, remarking "I really must be getting home: the night-air doesn't suit my throat!" And a Canary called out in a trembling voice, to its children, "Come away, my dears! It's high time you were all in bed!" On various pretexts they all moved off, and Alice was soon left alone.

10.2 SHETLAND SCOTS (LAUREEN JOHNSON)

"My tale," said da Moose, turnin ta Alice wi a seich, "is lang, laek me tail—an sad."

"He truly is a lang tail," said Alice, lookin doon an winderin at da Moose's tail; "but why does du say he's sad?" An shö keepit on axin hersel dat while da Moose wis spaekin, so at her idea o da tale wis somethin laek dis:— [...]

"Du's no peyin attention!" said da Moose ta Alice, aafil siccar. "Whit's du tinkin aboot?"

"A'm aafil sorry," said Alice, braaly sidden apon. "Du wis wun ta da fift bend, I tink."

"I wis *not*!" cried da Moose, sharp an aafil tirn.

"A knot!" said Alice, aye ready ta mak hersel ösfil, an shö lookit aboot her, anxious ta fin dis knot. "Oh, lat me help ta lowse him!"

"A'll dö naethin o da kind," said da Moose, risin an walkin awa. "Du's makkin a föl o me wi aa dis bruck du's spaekin!"

"I didna mean it!" poor Alice plötit. "But du's dat aesy offendit, du kens!"

Aa da answer shö got fae da Moose wis a girn.

"Please come back an feenish dee story!" Alice cried efter him; an da rest o dem said, aa at ee time, "Yes, will du, please!" but da Moose only shook his head, ill-naitered-wye, an walkit a coarn faster.

"Whit a peety he widna bide!" said da Lory wi a seich, as shön as he wis fairly oot o sicht; an an aald Crab took da chance o sayin tae her dochter, "Ah my lass! Lat dis be a lesson ta dee never ta loss *dy* temper!"

"Hadd dee wheesht, Mam!" said da young Crab, kinda snippit. "Du's enyoch ta try da patience o a lempit!"

"I wiss I hed wir Dinah here, I truly dö!" said Alice oot lood, spaekin ta naebody in parteeklar. "Shö wid shön fetch him back!"

"An wha is Dinah, if I micht ventir ta ax?" said da Lory.

Alice wis aaber ta answer, for shö wis aye ready ta spaek aboot her pet: "Dinah is wir cat. An shö's datten a guid haand at catchin mice, you hae nae idea. An oh, I wiss you saa her efter da birds! Feth, shö wid aet a peerie bird as shön as look at him!"

Dis set da hale baand in a braa steer. Some o da birds flaachtered aff wi dat sam: ee aald magpie startit rowin himsel up aafil tentily an sayin, "I doot A'll hae ta geng hame; da nicht-air doesna dö wi my trot!" An a Canary cried oot tae her bairns wi a voice at wis juist trimmlin, "Come you, bairns! Hit's time noo at you wir aa i your beds!" Some gae ee raeson an some anidder, but dey aa guid, an Alice wis shön aa on her ain.

"My tale," said the Moose, turnin tae Alice wi a sich, "is lang, like ma tail—and sad."

"He truly is a lang tail," said Alice, leukin doun and winderin at the Moose's tail; "but why daes thoo say he's sad?" And she keepit on aksin hersel that while the Moose wis speakin, so 'at her idea o the tale wis something like this:— […]

"Thoo's no peyin attention!" said the Moose tae Alice, awful siccar. "Whit's thoo thinkin aboot?"

"I'm awful sorry," said Alice, brawly sudden upon. "Thoo wis wun tae the fift bend, I think."

"I wis *not!*" cried the Moose, sharp and awful tirren.

"A knot!" said Alice, aye ready tae mak hersel uissful, and she leukit aboot her, anxious tae find this knot. "Oh, lat me help tae lowse him!"

"I'll dae naething o the kind," said the Moose, risin and walkin awa. "Thoo's makkin a fuil o me wi aw this bruck thoo's speakin!"

"I didna mean it!" puir Alice pluitit. "But thoo's that easy offendit, thoo kens!"

Aw the answer she got fae the Moose wis a girn.

"Please come back and feenish thee story!" Alice cried efter him; and the rest o thaim said, aw at ae time, "Yes, will thoo, please!" but the Moose only sheuk his heid, ill-naitured-wey, and walkit a corn faster.

"Whit a peety he wadna bide!" said the Lory wi a sich, as suin as he wis fairly oot o sicht; and an auld Crab teuk the chance o sayin tae her dochter, "Ah my lass! Lat this be a lesson tae thee never tae loss *thy* temper!"

"Haud thee wheesht, Mam!" said the young Crab, kind o snippit. "Thoo's eneuch tae try the patience o a lempet!"

"I wiss I haed wir Dinah here, I truly dae!" said Alice oot loud, speakin tae naebody in parteecular. "She wad suin fetch him back!"

"And wha is Dinah, if I micht ventur tae aks?" said the Lory.

Alice wis aaber tae answer, for she wis aye ready tae speak aboot her pet: "Dinah is wir cat. And she's thattan a guid haund at catchin mice, you hae nae idea. And oh, I wiss you saw her efter the birds! Feth, she wad eat a peerie bird as suin as leuk at him!"

This set the hale baund in a braw steer. Some o the birds flauchtered aff wi that same: ae auld magpie startit rowin himsel up awful tentily and sayin, "I dout I'll hae tae gang hame; the nicht-air daesna dae wi my throat!" And a Canary cried oot tae her bairns wi a voice 'at wis juist trimmlin, "Come you, bairns! Hit's time nou 'at you war aw in your beds!" Some gae ae raison and some anither, but thay aw gaed, and Alice wis suin aw on her ain.

10.3 ORKNEY SCOTS (DONNA HEDDLE)

"Mine is a ferfil long, sad tale!" yarpid the Moose, turnan tae Alice wae a gret sich.

"Hid *is* a long tail, right enough," said Alice, lukking doon wae winder at the Moose's tail; "but whit wey deu thoo caa hid sad?" And sheu jalousid aboot hid while the Moose wis spikan, so hur notion o the tale wis sometheen this wey:—[…]

"Thoor no watchan!" yarpid the Moose tae Alice in a tirr. "Er thoo in a dwam?"

"Dinno be grabbit," said Alice aafil peaceably: "thoo hid wun tae the fifth lirk, hid thoo no?"

"Ah hid *not*!" golderid the Moose, aafil tirrie.

"A knot!" said Alice, aye ready tae mak hursael a help, and lukking ferfully aboot hands. "Oh, deu let me gie thee a haund tae undae hid!"

"Ah shall hiv feentie-thing wae hid tae deu," said the Moose, gittan up and walkan awey. "Thoo mittle me by spaekan sic haivers!"

"Ah deudna mean hid!" gret puir peedie Alice. "But thoo're aafil easy pit up the spoot, thoo kens!"

The ill-nettered Moose juist naurit.

"Plaese come back and feenish thoor tale!" Alice caad eftir hid; and the fock all golderid, "Aye deu, beuy, for a mercy!" but the Moose geed his heid a dilder in a gey twartie wey, and pattlid a peedie bit queeker.

"Whit a peety hid widna bide!" sichid the Lory, as seun as hid wis ferly awey; and an owld Partan hid a spaek tae hur dowter "Ah, me bonnie lass! Let this be a lesson tae thee nivver tae get *thoor* dander up!"

"Haad thoor wheest, Mither!" said the peedie Partan, ferly girnie. "Thoo wid scunner an oyster!"

"Ah wish Ah hid wur Dinah aboot hands, Ah ken Ah dae!" said Alice alood, spaekan tae naebody in parteeclar. "Sheu'd soon fetch it back!"

"And whar is Dinah, gin Ah can speir?" said the Lory.

Alice wis yivverie tae spaek, for sheu wis alwis mad for spaekan aboot hur ketleen: "Dinah's wur cat. And sheu's sic a grand wan for catchan mice ye can't jalouse! And oh, Ah wish ye could see her eftir the birds! Why, sheu'll aet a peedie bird as queek as lukk at hid!"

Sic a spaek ferly raffled the fock. Twartree o the birds herried aff at wance: wan owld Magpie stairtit happan hidsel up aafil weel, yarpan, "*Ah* really maun be gittan up-bye; the night-air disna suit me thrapple!" and a Canary caad oot in a wafflie wey tae hids bairns, "Come awey, bairns! Hid's high time ye wur aal in thoor beds!" On a dose o ploys they aal trampit awey, and in a peedie blink Alice wis by hur leen.

"Mine is a fair full long, sad tale!" yirpit the Moose, turnin tae Alice wi a great sich.

"Hit is a long tail, right enough," said Alice, leukin doun wi winder at the Moose's tail; "but whit wey dae thou caw hit sad?" And she jaloused aboot hit while the Moose wis speakin, so her notion o the tale wis something this wey:—[...]

"Thoo're no watchin!" yirpit the Moose tae Alice in a tirr. "Are thoo in a dwaum?"

"Dinna be grabbit," said Alice awful peaceably: "thoo haed wun tae the fifth lirk, haed thoo no?"

"I haed not!" goldered the Moose, awful tirry.

"A knot!" said Alice, aye ready tae mak hersel a help, and leukin fearfully aboot haunds. "Oh, dae let me gie thee a haund tae undae hit!"

"I shall hiv fientie-thing wi hit tae dae," said the Moose, gittin up and walkin awey. "Thoo mittle me by speakin sic haivers!"

"I daedna mean hit!" great puir peedie Alice. "But thoo're awful easy pit up the spoot, thoo kens!"

The ill-naitured Moose juist nurrit.

"Please come back and feenish thoor tale!" Alice cawed efter hit; and the fowk all goldered, "Aye dae, boy, for a mercy!" but the Moose gied his heid a dilder in a gey thwartie wey, and pattelt a peedie bit quicker.

"Whit a peety hit wadna bide!" sichit the Lory, as suin as hit wis fairly awey; and an auld Partan haed a speak tae her dowter "Ah, ma bonnie lass! Let this be a lesson tae thee niver tae get *thoor* dander up!"

"Haud thoor wheesht, Mither!" said the peedie Partan, fairly girnie. "Thoo wad scunner an oyster!"

"I wish I haed wir Dinah aboot haunds, I ken I dae!" said Alice alood, speakin tae naebody in parteecular. "She'd suin fetch it back!"

"And whaur is Dinah, gin I can speir?" said the Lory.

Alice wis aiverie tae speak, for she wis allways mad for speakan aboot her kittlin: "Dinah's wir cat. And she's sic a grand wan for catchin mice ye can't jalouse! And oh, I wish ye coud see her efter the birds! Why, she'll eat a peedie bird as quick as leuk at hit!"

Sic a speak fairly raivelt the fowk. Twa or three o the birds hurried aff at wance: wan auld Magpie stertit happin hitsel up awful weel, yirpin, "*I* really maun be gittin upby; the night-air disna suit ma thrapple!" and a Canary cawed oot in a wafflie wey tae hits bairns, "Come awey, bairns! Hit's high time ye war all in thoor beds!" On a dose o ploys they all trampit awey, and in a peedie blink Alice wis by her lane.

10.4 CAITHNESS SCOTS (CATHERINE BYRNE)

"Mine is a long an a sad tale!" sade e Moose, turnan till Alice, an sighan.

"Id *is* a long tail, certainly," sade Alice, lookan doon wi winder at e Moose's tail; "but why do ee call id sad?" An she kept on puzzlan aboot id while e Moose wis speakan, so at her idea o e tale wis somethin lek is:— [...]

"Ee are no attendan!" sade e Moose till Alice severely. "What are ee thinkan o?"

"A beg yer pardon," sade Alice awful humbly: "ee hed got till e fifth bend, A think?"

"A hedna!" cowned e Moose, sharply an awful mad.

"A knot!" sade Alice, always ready till make hersel useful, an lookan anxiously aboot her. "Oh, do lit me help till loosen id!"

"A'll do nothin o e sort," sade e Moose, gettan up an walkan awy. "Ee insult me by talkan such nonsense!"

"A didna mean id!" pleaded poor Alice. "But ye're so easily offended, ee ken!"

E Moose only growled in reply.

"Please come back, an feenish yer story!" Alice called efter id. An e ithers all joined in chorus, "Yis, please do!" But e Moose only shook ids hied impatiently, an walked a peedy bit quicker.

"What a pity id widna stay!" sighed e Lory, as soon as id wis quite oot o sicht. An an owld Crab took e opportunity o sayan till her douchter "Ah, ma dear! Lit iss be a lesson till ee never till lose *yer* temper!"

"Howld yer tongue, Ma!" sade e Crab, a bittie snappishly. "Ye're enough till try e patience o an oyster!"

"A wish A hed wur Dinah here, A ken A do!" sade Alice oot loud, addressan nobody in particular. "*She'd* soon fetch id back!"

"An who is Dinah, if A micht venture till ask e question?" sade e Lory.

Alice replied eagerly, for she wis always ready till talk aboot her pet: "Dinah's wur cat. An she's such a great wan for catchan mice ee canna think! An oh, A wish ee could see her efter e burds! Why, she'll eit a peedy burd as soon as look at id!"

Iss speech caused a remarkable sensation amang e party. Some o e burds hurried off at wance: wan owld Magpie began wrappan idsell up awful carefully, remarkan, "A really mosst be gettan hom; e nicht-air disna suit ma throat!" An a Canary called oot in a tremblan voice till ids bairns, "Come aweiy, ma dears ! Id's high time ee were all in bed!" On various pretexts they all moved off, an Alice wis soon left on her own.

"Mine is a long and a sad tale!" said the Moose, turnin til Alice, and sighin.

"It *is* a long tail, certainly," said Alice, leukin doun wi winder at the Moose's tail; "but why do ye call it sad?" And she kept on puzzlin aboot it while the Moose wis speakin, so 'at her idea o the tale wis something like this:— [...]

"Ye are no attendin!" said the Moose til Alice severely. "What are ye thinkin o?"

"I beg yer pardon," said Alice awful humbly: "ye haed got til the fifth bend, I think?"

"I haedna!" cowned the Moose, sharply and awful mad.

"A knot!" said Alice, always ready til make hersel useful, and leukin anxiously aboot her. "Oh, do lat me help til loosen it!"

"I'll do nothing o the sort," said the Moose, gettin up and walkin awey. "Ye insult me by talkin such nonsense!"

"I didna mean it!" pleaded poor Alice. "But ye're so easily offended, ye ken!"

The Moose only growled in reply.

"Please come back, and feenish yer story!" Alice called efter it. And the ithers all joined in chorus, "Yes, please do!" But the Moose only sheuk its heid impatiently, and walked a peedie bit quicker.

"What a pity it wadna stay!" sighed the Lory, as soon as it wis quite oot o sicht. And an auld Crab teuk the opportunity o sayin til her dochter "Ah, ma dear! Lat this be a lesson til ye never til lose *yer* temper!"

"Hold yer tongue, Ma!" said the Crab, a bittie snappishly. "Ye're enough til try the patience o an oyster!"

"I wish I haed wir Dinah here, I ken I do!" said Alice oot loud, addressin nobody in particular. "*She'd* soon fetch it back!"

"And who is Dinah, if I micht venture til ask the question?" said the Lory.

Alice replied eagerly, for she wis always ready til talk aboot her pet: "Dinah's wir cat. And she's such a great wan for catchin mice ye canna think! And oh, I wish ye coud see her efter the birds! Why, she'll eat a peedie bird as soon as leuk at it!"

This speech caused a remarkable sensation amang the party. Some o the birds hurried off at wance: wan auld Magpie began wrappin itsel up awful carefully, remarkin, "I really must be gettin home; the nicht-air disna suit ma throat!" And a Canary called oot in a tremblin voice til its bairns, "Come awey, ma dears ! It's high time ye were all in bed!" On various pretexts thay all moved off, and Alice wis soon left on her own.

10.5 NORTH-EAST SCOTS (J. DERRICK MCCLURE)

"My tale's a lang een an a dowie!" said the Mous, turnin tae Ailice wi a saich.

"Certies it's a lang een,", said Ailice, gomin doun bambaizit at the Mous's tail, "but fit wye dae ye say it's dowie?" An she heeld on wi ferliein at it aa the file the Mous wes spickin, sae as her consait o the tale wes a bittie like iss:— […]

"Ye're nae takin tent!" said the Mous tae Ailice, fell stern-like. "Fit are ye thinkin about?"

"I'm rael sorry," said Ailice hummlie. "Ye'd wan tae the fift link, hed ye nae?

"Naethin o the sort!" scraich't the Mous, in a fair ill teen.

"Ye'd hae me tae sort it for ye?" speir't Ailice, aye wullin tae mak hersel eesefu, an teetit thochtilie aa roun about her. "Here till I gie ye a hann!"

"Na, ye'll dee nae siccan thing!" said the Mous, risin an stilpin awaa. "Ye jist set my birse up wi your haverin!"

"I didna mean tae!" priggit peer Ailice. "But ye're aat quick tae fung, ye ken!"

The Mous gied nae answer but a gurr.

"Wull ye nae come back an feinish your story?" Ailice cried efter it. An aa the idders jyn't in thegidder, "Aye, dee, gin ye please!" But the Mous jist sheuk its heid in a fuff an mairch't awaa the quicker.

"Fit a peity it wadna bide!" souch't the Lory, as seen as it wes out o sicht. An an aal Partan tyeuk the chunce o sayin tae her dother, "Aye, my daatie! Tak iss as a lesson aye tae keep a caam souch!"

"Haud your tung, Ma!" said the ying Partan, a wee thing capernicious-like. "Ye wad gar an eyster loss the heid!"

"I wuss I hed our Tibbie here, atweel I dee!" said Ailice out loud, nae spickin tae onybody in parteiclar. "She wadna be lang o fessin it back!"

"An fa's Tibbie, mith I be sae baal as tae speir?" said the Lory.

Ailice wes gleg tae answer, for she wes aye aiverie tae spick about her pet. "Tibbie's our cat. An ye've niver seen sic a bonnie een for nabbin mousies! An och, I wuss ye cwid see her gyaan efter the birdies! Fegs, she'll aet a wee birdie as seen's she gets a scunce o't!"

Iss speil pit the bourachie in a byordnar feem. Some o the birds gaed breeshlin aff richt awaa: ae aal Pyot set tae happin itsel rael tentilie, sayin "I raelly beed tae be takin the gait hame nou, the nicht air's nae gweed for my thrapple!" An a Canary wheepl't out in a chitterin vyce tae its littleens, "Come awaa nou, my bairnikies! It's time ye war aa in your bed!" On ae exceese or anidder they aa hushl't aff, an it wesna lang or Ailice wes aa her leen.

"My tale's a lang ane and a dowie!" said the Moose, turnin tae Ailice wi a sich.

"Certies it's a lang ane,", said Ailice, goamin doun bumbaise't the Moose's tail, "but whit wey dae ye say it's dowie?" And she huild on wi ferliein at it aw the while the Moose wis speakin, sae as her conceit o the tale wis a bittie like this:— […]

"Ye're nae takkin tent!" said the Moose tae Ailice, fell stern-like. "Whit are ye thinkin aboot?"

"I'm real sorry," said Ailice hummly. "Ye'd wan tae the fift link, haed ye nae?

"Naething o the sort!" skreicht the Moose, in a fair ill teen.

"Ye'd hae me tae sort it for ye?" speirt Ailice, aye willin tae mak hersel uissfu, and teetit thochtily aw roond aboot her. "Here til I gie ye a haund!"

"Na, ye'll dae nae siccan thing!" said the Moose, risin and stilpin awa. "Ye juist set my birse up wi your haiverin!"

"I didna mean tae!" priggit puir Ailice. "But ye're 'at quick tae fung, ye ken!"

The Moose gied nae answer but a gurr.

"Will ye nae come back and feenish your story?" Ailice cried efter it. And aw the ithers jyne't in thegither, "Aye, dae, gin ye please!" But the Moose juist sheuk its heid in a fuff and maircht awa the quicker.

"Whit a peety it wadna bide!" soucht the Lory, as suin as it wis oot o sicht. And an auld Partan teuk the chance o sayin tae her dochter, "Aye, my dautie! Tak this as a lesson aye tae keep a caum souch!"

"Haud your tounge, Ma!" said the young Partan, a wee thing capernicious-like. "Ye wad gar an eyster loss the heid!"

"I wiss I haed oor Tibbie here, atweel I dae!" said Ailice oot lood, nae speakin tae onybody in parteecular. "She wadna be lang o feshin it back!"

"And wha's Tibbie, micht I be sae bauld as tae speir?" said the Lory.

Ailice wis gleg tae answer, for she wis aye aiverie tae speak aboot her pet. "Tibbie's oor cat. And ye've niver seen sic a bonnie ane for nabbin moosies! And och, I wiss ye coud see her gaun efter the birdies! Fegs, she'll eat a wee birdie as suin's she gets a scance o't!"

This speel pit the boorachie in a byordinar fume. Some o the birds gaed breeshlin aff richt awa: ae auld Pyot set tae happin itsel real tentily, sayin "I really buid tae be takin the gate hame nou, the nicht air's nae guid for my thrapple!" And a Canary wheepelt oot in a chitterin vyce tae its little anes, "Come awa nou, my bairnockies! It's time ye war aw in your bed!" On ae excuiss or anither thay aw hushelt aff, and it wisna lang or Ailice wis aw her lane.

10.6 FIFE SCOTS (TOM HUBBARD)

"Mines is an awfy lang and sad tale," says the Moose, turnin ti Alice, and sighin like.

"Hit's a lang tail, nae doobt aboot that," says Alice, lookin doon and wunnerin at the Moose's tail, "but why dae ye cry hit sad?" And she kept on puzzlin aboot hit while the Moose wis speakin, sae her notion o the tale wis somehin like this:—[…]

"Ye're no lissnin!" says the Moose ti Alice, his dander fair up. "Whit are ye thinkin o?"

"Sorry," says Alice, awfy humble likes, "ye've got ti the fift bend, huv ye no?"

"Ah definitely had *not*!" cries the Moose, gey sharp and aw het up.

"A *knot*, ye say?" said Alice, aye ready ti mak hersel yuisfu, and lookin awfy anxious like aboot her. "Here, let me undae hit!"

"Ah'll dae nuhhin o the sort," said the Moose, gittin up and walkin awaw. "Ye're insultin me, talkin aw thae blethers!"

"Ah didnae mean hit!" puir Alice fair begged him. "But ye're awfy quick ti tak the huff, kén!"

The Moose juist growled in reply.

"Och juist come back and finish yer story!" Alice cried oot at hit. And the ithers jyned in a chorus. "Ay, come on, please, eh?" But the Moose juist shook hits heid impatient like, and walked a wee bit quicker.

"Thaht's an awfy pity likes, hit wuidnae byde!" sighed the Lory, as süne as the Moose wis oot o sicht. And an auld Crab tuik the chaunce o sayin ti her dochter "Och hen! Thaht'll learn ye, no ti lose yer temper like thon Moose!"

"Juist shut it Mum, eh?" says the young Crab, bein gey snippy, "Kén, ye'd try the patience o an oyster!"

"Ah wish Ah hud oor Zoë here, Ah really dae!" said Alice, oot lood, no speakin ti onybody in particular. "*She'd* süne fetch hit back!"

"And wha's this Zoë when she's at hame?" said the Lory.

Alice replied, aw eager like, fir she wis aye gleg ti talk aboot her pet. "Zoë's oor cat. And she's a champion at catchin mice, thaht's fir shair! Och, Ah wish ye cuid see her efter the birds! Ay, she'll eat a wee bird süne as look at hit!"

This speech fair caused some sensation amang aw thaht lot. Some o the birds hurried aff at wance: wan auld Magpie stertit wrappin hitsel up awfy carefu like, sayin by-the-by: "Hei, Ah've really got ti git hame, the nicht-air isnae guid fir ma thrapple!" And a Canary cried oot in a richt tremmlin voice, ti hits bairns, "Come on, youse yins! Hit's high time youse wis aw in yer beds!" Wi various excuses they aw breenged aff, and Alice wis left aw her lane.

"Mines is an awfu lang and sad tale," says the Moose, turnin tae Alice, and sighin like.

"Hit's a lang tail, nae doot aboot that," says Alice, leukin doun and wunnerin at the Moose's tail, "but why dae ye cry hit sad?" And she kept on puzzlin aboot hit while the Moose wis speakin, sae her notion o the tale wis something like this:—[...]

"Ye're no listenin!" says the Moose tae Alice, his dander fair up. "Whit are ye thinkin o?"

"Sorry," says Alice, awfu humble likes, "ye'v got tae the fift bend, hiv ye no?"

"I definitely haed not!" cries the Moose, gey sharp and aw het up.

"A knot, ye say?" said Alice, aye ready tae mak hersel uissfu, and leukin awfu anxious like aboot her. "Here, let me undae hit!"

"I'll dae naething o the sort," said the Moose, gettin up and walkin awa. "Ye're insultin me, talkin aw thae blethers!"

"I didna mean hit!" puir Alice fair beggit him. "But ye're awfu quick tae tak the huff, ken!"

The Moose juist growled in reply.

"Och juist come back and finish yer story!" Alice cried oot at hit. And the ithers jyned in a chorus. "Ay, come on, please, eh?" But the Moose juist sheuk hits heid impatient like, and walked a wee bit quicker.

"That's an awfu pity likes, hit wadna bide!" sighed the Lory, as suin as the Moose wis oot o sicht. And an auld Crab teuk the chance o sayin tae her dochter "Och hen! That'll learn ye, no tae lose yer temper like thon Moose!"

"Juist shut it Mum, eh?" says the young Crab, bein gey snippy, "Ken, ye'd try the patience o an oyster!"

"I wish I haed oor Zoë here, I really dae!" said Alice, oot lood, no speakin tae onybody in particular. "*She'd* suin fetch hit back!"

"And wha's this Zoë when she's at hame?" said the Lory.

Alice replied, aw eager like, for she wis aye gleg tae talk aboot her pet. "Zoë's oor cat. And she's a champion at catchin mice, that's for shuir! Och, I wish ye coud see her efter the birds! Ay, she'll eat a wee bird suin as leuk at hit!"

This speech fair caused some sensation amang aw that lot. Some o the birds hurried aff at wance: wan auld Magpie stertit wrappin hitsel up awfu carefu like, sayin by-the-by: "Hey, I'v really got tae git hame, the nicht-air isna guid for ma thrapple!" And a Canary cried oot in a richt tremmlin voice, tae hits bairns, "Come on, youse anes! Hit's high time youse wis aw in yer beds!" Wi various excuses they aw breenged aff, and Alice wis left aw her lane.

10.7 SOUTH-EAST CENTRAL SCOTS (SANDY FLEEMIN)

"Mines is a lang an dowie tale!" says the Moose, turnin tae Ailice an lattin oot a sich.

"It *is* a lang tail, my certy," says Ailice, keekin doun an wunnerin at the Moose's tail; but what are ye caain it dowie for?" An she kept on wunnerin aboot it the time the Moose wis spaekin, sae's her idea o the tale wis kin o like this:— […]

"Ye're no listenin!" says the Moose tae Ailice, severe-like. "What are ye thinkin aboot?"

"I beg yer pairdon," says Ailice gey hummled: "ye haed gotten tae the fifth bend, I think?"

"I haed *nut*!" cried the Moose gey short an fair wud.

"A nut!" says Ailice, aye ready tae mak hersel some uise, an keekin nervish aboot her. "Aw, g'on an lat me crack it!"

"I'se dae naething the like," says the Moose, gittin up an walkin awa. "I'm black affrontit at sic bletheration!"

"I didna mean it!" puir Ailice pleadit. "But ye'r that kittle, ye ken!"

The Moose juist growled at this.

"Come on back an feenish yer story!" Ailice cried efter it. An aabody jyned in the chorus "Ay, come on an dae that!" But the Moose juist sheuk its heid impatient, an walkit a bittie mair swippert.

"What a peety it wadna bide!" siched the Lory, the meenit it wis awa oot o sicht. An an auld Partan teuk the chance tae say tae her dochter "Weel, hen! Lat this be a lesson tae ye never tae loss *your* heid!"

"Haud yer wheesht, Ma!" says the young Partan, a bittie short wi her. Ye'd try the patience o an eyster!"

"I wish I haed oor Dinah here, I ken I div!" says Ailice oot lood, addressin naebody in parteeclar. "*She'd* fesh it back suin eneuch!"

"An wha's this Dinah, gin I micht anter tae pit the question?" says the Lory.

Ailice replied fair eident, the wey she wis aye set tae spaek aboot her pet: "Dinah's oor cat. An she's sic a capital ane for catchin mice, ye'd never think! An och, I wish ye could see her efter the birds! Ye ken, she'll aet a wee birdie as suin as keek at it!"

At this the pairty wis sair pitten aboot. Some o the birds wis oot o't strechtawa: ae auld Magpie startit happin itsel juist canny, chancin tae say, "I'll shuirly hae tae awa hame: the nicht-air daes my throat nae guid!" An a Canary cried oot in a trumlin vyce, til its bairns, "C'awa, my dearies! It's hie time ye wis aa in yer beds!" On a variorum o pretexts they wis aa suin awa, an Ailice wis left aa hersel.

"Mines is a lang and dowie tale!" says the Moose, turnin tae Ailice and lattin oot a sich.

"It *is* a lang tail, my certe," says Ailice, keekin doun and wunnerin at the Moose's tail; but what are ye cawin it dowie for?" And she kept on wunnerin aboot it the time the Moose wis speakin, sae's her idea o the tale wis kin o like this:— [...]

"Ye're no listenin!" says the Moose tae Ailice, severe-like. "What are ye thinkin aboot?"

"I beg yer pairdon," says Ailice gey hummled: "ye haed gotten tae the fifth bend, I think?"

"I haed *nut!*" cried the Moose gey short and fair wuid.

"A nut!" says Ailice, aye ready tae mak hersel some uiss, and keekin nervish aboot her. "Aw, g'on and lat me crack it!"

"I s' dae naething the like," says the Moose, gittin up and walkin awa. "I'm black affrontit at sic bletheration!"

"I didna mean it!" puir Ailice pleadit. "But ye're that kittle, ye ken!"

The Moose juist growled at this.

"Come on back and feenish yer story!" Ailice cried efter it. And awbody jyned in the chorus "Ay, come on and dae that!" But the Moose juist sheuk its heid impatient, and walkit a bittie mair swippert.

"What a peety it wadna bide!" siched the Lory, the meenit it wis awa oot o sicht. And an auld Partan teuk the chance tae say tae her dochter "Weel, hen! Lat this be a lesson tae ye never tae loss *your* heid!"

"Haud yer wheesht, Ma!" says the young Partan, a bittie short wi her. Ye'd try the patience o an eyster!"

"I wish I haed oor Dinah here, I ken I div!" says Ailice oot lood, addressin naebody in parteecular. "*She'd* fesh it back suin eneuch!"

"And wha's this Dinah, gin I micht anter tae pit the question?" says the Lory.

Ailice replied fair eydent, the wey she wis aye set tae speak aboot her pet: "Dinah's oor cat. And she's sic a capital ane for catchin mice, ye'd never think! And och, I wish ye coud see her efter the birds! Ye ken, she'll eat a wee birdie as suin as keek at it!"

At this the pairty wis sair pitten aboot. Some o the birds wis oot o't strechtawa: ae auld Magpie startit happin itsel juist canny, chancin tae say, "I'll shuirly hae tae awa hame: the nicht-air daes my throat nae guid!" And a Canary cried oot in a trimmlin vyce, til its bairns, "C'awa, my dearies! It's hie time ye wis aw in yer beds!" On a variorum o pretexts thay wis aw suin awa, and Ailice wis left aw hersel.

10.8 SYNTHETIC SCOTS (ANDREW MCCALLUM)

"Mine is a lang an dulesome tale!" quo the Moose, tirnin til Ailis wi a sich.

"Certes, it *is* a lang tail," quo Ailis, leukin doun dumfoondert at the Moose's tail. "But whit dae ye caa it dulesome for?" An she kep on settin her brains asteep owre the maiter aa the time that the Moose was speikin, sae that her idea o the tale was somethin lik this:— [...]

"Yer no peyin heed!" quo the Moose, snell, til Ailis. "Whit are ye thinkin on?"

"I beseek yer pardon," quo Ailis, sair hummelt. "Ye haed won til the fift bucht, I wat?"

"I haed *not*!" the Moose cried shairp an atterie.

"A knot!" quo Ailis, leukin fondly aboot her, ay redd ti mak hersel aisefou. "Oh, dae lat me help ye unfankle it!"

"I sall dae nae sic thing," quo the Moose, risin an waukin awaa. "Ye miscaa me bi speikin sic snash!"

"I daedna mynt it!" puir Ailis pled. "But ye're owre easy riled, ye ken!"

The Moose juist gurlt back.

"Please come back an feenish yer story!" Ailis cried ahint it. An the ithers aa jynt in, "Aye, *please!*" But the Moose juist shakkit its heid fuffie-lik, an waukit on a bit swither.

"Whit a peety it wadna bide!" the Paurit soucht, as suin as it was richt oot o sicht. An an auld Catterkeavie takkit the chaunce o sayin ti her dochter, "Ay, my dear! Lat this be a lesson ti ye, niver ti los *your* heid!"

"Haud yer wheesht, Maw!" quo the young Keavie, a wee bit nippie. "Ye're eneuch ti try the tholin o an eyster!"

"I wiss that I haed oor Dinah here, that I dae!" quo Ailis lood oot, ti naebody in particklar. "*She'd* suin fesh it back!"

"An wha is *Dinah*, gin ye please?" the Paurit speirt.

Ailis spak back willintly, for she was ay redd ti speik anent her dautie. "Dinah's oor pousie. An she's sic a guid ane for clauchtin mooses, ye wadna think! An och, I wiss that ye cud see her huntin the birds! Fegs, she'll eat a wee bird as suin as leuk at it!"

Thir wirds gart an unco flocht amang the coer. Twa-three o the birds breeshelt awaa at aince. Ane auld Pyat stertit happin itsel up gey cannily, sayin, "I ralely maun be winnin hame. My thrapple canna be daein wi the nicht-air!" An a Canary peepit oot in a chitterin vyce til its bairns, "C'wa, my dearies! It's hie time ye war aa in yer beds!" On sindrie whimples they aa flittit awaa, an Ailis was suin left on her lane.

"Mine is a lang and dulesome tale!" quo the Moose, turnin til Ailice wi a sich.

"Certes, it *is* a lang tail," quo Ailice, leukin doun dumfoondert at the Moose's tail. "But whit dae ye caw it dulesome for?" And she kept on settin her brains asteep ower the maiter aw the time that the Moose was speakin, sae that her idea o the tale was something like this:— [...]

"Ye're no peyin heed!" quo the Moose, snell, til Ailice. "Whit are ye thinkin on?"

"I beseek yer pardon," quo Ailice, sair hummelt. "Ye haed won til the fift bucht, I wat?"

"I haed *not!*" the Moose cried shairp and atterie.

"A knot!" quo Ailice, leukin fondly aboot her, ay redd tae mak hersel uissfu. "Oh, dae lat me help ye unfankle it!"

"I sall dae nae sic thing," quo the Moose, risin and walkin awa. "Ye miscaw me by speakin sic snash!"

"I daedna mynt it!" puir Ailice pled. "But ye're ower easy riled, ye ken!"

The Moose juist gurlt back.

"Please come back and feenish yer story!" Ailice cried ahint it. And the ithers aw jynt in, "Aye, *please!*" But the Moose juist shakkit its heid fuffie-like, and walkit on a bit swither.

"Whit a peety it wadna bide!" the Paurit soucht, as suin as it was richt oot o sicht. And an auld Catterkeavie takkit the chance o sayin tae her dochter, "Ay, my dear! Lat this be a lesson tae ye, niver tae loss *your* heid!"

"Haud yer wheesht, Maw!" quo the young Keavie, a wee bit nippie. "Ye're eneuch tae try the tholin o an eyster!"

"I wiss that I haed oor Dinah here, that I dae!" quo Ailice lood oot, tae naebody in particular. "*She'd* suin fesh it back!"

"And wha is *Dinah*, gin ye please?" the Paurit speirt.

Ailice spak back willintly, for she was aye redd tae speik anent her dautie. "Dinah's oor pousie. And she's sic a guid ane for clauchtin mooses, ye wadna think! And och, I wiss that ye coud see her huntin the birds! Fegs, she'll eat a wee bird as suin as leuk at it!"

Thir wirds gart an unco flocht amang the core. Twa-three o the birds breeshelt awa at ance. Ane auld Pyot stertit happin itsel up gey cannily, sayin, "I really maun be winnin hame. My thrapple canna be daein wi the nicht-air!" And a Canary peepit oot in a chitterin vyce til its bairns, "C'wa, my dearies! It's hie time ye war aw in yer beds!" On sindry whimples thay aw flittit awa, and Ailice wis suin left on her lane.

10.9 BORDERS SCOTS (CAMERON HALFPENNY)

"Mine is a lang an a sad tale!" said th Moose, turnin tae Ahlice, an sighin.

"Eet *is* a lang tail, richt enough," said Ahlice, lookin doon wi wunder at th Moose's tail; "but how div ee ca eet sad?" An she kept oan puzzlin aboot eet while th Moose was speakin, sae that hur idea o th tale was somethin lik this:— [...]

"Ee're no listenin!" said th Moose tae Ahlice sternly. "Whit are ee hinkin o?"

"Ah beg eer pairdon," said Ahlice awfy humbly: "ee hed got tae th fifth bend, Ah hink?"

"Ah hed *not*!" cried th Moose, shairply an fair beelin.

"A knot!" said Ahlice, ay ready tae mak hersel yisfi, an lookin anxiously aboot hur. "Och, dae let iz help tae undae eet!"

"Ah wull dae nithin o th sort," said th Moose, gettin up an saunterin awa. "Ee insult iz b' talkin sic nonsense!"

"Ah didnae mean eet!" pleaded pair Ahlice. "But ee're sae easily offended, ee ken!"

Th Moose jist growled in reply.

"Please come back, an feeneesh eer story!" Ahlice ca'ed efter eet. An th ithers aw joined in chorus, "Aye, please dae!" But th Moose only shook eets heid impatiently, an walked a wee bit quicker.

"Whit a pity eet wouldnae stei!" sighed th Lory, as sin as eet was quite oot o sicht. An an auld Crab took th opportunity o sayin tae hur dauchter "Ah, ma dear! Let this b' a lesson tae ee ne'er tae lose *eer* temper!"

"Haud eer tongue, Ma!" said th young Crab, a bit nippy lik. "Ee'r enough tae try th patience o an oyster!"

"Ah wish Ah hed oor Dinah here, Ah ken Ah dae!" said Ahlice aloud, addressin naebody in particular. "*She'd* sin fetch eet back!"

"An whae is Dinah, if Ah might venture tae ask th queestion?" said th Lory.

Ahlice replied eagerly, fur she was ay ready tae talk aboot hur pet: "Dinah's oor cat. An she's sic a teesh yin fur catchin mice ee cannae imagine! An och, Ah wish ee could say hur efter th birds! Jings, she'll scoff a wee bird as sin as keek at eet!"

This speech caused a richt cafuffle amang th crood. Some o th birds hurried off at yince: yin auld Magpie sterted wrappin itsel up awfy carefully, remarkin, "Ah really must b' gettin hame; th nicht-air disnae suit ma throat!" An a Canary ca'ed oot in a tremblin voice tae eets bairns, "Come oan, ma dears! Eet's high time ee were aw in bed!" Wi various excuses they aw moved off, an Ahlice was sin left alane.

"Mine is a lang and a sad tale!" said the Moose, turnin tae Alice, and sighin.

"It *is* a lang tail, richt enough," said Alice, leukin doun wi wonder at the Moose's tail; "but hou div ye caw it sad?" And she kept on puzzlin aboot it while the Moose was speakin, sae that her idea o the tale was something like this:— […]

"Ye're no listenin!" said the Moose tae Alice sternly. "Whit are ye thinkin o?"

"I beg yer pairdon," said Alice awfu humbly: "ye haed got tae the fifth bend, I think?"

"I haed *not!*" cried the Moose, shairply and fair bealin.

"A knot!" said Alice, aye ready tae mak hersel uissfu, and leukin anxiously aboot her. "Och, dae let us help tae undae it!"

"I will dae naething o the sort," said the Moose, gettin up and saunterin awa. "Ye insult us by talkin sic nonsense!"

"I didna mean it!" pleaded puir Alice. "But ye're sae easily offended, ye ken!"

The Moose juist growled in reply.

"Please come back, and feenish yer story!" Alice cawed efter it. And the ithers aw joined in chorus, "Aye, please dae!" But the Moose only sheuk its heid impatiently, and walked a wee bit quicker.

"Whit a pity it wadna stey!" sighed the Lory, as suin as it was quite oot o sicht. And an auld Crab teuk the opportunity o sayin tae her dochter "Ah, ma dear! Let this be a lesson tae ye ne'er tae lose *yer* temper!"

"Haud yer tongue, Ma!" said the young Crab, a bit nippy like. "Ye're enough tae try the patience o an oyster!"

"I wish I haed oor Dinah here, I ken I dae!" said Alice alood, addressin naebody in particular. "*She'd* suin fetch it back!"

"And wha is Dinah, if I might venture tae ask the quaisten?" said the Lory.

Alice replied eagerly, for she was aye ready tae talk aboot her pet: "Dinah's oor cat. And she's sic a teesh ane for catchin mice ye canna imagine! And och, I wish ye coud see her efter the birds! Jings, she'll scoff a wee bird as suin as keek at it!"

This speech caused a richt carfuffle amang the croud. Some o the birds hurried off at ance: ane auld Magpie sterted wrappin itsel up awfu carefully, remarkin, "I really must be gettin hame; the nicht-air disna suit ma throat!" And a Canary cawed oot in a tremblin voice tae its bairns, "Come on, ma dears! It's high time ye were aw in bed!" Wi various excuses thay aw moved off, and Alice was suin left alane.

10.10 WEST-CENTRAL SCOTS (JAMES ANDREW BEGG)

"Weel, mine's is a lang an dowie tail!" said the Mous, turnin tae Alison wi a souch.

"It's a lang tail, for shuir," said Alison luikin doun in wunner at the Mous's tail; "but for why dae ye caa it dowie?" An she kep on thinkin aboot it that muckle while the Mous wis speikin, that her norie o the tale went somethin like this:— […]

"Ye're no listenin!" boufft the Mous tae Alison. "Whit are ye thinkin aboot?"

"I'm awfy sorry," said Alison, fair hummlt: "ye had gotten tae the fifth bend, I think?"

"I had not!" cried the Mous, gey angert an sherp.

"A knot!" said Alison, aye ready tae dae somethin uisefu, an cannily luikin rounaboot her. "Can I gie ye a haun tae unfankle it?"

"Ye'll dae naethin o the kind," said the Mous, staunin up an walkin awa. "Ye affront me wi yer daft blethers!"

"I didnae mean tae!" pleaded puir Alison. "But ye tak the pet ower easy, ye ken!"

The Mous juist gied a grumph.

"Och, please come on back an feenish yer story!" Alison cried efter it. An the ithers aa jyned in, "Aye, ple-e-e-ase!" but the Mous juist shouglt its heid in a richt tid, an walked awa even smerter.

"Whit a peety it widnae stey!" soucht the Lory, as shuin as it wis awa oot o sicht. An an auld Partan tuik the chance tae tell her dochter "Weel, hen! Let that be a lesson tae ye never tae loss the heid!"

"Haud yer wheesht, Mither!" said the wee lassie Partan, nippy-like. "Yer threipin-on wad try the patience o an oyster!"

"Aw, I wish I had oor Dinah here, I ken I dae!" said Alison oot loud, tae naebody in parteecular. "She'd shuin fetch it back!"

"An whae's Dinah, when she's at hame?" said the Lory.

Alison wis gleg wi her reply, for she wis aye keen tae talk aboot her cheetie-cat: "Dinah's oor cat. An she's sic a guid yin for catchin mice, I'll tell ye! An wo-och, ye shuid see her efter the burds! Jings! she'll swallie a wee burd as shuin's luik at it!"

This speech steirt up a richt carfuffle amang the getherin. Some o the burds scurrit awa at yince; yin auld Magpie stertit tae hap itsel up weel, mutterin: "I'd better be awa hame, this cauld nicht-air disnae dae wi my thrapple!" An a Canary cried oot in a trimmlin vyce tae its weans, "Come awa, bairns! It's high time ye were aa in yer beds!" Wi thae excuses, they aa tootlt aff, an Alison wis shuin left ahint, aa her lane.

"Weel, mines is a lang and dowie tail!" said the Moose, turnin tae Alison wi a souch.

"It's a lang tail, for shuir," said Alison leukin doun in wunner at the Moose's tail; "but for why dae ye caw it dowie?" And she kept on thinkin aboot it that muckle while the Moose wis speakin, that her norrie o the tale went something like this:— […]

"Ye're no listenin!" bowft the Moose tae Alison. "Whit are ye thinkin aboot?"

"I'm awfu sorry," said Alison, fair hummelt: "ye had gotten tae the fifth bend, I think?"

"I haed not!" cried the Moose, gey angert and shairp.

"A knot!" said Alison, aye ready tae dae something uissfu, and cannily leukin roond aboot her. "Can I gie ye a haund tae unfankle it?"

"Ye'll dae naething o the kind," said the Moose, staundin up and walkin awa. "Ye affront me wi yer daft blethers!"

"I didna mean tae!" pleaded puir Alison. "But ye tak the pet ower easy, ye ken!"

The Moose juist gied a grumph.

"Och, please come on back and feenish yer story!" Alison cried efter it. And the ithers aw jyned in, "Aye, ple-e-e-ase!" but the Moose juist shoogelt its heid in a richt tid, and walked awa even smairter.

"Whit a peety it wadna stey!" soucht the Lory, as suin as it wis awa oot o sicht. And an auld Partan teuk the chance tae tell her dochter "Weel, hen! Let that be a lesson tae ye never tae loss the heid!"

"Haud yer wheesht, Mither!" said the wee lassie Partan, nippy-like. "Yer threapin-on wad try the patience o an oyster!"

"Aw, I wish I haed oor Dinah here, I ken I dae!" said Alison oot lood, tae naebody in parteecular. "She'd suin fetch it back!"

"And wha's Dinah, when she's at hame?" said the Lory.

Alison wis gleg wi her reply, for she wis aye keen tae talk aboot her cheetie-cat: "Dinah's oor cat. And she's sic a guid ane for catchin mice, I'll tell ye! And wo-och, ye shuid see her efter the birds! Jings! she'll swallae a wee bird as suin's leuk at it!"

This speech steert up a richt carfuffle amang the gaitherin. Some o the birds scurrit awa at ance; ane auld Magpie stertit tae hap itsel up weel, mutterin: "I'd better be awa hame, this cauld nicht-air disna dae wi my thrapple!" And a Canary cried oot in a tremmlin vyce tae its weans, "Come awa, bairns! It's high time ye were aw in yer beds!" Wi thae excuses, thay aw tootelt aff, and Alison wis suin left ahint, aw her lane.

10.11 GLASWEGIAN SCOTS (THOMAS CLARK)

"Och, ma tale's an awfy long yin, an sad!" said the Moose, turnin tae Alice, an sighin.

"It's lang enough, awright," said Alice, lookin doon at the Moose's tail wae wunner; "bit how's it sad?" An she kept oan puzzlin aboot it while the Moose wis talkin, so her idea ae the tale wound up suhin like this:— [...]

"Ye're no even listenin!" said the Moose tae Alice huffily. "Ye're hinkin aboot suhin else!"

"Och, sorry, sorry," said Alice, awfy humble, like: "ye'd goat tae aboot the fifth bend, eh no?"

"Ye've no been listenin tae a single hing!" shoutit the Moose furiously.

"Tanglit string!" said Alice, ayeweys ready tae make hersel useful, an lookin anxiously aboot her. "Show us whaur it is an ah'll help ye!"

"That'll be shinin bright," said the Moose, gittin up an walkin awey. "Ye're jist takin the mick, noo!"

"Ah didnae mean it!" pleadit Alice. "Bit ye take the huff that easy, like!"

The Moose only growlt in reply.

"Och, moan back, eh, feeneesh yer story!" Alice shoutit efter it. An the ithers aw joint in in chorus, "Aye, moan back!" Bit the Moose only shook its heid impatiently, an walked a wee bit quicker.

"Whit a pity it widnae stey!" sighed the Lory, soon as it wis quite oot ae sight. An an auld Crab took the chance ae sayin tae her daughter "Och, hen! Hope ah never see *you* loasin the heid like that!"

"Clamp it, Maw!" said the wee Crab, a bit snappishly. "Ye'd try the patience ae an oyster, so ye wid!"

"Ah wish ah hid oor Dinah here, so ah dae!" said Alice alood, talkin tae naebdy in particular. "*She'd* hiv him back pronto!"

"An wha's Dinah, when she's at hame?" said the Lory.

Alice replied eagerly, cause she wis ayeweys up fur a blether aboot her pet: "Dinah's oor cat. An she's the best moose-catcher ye've ever seen! Honestly, ah wish ye could see her efter the birds! She'll jist eat a wee bird soon as look at it!"

This speech goat a fair reaction frae the assembly. Some ae the birds hurrit oaf straight away: wan auld Magpie stairtit wrappin itsel up awfy carefully, sayin, "Well, s'aboot time ah wis hittin the dusty trail; the nights are fair drawin in!" An a Canary cawed oot tae its weans in a tremblin voice, "Right youse lot, time tae go! That's well past yer bedtime!" Oan various pretexts they aw took aff, an Alice wis soon left oan her ding.

"Och, ma tale's an awfu long ane, and sad!" said the Moose, turnin tae Alice, and sighin.

"It's lang enough, awright," said Alice, leukin doun at the Moose's tail wi wunner; "but how's it sad?" And she kept on puzzlin aboot it while the Moose wis talkin, so her idea o the tale wound up something like this:—

[...]

"Ye're no even listenin!" said the Moose tae Alice huffily. "Ye're thinkin aboot something else!"

"Och, sorry, sorry," said Alice, awfu humble, like: "ye'd got tae aboot the fifth bend, eh no?"

"Ye'v no been listenin tae a single thing!" shoutit the Moose furiously.

"Tangelt string!" said Alice, ayeweys ready tae make hersel useful, and leukin anxiously aboot her. "Show us whaur it is and I'll help ye!"

"That'll be shinin bright," said the Moose, gettin up and walkin away. "Ye're juist takin the mick, nou!"

"I didna mean it!" pleadit Alice. "But ye take the huff that easy, like!"

The Moose only growlt in reply.

"Och, 'm'on back, eh, feenish yer story!" Alice shoutit efter it. And the ithers aw joint in in chorus, "Aye, 'm'on back!" But the Moose only sheuk its heid impatiently, and walked a wee bit quicker.

"Whit a pity it wadna stey!" sighed the Lory, soon as it wis quite oot o sight. And an auld Crab teuk the chance o sayin tae her daughter "Och, hen! Hope I never see *you* lossin the heid like that!"

"Clamp it, Maw!" said the wee Crab, a bit snappishly. "Ye'd try the patience o an oyster, so ye wad!"

"I wish I haed oor Dinah here, so I dae!" said Alice alood, talkin tae naebody in particular. "*She'd* hiv him back pronto!"

"And wha's Dinah, when she's at hame?" said the Lory.

Alice replied eagerly, 'cause she wis ayeweys up for a blether aboot her pet: "Dinah's oor cat. And she's the best moose-catcher ye'v ever seen! Honestly, I wish ye coud see her efter the birds! She'll juist eat a wee bird soon as leuk at it!"

This speech got a fair reaction frae the assembly. Some o the birds hurrit off straight away: wan auld Magpie stertit wrappin itsel up awfu carefully, sayin, "Well, 's aboot time I wis hittin the dusty trail; the nights are fair drawin in!" And a Canary cawed oot tae its weans in a tremblin voice, "Right youse lot, time tae go! That's well past yer bedtime!" On various pretexts thay aw teuk aff, and Alice wis soon left on her ding.

10.12 GALLOWAY SCOTS (STUART PATERSON)

"Mine's a gey lang an dowie tale!" said the Moose birlin roon tae Alice an sichin awa.

"It's a lang tail fir shair," said Alice, luikin doon wi wunner at the Moose's tail; "but hoo come ye cry it dowie?" An she cairrit oan wunnerin aboot it whiles the Moose wis bletherin, sae hoo she thocht o the tale wis a wee sint lik this:— [...]

"Ye'r no luggin in!" the Moose said scunnertlie tae Alice. "Whit ye dwallin oan?"

"Ah'm affy sorry," said Alice richt hummlie: "ye'd got tae the fifth corner Ah jalouse?"

"Naw Ah hadnae!" skreiched the Moose, fair beelin an wi a pettit lip.

"A knot!" Alice said, aye happy tae len a haun an luikin aboot the place a bit fashed. "Ocht let me help ye undae it!"

"Ah'll no let ye dae yon at aw!" said the Moose, staunin up an dannerin awa. "Ye mak me feel got at haverin lik yon!"

"Ah didnae mean tae dae yon!" puir Alice pleadit. "But ye feel got at deid easy ye ken!"

The Moose did nocht but girn back at her.

"Jist come back an feenish yer tale eh!" Alice skreiched owre tae it; an aw o them jyned in chorus, "Aye, gan oan, please dae!" but the Moose jist shook its heid in a turravee an dannered oan a bit faster.

"Sic a shame it widnae stey!" siched the Lorie suin as the Moose wis awa oot o sicht; an an auld Partan taen a meenit tae say tae her dochter "Ocht hen! Hope aw thir maks ye ken no tae loss yer *ain* heid!"

"Haud yer wheesht Mither!" the Partan wean said fair scunnert. "Ye cuid mak a freenlie Oyster feel hatttered!"

"Ah weesh oor Dinah wis here wi me, Ah ken Ah dae!" Alice said oot lood, bletherin tae naebody bar hersel. "She'd no be lang bringin it back!"

"Sae whae's Dinah, gin ye dinnae mind me askin?" said the Lorie.

Alice wis aye deid chuffed tae blether aboot her pet an said back blythelie: "Dinah is oor cat. An ye widnae believe hoo guid she is at catchin the moosies! Ocht, Ah weesh ye cuid see her gan fir the birds! She'll scran a wee bird suin as luik at it!"

The wey Alice said thon had a richt effect oan the pairty. A few wee birds skittered aff richt awa: yin auld Pyat stertit happin itsel gey weel, sayin, "Ah'd best be getting hame; the nicht air isnae guid fir ma trapple!" an a Canary cried oot feart tae its weans, "Richto, aff we gan ma wee sowls! Aboot time ye were aw cooried up in yer beds!" They aw stertit gan aff tae their ain bits, an Alice wis suin ootby oan her ain.

"Mine's a gey lang and dowie tale!" said the Moose birlin roond tae Alice and sichin awa.

"It's a lang tail for shuir," said Alice, leukin doun wi wunner at the Moose's tail; "but hou come ye cry it dowie?" And she cairit on wunnerin aboot it whiles the Moose wis bletherin, sae hou she thocht o the tale wis a wee scent like this:— […]

"Ye're no luggin in!" the Moose said scunnertly tae Alice. "Whit ye dwallin on?"

"I'm awfu sorry," said Alice richt hummly: "ye'd got tae the fifth corner I jalouse?"

"Naw I haedna!" skreiched the Moose, fair bealin and wi a pettit lip.

"A knot!" Alice said, aye happy tae len a haund and leukin aboot the place a bit fashed. "Ocht let me help ye undae it!"

"I'll no let ye dae yon at aw!" said the Moose, staundin up and daunderin awa. "Ye mak me feel got at haiverin like yon!"

"I didna mean tae dae yon!" puir Alice pleadit. "But ye feel got at deid easy ye ken!"

The Moose did nocht but girn back at her.

"Juist come back and feenish yer tale eh!" Alice skreiched ower tae it; and aw o them jyned in chorus, "Aye, gan on, please dae!" but the Moose juist sheuk its heid in a tirrivee and daundered on a bit faster.

"Sic a shame it wadna stey!" siched the Lorie suin as the Moose wis awa oot o sicht; and an auld Partan taen a meenit tae say tae her dochter "Ocht hen! Hope aw thir maks ye ken no tae loss yer ain heid!"

"Haud yer wheesht Mither!" the Partan wean said fair scunnert. "Ye coud mak a freendly Oyster feel hattered!"

"I weesh oor Dinah wis here wi me, I ken I dae!" Alice said oot lood, bletherin tae naebody baur hersel. "She'd no be lang bringin it back!"

"Sae wha's Dinah, gin ye dinna mind me askin?" said the Lorie.

Alice wis aye deid chuffed tae blether aboot her pet and said back blithely: "Dinah is oor cat. And ye wadna believe hou guid she is at catchin the moosies! Ocht, I weesh ye coud see her gaun for the birds! She'll scran a wee bird suin as leuk at it!"

The wey Alice said thon haed a richt effect on the pairty. A few wee birds skittered aff richt awa: ane auld Pyot stertit happin itsel gey weel, sayin, "I'd best be getting hame; the nicht air isna guid for ma thrapple!" and a Canary cried oot feart tae its weans, "Richto, aff we gan ma wee sowels! Aboot time ye were aw couried up in yer beds!" They aw stertit gaun aff tae their ain bits, and Alice wis suin ootby on her ain.

10.13 ULSTER SCOTS (ANNE MORRISON-SMYTH)

"Mine's a lang sad tale!" said the Moose, turnin tae Alice, an sighin.

"It's a lang tail, richt enuch," said Alice, lukin doon an wunnerin aboot the Moose's tail; "but why ir yae caalin it sad?" An shae kept on switherin aboot it whin the Moose wus taakin, so hir thocht o the story went lik this:— […]

"Yae'r naw listenin!" said the Moose tae Alice, really cross. "What ir yae thinkin o?"

"What dae yae say," said Alice humbly: "yae had got tae the fifth bend, A think?"

"A had *not!*" gret the Moose, shairply an wile angry.

"A knot!" said Alice, aye makin hirsel useful, an lukin nervously roon hir. "Aw, let mae help yae tae open it!"

"A'll dae naethin o the soart," said the Moose, gittin up an waakin awa. "Yae insult mae wi yer santerin!"

"A didnae mean it!" pleadet Alice. "But yae'r wile easy offendet, yae know!"

The Moose jest growlt in reply.

"Please come baak an finish yer story!" Alice guldert efter it. An the rest aal joint in "Ay, please dae!" But the Moose jest shuk its heid impatiently an waakt a weethin quicker.

"It's a pity it wudnae stye!" sighed the Lory, is shane is it wus oot o sicht. An an oul Crab tuk the chance o sayin tae hir dochter "Aw, mae dear! Let this bae a lesson tae yae naw tae iver loass *yer* temper!"

"Houl yer wheesht, Ma!" said the yeng Crab, a weethin shairp. "Yae'r enuch tae try the patience o a oyster!"

"A wish A had oor Dinah here, A know A dae!" said Alice oot loud, naw taakin tae onieboadie in particular. "*Shae* wud shane bring it baak!"

"An wha's Dinah, if A'm allood tae ax?" said the Lory.

Alice answert him brev an quick, fur shae wus aye ready tae taak aboot hir pet: "Dinah's oor cat. An shae's that guid at catchin mice, yae cannae think! An boys, A wish yae seen hir efter burds! Shae'll ait a burd is shane is luk at it!"

This statement caased a wile strange feelin amang the pairty. Some o the burds tuk aff richt awa, yin oul Magpie stairtet wrappin itsel up wile cairfully, sayin, "A'll really hae tae git hame: that nicht-air disnae dae mae thrapple onie guid!" An a canary caalt oot in a shaky voice, tae its weeyins. "Come on, weeyins! It's aboot time yaes wur aal in bed!" Fur different raisons they aal moved awa, an Alice wus shane left hirsel.

"Mine's a lang sad tale!" said the Moose, turnin tae Alice, and sighin.

"It's a lang tail, richt eneuch," said Alice, leukin doun and wunnerin aboot the Moose's tail; "but why are ye callin it sad?" And she kept on switherin aboot it whan the Moose wis talkin, so her thocht o the story went like this:— [...]

"Ye're no listenin!" said the Moose tae Alice, really cross. "What are ye thinkin o?"

"What dae ye say," said Alice humbly: "ye haed got tae the fifth bend, I think?"

"I haed *not!*" grat the Moose, shairply and wild angry.

"A knot!" said Alice, aye makin hersel useful, and leukin nervously roond her. "Aw, let me help ye tae open it!"

"I'll dae naething o the sort," said the Moose, gettin up and walkin awa. "Ye insult me wi yer saunterin!"

"I didna mean it!" pleadit Alice. "But ye're wild easy offendit, ye knaw!"

The Moose juist growlt in reply.

"Please come back and finish yer story!" Alice goldert efter it. And the rest all joint in "Ay, please dae!" But the Moose juist sheuk its heid impatiently and walked a wee thing quicker.

"It's a pity it wadna stey!" sighed the Lory, as suin as it wis oot o sicht. And an auld Crab teuk the chance o sayin tae her dochter "Aw, ma dear! Let this be a lesson tae ye no tae iver loss *yer* temper!"

"Hold yer wheesht, Ma!" said the young Crab, a wee thing shairp. "Ye're eneuch tae try the patience o a oyster!"

"I wish I had oor Dinah here, I knaw I dae!" said Alice oot loud, no talkin tae onybody in particular. "*She* wad suin bring it back!"

"And wha's Dinah, if I'm alloued tae aks?" said the Lory.

Alice answert him brave and quick, for she wis aye ready tae talk aboot her pet: "Dinah's oor cat. And she's that guid at catchin mice, ye canna think! And boys, I wish ye seen her efter birds! She'll eat a bird as suin as leuk at it!"

This statement caused a wild strange feelin amang the pairty. Some o the birds teuk aff richt awa, ane auld Magpie stertit wrappin itsel up wild carefully, sayin, "I'll really hae tae get hame: that nicht-air disna dae ma thrapple ony guid!" And a canary callt oot in a shaky voice, tae its wee anes. "Come on, wee anes! It's aboot time yese war all in bed!" For different raisons thay all moved awa, and Alice wis suin left hersel.

10.14 SUMMARY FOR COMPARISON
10.14.1 Lewis Carroll
This speech caused a remarkable sensation among the party. Some of the birds hurried off at once: one old Magpie began wrapping itself up very carefully, remarking "I really must be getting home: the night-air doesn't suit my throat!" And a Canary called out in a trembling voice, to its children, "Come away, my dears! It's high time you were all in bed!" On various pretexts they all moved off, and Alice was soon left alone.

10.14.2 Laureen Johnson
This set the hale baund in a braw steer. Some o the birds flauchtered aff wi that same: ae auld magpie startit rowin himsel up awful tentily and sayin, "I dout I'll hae tae gang hame; the nicht-air daesna dae wi my throat!" And a Canary cried oot tae her bairns wi a voice 'at wis juist trimmlin, "Come you, bairns! Hit's time nou 'at you war aw in your beds!" Some gae ae raison and some anither, but thay aw gaed, and Alice wis suin aw on her ain.

10.14.3 Donna Heddle
Sic a speak fairly raivelt the fowk. Twa or three o the birds hurried aff at wance: wan auld Magpie stertit happin hitsel up awful weel, yirpin, "I really maun be gittin upby; the night-air disna suit ma thrapple!" and a Canary cawed oot in a wafflie wey tae hits bairns, "Come awey, bairns! Hit's high time ye war all in thoor beds!" On a dose o ploys they all trampit awey, and in a peedie blink Alice wis by her lane.

10.14.4 Catherine Byrne
This speech caused a remarkable sensation amang the party. Some o the birds hurried off at wance: wan auld Magpie began wrappin itsel up awful carefully, remarkin, "I really maun be gettin home; the nicht-air disna suit ma throat!" And a Canary called oot in a tremblin voice til its bairns, "Come awey, ma dears ! It's high time ye were all in bed!" On various pretexts thay all moved off, and Alice wis soon left on her own.

10.14.5 J. Derrick McClure
This speel pit the boorachie in a byordinar fume. Some o the birds gaed breeshlin aff richt awa: ae auld Pyot set tae happin itsel real tentily, sayin, "I really buid tae be takin the gate hame nou, the nicht-air's nae guid for my thrapple!" And a Canary wheepelt oot in a chitterin vyce tae its little anes, "Come awa nou, my bairnockies! It's time ye war aw in your bed!" On ae excuiss or anither thay aw hushelt aff, and it wisna lang or Ailice wis aw her lane.

10.14.6 Tom Hubbard
This speech fair caused some sensation amang aw that lot. Some o the birds hurried aff at wance: wan auld Magpie stertit wrappin hitsel up awfu carefu like, sayin by-the-by: "Hey, I'v really got ae git hame, the nicht-air isna guid for ma thrapple!" And a Canary cried oot in a richt tremmlin voice, tae hits bairns, "Come on, youse anes! Hit's high time youse wis aw in yer beds!" Wi various excuses they aw breenged aff, and Alice wis left aw her lane.

10.14.7 Sandy Fleemin
At this the pairty wis sair pitten aboot. Some o the birds wis oot o't strechtawa: ae auld Magpie startit happin itsel juist canny, chancin tae say, "I'll shuirly hae tae

awa hame: the nicht-air daes my throat nae guid!" And a Canary cried oot in a trimmlin vyce, til its bairns, "C'awa, my dearies! It's hie time ye wis aw in yer beds!" On a variorum o pretexts thay wis aw suin awa, and Ailice wis left aw hersel.

10.14.8 Andrew McCallum

Thir wirds gart an unco flocht amang the core. Twa-three o the birds breeshelt awa at ance. Ane auld Pyot stertit happin itsel up gey cannily, sayin, "I really maun be winnin hame. My thrapple canna be daein wi the nicht-air!" And a Canary peepit oot in a chitterin vyce til its bairns, "C'wa, my dearies! It's hie time ye war aw in yer beds!" On sindry whimples thay aw flittit awa, and Ailice wis suin left on her lane.

10.14.9 Cameron Halfpenny

This speech caused a richt carfuffle amang the croud. Some o the birds hurried off at ance: ane auld Magpie sterted wrappin itsel up awfu carefully, remarkin, "I really must be gettin hame; the nicht-air disna suit ma throat!" And a Canary cawed oot in a tremblin voice tae its bairns, "Come on, ma dears! It's high time ye were aw in bed!" Wi various excuses thay aw moved off, and Alice was suin left alane.

10.14.10 James Andrew Begg

This speech steert up a richt carfuffle amang the gaitherin. Some o the birds scurrit awa at ance; ane auld Magpie stertit tae hap itsel up weel, mutterin: "I'd better be awa hame, this cauld nicht-air disna dae wi my thrapple!" And a Canary cried oot in a tremmlin vyce tae its weans, "Come awa, bairns! It's high time ye were aw in yer beds!" Wi thae excuses, thay aw tootelt aff, and Alison wis suin left ahint, aw her lane.

10.14.11 Thomas Clark

This speech got a fair reaction frae the assembly. Some o the birds hurrit off straight away: wan auld Magpie stertit wrappin itsel up awfu carefully, sayin, "Well, 's aboot time I wis hittin the dusty trail; the nights are fair drawin in!" And a Canary cawed oot tae its weans in a tremblin voice, "Right youse lot, time tae go! That's well past yer bedtime!" On various pretexts thay aw teuk aff, and Alice wis soon left on her ding.

10.14.12 Stuart Paterson

The wey Alice said thon haed a richt effect on the pairty. A few wee birds skittered aff richt awa: ane auld Pyot stertit happin itsel gey weel, sayin, "I'd best be getting hame; the nicht air isna guid for ma thrapple!" and a Canary cried oot feart tae its weans, "Richto, aff we gan ma wee sowels! Aboot time ye were aw couried up in yer beds!" They aw stertit gaun aff tae their ain bits, and Alice wis suin ootby on her ain.

10.14.13 Anne Morrison-Smyth

This statement caused a wild strange feelin amang the pairty. Some o the birds teuk aff richt awa: ane auld Magpie stertit wrappin itsel up wild carefully, sayin, "I'll really hae tae get hame: that nicht-air disna dae ma thrapple ony guid!" And a canary callt oot in a shaky voice, tae its wee anes. "Come on, wee anes! It's aboot time yese war all in bed!" For different raisons thay all moved awa, and Alice wis suin left hersel.

11
BIBLIOGRAPHY

Agutter, Alex. 1987. "A taxonomy of Older Scots orthography" in Caroline Macafee and Iseabail Macleod, eds. *The Nuttis Schell: Essays on the Scots Language Presented to A. J. Aitken*. Aberdeen: Aberdeen University Press, 75–82.

Aitken, A. J. 1977. "How to pronounce Older Scots" in A. J. Aitken *et al.*, eds. *Bards and Makars: Scottish Language and Literature, Medieval and Renaissance*, Glasgow: Glasgow University Press, 1–21.

——, Matthew McDiarmid, and Derick Thomson, eds. 1977. *Bards and Makars: Scottish Language and Literature, Medieval and Renaissance*, Glasgow: Glasgow University Press.

——. 1981a. "The Good Old Scots Tongue" in Einar Haugen *et al.*, eds. *Minority Languages Today*. Edinburgh: Edinburgh University Press, 72–90.

——. 1981b. "The Scottish Vowel Length Rule" in Michael Benskin and M. L. Samuels, eds. *So Meny People, Longages and Tonges: Philological Essays in Scots and Mediaeval English Presented to Angus McIntosh*, Edinburgh: The Middle English Dialect Project, 131–157.

——. 1984. "Scottish accents an dialects" in Peter Trudgill ed. *Language in the British Isles*. Cambridge: Cambridge University Press, 94–114.

——. 1985. "The Pronunciation of Entries for the CSD" in Richard W. Bailey, ed. *Dictionaries 7: Journal of the Dictionary Society of North America*.

——. 2002. "A history of Scots to 1700" in William Craigie and A. J. Aitken, eds. (1931–2002).

—— and Caroline Macafee, eds. 2002. *The Older Scots Vowels: A History of the Stressed Vowels of Older Scots from the Beginnings to the Eighteenth Century*, Scottish Text Society.

Allan, Alasdair. 1995. "Scots spellin: Ettlin efter the quantum lowp", *English World-Wide* 16:1, 61–103.

Allerton, D. J. 1982. "Orthography and Dialect: How can different regional pronunciations be accommodated in a single orthography?" in *Standard Languaes Spoken and Written*. Manchester: Manchester University Press.

Bailey, Richard. 1987. "Teaching the vernacular: Scotland, schools, and linguistic diversity" in Caroline Macafee and Iseabail Macleod, eds. *The Nuttis Schell: Essays on the Scots Language presented to A. J. Aitken*. Aberdeen: Aberdeen University Press, 131–142.

Benskin, Michael and M. L. Samuels, eds. 1981. *So Meny People, Longages and Tonges: Philological Essays in Scots and Mediaeval English Presented to Angus McIntosh*. Edinburgh: Middle English Dialect Project .

Braidwood, John. 1964. "Ulster and Elizabethan English" in G. Brendan Adams, ed. *Ulster Dialects: An Introductory Symposium*, Cultra: Ulster Folk Museum, 5–109.

———. 1975. *The Ulster Dialect Lexicon: An Inaugural Lecture Delivered Before the Queen's University of Belfast on 23 April, 1969*. Belfast: Queen's University.

Brett, David. 1999. *The Plain Style: Reformation, Culture and the Crisis of Protestant Identity*, Belfast: Black Square Books.

Cairns Speitel, Pauline, Marace Dareau, Alison Grant, and Chris Robinson, eds. 2017. *The Concise Scots Dictionary*. Second edition. Edinburgh: Edinburgh University Press.

Carroll, Lewis. 2011. *Ailice's Àventurs in Wunnerland*. Translated into South-East Central Scots by Sandy Fleemin. Cathair na Mart: Evertype. ISBN 978-1-904808-64-0.

———. 2012. *Ailice's Anters in Ferlielann*. Translated into North-East Scots by Derrick McClure. Cathair na Mart: Evertype. ISBN 978-1-78201-016-6.

———. 2012. *Alice's Adventirs in Wonderlaand*. Translated into Shetland Scots by Laureen Johnson. Cathair na Mart: Evertype. ISBN 978-1-78201-008-1.

———. 2013. *Ailis's Anterins i the Laun o Ferlies*. Translated into Synthetic Scots by Andrew McCallum. Cathair na Mart: Evertype. ISBN 978-1-78201-026-5.

———. 2013. *Alice's Carrànts in Wunnerlan*. Translated into Ulster Scots by Anne Morrison-Smyth. Second edition. Cathair na Mart: Evertype. ISBN 978-1-78201-011-1.

———. 2014. *Alice's Adventirs in Wunnerlaun*. Translated into Glaswegian Scots by Thomas Clark. Cathair na Mart: Evertype. ISBN 978-1-78201-070-8.

———. 2014. *Alice's Mishanters in e Land o Farlies*. Translated into Caithness Scots by Catherine Byrne. Cathair na Mart: Evertype. ISBN 978-1-78201-060-9.

———. 2014. *Alison's Jants in Ferlieland*. Translated into West-Central Scots by James Andrew Begg. Cathair na Mart: Evertype. ISBN 978-1-78201-084-5.

———. 2015. *Ahlice's Adveenturs in Wunderlaant*. Translated into Border Scots by Cameron Halfpenny. Cathair na Mart: Evertype. ISBN 978-1-78201-087-6.

Carter, Jennifer J. and Joan H. Pittock, eds. 1987. *Aberdeen and the Enlightenment*. Aberdeen: Aberdeen University Press.

Cockburn H. 1874. *Journal, 1831–1854*. Edinburgh: Edmonston and Douglas.

Connolly, R. J. 1981. *An Analysis of Some Linguistic Information Obtained from Eighteenth and Nineteenth Century Ulster Poetry*. Unpublished Thesis, Queen's University of Belfast.

Corbett, John, Derrick McClure, and Jane Stuart-Smith, eds. 2003. *The Edinburgh Companion to Scots*. Edinburgh: Edinburgh University Press. ISBN 0-7486-1596-2.

Craigie, William. 1924. "The present state of the Scots tongue" in W. A. Craigie *et al.*, eds. *The Scottish Tongue: A Series of Lectures on the Vernacular Language of Lowland Scotland delivered to the members of the Vernacular Circle of the Burns Club of London*. London: Cassell and Company, 3–46.

———. 1927. *English Spelling Its Rules and Reasons*. Crofts, New York, Reprint 1969.

———. 1942. *Problems of Spelling Reform*. Folcroft Press, Folcroft PA, Reprint 1969.

———. 1944. *Some Anomalies of Spelling*. Folcroft Press, Folcroft PA, Reprint 1969.

———. *et al.*, eds. 1931–2002. *A Dictionary of the Older Scottish Tongue, from the 12th Century to the End of the 17th*. Oxford: Oxford University Press.

Crystal, David. 1995. *The Cambridge Encyclopedia of the English Language*. Cambridge University Press.

Dieth, Eugen. 1932. *A Grammar of the Buchan Dialect*. Cambridge: Heffer & Sons.

Donaldson, William. 1986. *Popular Literature in Victorian Scotland:Language, Fiction and the Press*. Aberdeen: Aberdeen University Press.

———. 1989. *The Language of the People: Scots Prose from the Victorian Revival*. Aberdeen: Aberdeen University Press.

Dossena, Marina. 2005. *Scotticisms in Grammar and Vocabulary*. Edinburgh: Birlinn.

Eagle, Andy and Falconer, Gavin. 2004. "Tha Boord of Ulstér-Scotch: An English Name for a Scots Organisation?" *Ulster Folklife* 50: Ulster Folk and Transport Museum, 99–109.

Ellis, Alexander J. 1890. *English Dialects and their Sounds and Homes*. London (Kraus Reprint Ltd. Vaduz 1965).

Falconer, Gavin. 2005. "Breaking Nature's Social Union: The Autonomy of Scots in Ulster" in John Kirk and Dónall Ó Baoill, eds., *Legislation, Literature and Sociolinguistics: Northern Ireland, the Republic of Ireland, and Scotland*. Belfast: Queen's University, 48–59.

Firchow, E. S. *et al.*, eds. 1972. *Studies by Einar Haugen*. (Janua Linguarum. Series Maior; 49) The Hague and Paris.

Flaws, Margaret and Lamb, Gregor. 1996. *The Orkney Dictionary*. Kirkwall: The Orkney Language and Culture Group.

Graham, William. 1997. *Scorn, My Inheritance*. Glasgow: Scotsoun.

Grant, William and James Main Dixon. 1921. *Manual of Modern Scots*. Cambridge: Cambridge University Press.

Grant, William *et al.*, eds. 1931–1975. *The Scottish National Dictionary*. 10 volumes. Edinburgh: Chambers.

Gregg, Robert. 1958. "Notes on the phonology of a County Antrim Scotch-Irish Dialect", *Orbis* 7:2, 392–406.

———. 1972. "The Scotch-Irish dialect boundaries in Ulster" in Martyn Wakelin, ed. *Patterns in the Folk Speech of the British Isles*. London: Athlone, 109–139.

Görlach, Manfred. 2002. *A Textual History of Scots*. Heidelberg: Carl Winter.

Haas, W. 1982. *Standard Languages Spoken and Written*. Manchester: Manchester University Press.

Hagan, Anette I. 2002. *Urban Scots Dialect Writing*. Bern: Lang.

Halliday, M. A. K. 1985. *Spoken and Written Language*. Oxford: Oxford University Press.

Harris, John. 1984. "English in the north of Ireland" in Peter Trudgill, ed. *Language in the British Isles*. Cambridge: Cambridge University Press, 115–134.

———. 1985. *Phonological Variation and Change. Studies in Hiberno-English*. Cambridge: Cambridge University Press.

Haugen, Einar. 1961. "Language Planning in Modern Norway" in *Scandinavian Studies 33*, 68–81.

——. 1974. "Dialect, language, Nation" in J. B. Pride and Janet Holmes, eds., *Sociolinguistics: Selected Readings*; Harmondsworth: Penguin Books 97–111.

——. 1977. "How should a dialect be written?" in *Dialect und Dialektologie Ergebnisse des Internationalen Symposiums "Zur Theorie des Dialekts"*. Wiesbaden: Steiner.

——. et al., eds. 1981. *Minority Languages Today*. Edinburgh: Edinburgh University Press.

Herbison, Ivan. 2005. "The Revival of Ulster Scots:Why Literary History Matters" in John Kirk and Dónall Ó Baoill, eds., *Legislation, Literature and Sociolinguistics: Northern Ireland, the Republic of Ireland, and Scotland*. Belfast: Queen's University, 77–85.

Hewitt, John. 1974. *Rhyming Weavers and Other Country Poets of Antrim and Down*. Belfast: Blackstaff Press.

Hickey, Raymond. 2004. "Irish English: Phonology" in Schneider *et al.*, eds. *A handbook of Varieties of English Vol. 1*. Berlin/New York: Mouton de Gruyter, 68–97.

——, ed. 2004. *Legacies of Colonial English: Studies in Transported Dialects*. Cambridge: Cambridge University Press, 59–81.

Hodgart, John and Iseabail Macleod. 1996. "Using The Scots School Dictionary", *Laverock*, 29–32.

Jack, Ronald D.S. 1997. "The Language of Literary Materials: Origins to 1700" in Charles Jones, ed. *The Edinburgh History of the Scots Language*. Edinburgh: Edinburgh University Press, 213–263.

Jakobsen, Jakob. 2021. *An Etymological Dictionary of the Norn Language in Shetland: A colour facsimile edition*. (Corpus Textuum Scoticorum; 1) Dundee: Evertype. ISBN 978-1-78201-243-6

Jamieson, J., 1879–1882. *An Etymological Dictionary of the Scottish Language*. 4 vols. Paisley: Alexander Gardner.

Jeffares, A. Norman, ed. 1969. *Scott's Mind and Art*. Edinburgh: Olver & Boyd.

Johnston, Paul. 1997a. "Older Scots phonology and its regional variation" in Charles Jones, ed. *The Edinburgh History of the Scots Language*. Edinburgh: Edinburgh University Press, 47–111.

——. 1997b. "Regional variation" in Charles Jones, ed. *The Edinburgh History of the Scots Language*. Edinburgh: Edinburgh University Press, 443–513.

Jones, Charles. 1995. *A Language Supressed: the Pronunciation of the Scots Language in the 18th Century*. Edinburgh, John Donald.

——, ed. 1997. *The Edinburgh History of the Scots Language*. Edinburgh: Edinburgh University Press.

——. 2002. *The English language in Scotland An Introduction to Scots*. Tuckwell, East Linton.

Kallen, Jeffrey L. 1999. in *English World Wide* 20:1, p.160.

Kirk, John M. 1977. "Contemporary Literary Writing" in Jeffrey Kallen, ed. *Focus on Ireland*. Amsterdam: Benjamins.

——. 2000. "The New Written Scots Dialect in Present-day Northern Ireland" in Magnus Ljung, ed. *Language Structure and Variation*. Sockholm: Almqvist & Wiksell, 121–138.

—— and Dónall Ó Baoill, eds. 2000. *Language and Politics: Northern Ireland, the Republic of Ireland, and Scotland*. Belfast: Queen's University.

—— and Dónall Ó Baoill, eds. 2005. *Legislation, Literature and Sociolinguistics: Northern Ireland, the Republic of Ireland, and Scotland*. Belfast: Queen's University.

Kloss, Heinz. 1952. *Die Entwicklung neuer germanischer Kultursprachen von 1800 bis 1950*. München: Pohl & Co.

Kniezsa, Veronika. 1997. "The origins of Scots orthography" in Charles Jones, ed. *The Edinburgh History of the Scots Language*. Edinburgh: Edinburgh University Press, 24–46.

Lorimer, W. L. 1985. *The New Testament in Scots*. Harmondsworth: Penguin.

Lovie, Rod *et al.* 1995. *Innin ti the Scots Leid/An Introduction to the Scots Language*. Aiberdeen Univairsitie Scots Leid Quorum.

Macafee, Caroline. 1985. "Review of the CSD" in Richard W. Bailey, ed. *Dictionaries 7: Journal of the Dictionary Society of North America*.

—— and Iseabail Macleod, eds. 1987. *The Nuttis Schell: Essays on the Scots Language presented to A. J. Aitken*. Aberdeen: Aberdeen University Press.

——, ed. 1996. *Concise Ulster Dictionary*. Oxford: Oxford University Press.

——. 2001. "Lowland Sources of Ulster Scots: Some Comparisons between Robert Gregg's data and the *Linguistic Atlas of Scotland* (Volume 3)" in John M. Kirk and Dónall Ó Baoill, eds. *Language Links The languages of Scotland and Ireland*. Belfast: Queen's University, 119–132.

——. 2003. "Studying Scots Vocabulary" in Corbett et al. 2003.

——. 2004. "Scots and Scottish English" in R. Hickey, ed. *Legacies of Colonial English: Studies in Transported Dialects*. Cambridge: Cambridge University Press, 59–81.

Mackie, Albert D. 1952. "Fergusson's Language: Braid Scots then and now" in Syndney Goodsir Smith, ed. *Robert Fergusson 1750–1774*. Edinburgh: Nelson, 124–147.

——. 1955. "The spelling of Scots", in *Lines Review* 9, 29–31. Includes the Scots Style Sheet.

——. 1961. "Some Notes on Scots Grammar", in *Lines Review* 17, 25–30.

Macleod, Iseabail. 1993. "Research in progress: some problems in Scottish lexicography", *English World-Wide* 14:1, 115–128.

——. 2000. "Spellin at the SNDA", *Lallans* 57, 65–66.

—— and Pauline Cairns, eds. 1993. *The Concise English-Scots Dictionary*. Edinburgh: Chambers.

——. 1996. *The Scots School Dictionary*, Edinburgh: Chambers.

Macleod, Iseabail and Pauline Cairns, eds. (2004). *The Essential Scots Dictionary*. Edinburgh: Edinburgh University Press.

Mac Póilin, Aodán. 1999. "Language, Identity and Politics in Northern Ireland" in *Ulster Folk Life* 45. Cultra: Ulster Folk & Transport Museum.

Mather, James Y. 1973. "The Scots we speak today" in A. J. Aitken, ed. *Lowland Scots*, Association for Scottish Literary Studies, Occasional papers 2, 56–68.

—— and H. H. Speitel. 1975, 1977, 1986. *The Linguistic Atlas of Scotland*. 3 volumes. London: Croom Helm.

McClure, J. Derrick. 1980. "The Spelling of Scots: A Phoneme-Based System", in *Scottish Literary Journal* 12, 25–29.

——. *et al*. 1980a. *The Scots Language: Planning for Modern Usage*. Edinburgh: Ramsay Head.

——. 1981. "The synthesisers of Scots" in Einar Haugen *et al*., eds. *Minority Languages Today*. Edinburgh: Edinburgh University Press, 91–99.

——. 1985. "The debate on Scots orthography" in Manfred Görlach, ed. *Focus on: Scotland*. Amsterdam: Benjamins, 203–209.

——. 1987. "Language and Genre in Allan Ramsay's 1721 Poems" in Jennifer J. Carter & Joan H. Pittock, eds. 1987. *Aberdeen and the Enlightenment*. Aberdeen: Aberdeen University Press, 261–269.

——. 1995. *Scots and its Literature*. Amsterdam: Benjamins.

——. 1997. "The spelling of Scots: a difficulty" in Edgar Schneider, ed. *Englishes around the World I. General Studies, British Isles, North America. Studies in Honour of Manfred Görlach*. Amsterdam/Philadelphia: Benjamins, 173–184.

——. 2000). *Language, Poetry and Nationhood Scots as a Poetic Language from 1878 to the Present*. East Linton: Tuckwell.

——. 2002). *Doric: The Dialect of North-East Scotland*. Amsterdam: Benjamins.

——. 2003). "The Language of Modern Scots Poetry" in Corbett, John, *et al*., eds. 2003. *The Edinburgh Companion to Scots*. Edinburgh: Edinburgh University Press, 210–232.

McIlvanney, Liam and Ray Ryan, eds. 2005. *Ireland and Scotland: culture and society, 1700–2000*. Dublin: Four Courts Press.

Meurmann-Solin, Anneli. 1993. *Variation and Change in Early Scottish Prose: Studies Based on the Helsinki Corpus of Older Scots*. Helsinki: Suomalainen Tiedeakatemia.

——. 1997. "Differentiation and Standardisation in Early Scots" in Charles Jones, ed. *The Edinburgh History of the Scots Language*. Edinburgh: Edinburgh University Press, 3–23.

Millar, Robert McColl. 2005. *Language, Nation and Power An Introduction*. Basingstoke: Palgrave Macmillan.

——. 2006. "'Burying Alive': Unfocussed Governmental Language Policy and Scots" in *Language Policy* 5:1, 63–86.

Milroy, James. 1982. "Some connections between Galloway and Ulster speech", in *Scottish Language* 1, 23–29.

Milroy, L. 1994. "Intepreting the role of extralinguistic variables in linguistic variation and change", in G. Melchers and N.-L. Johanneson (eds), *Non-Standard Varieties of Language*. Stockholm: Almqvist and Wiksell, 131–45.

Müller, Paul. 1908. *Die Sprache der Aberdeener Urkunden des Sechszehnten Jahrhunderts*. Berlin: Meyer & Müller.

Murison, David. 1969. "The Two Languages in Scott" in A. Norman Jeffares, ed. *Scott's Mind and Art*. Edinburgh: Olver & Boyd, 206–229.

——. 1977. *The Guid Scots Tongue*. Edinburgh: Blackwood & Sons.

————. 1987. "Scottish lexicography" in Caroline Macafee and Iseabail Macleod, eds. *The Nuttis Schell: Essays on the Scots Language presented to A. J. Aitken*. Aberdeen: Aberdeen University Press, 17–24.

Murray, James. 1870–72, 1873. *The Dialect of the Southern Counties of Scotland*. London: Philological Society.

Niven, Liz and Robin Jackson, eds. 1998. *The Scots Language: Its Place in Education*. Newton Stewart: Watergaw.

Ó Baoill, Dónall P. 1990. "Language contact in Ireland: The Irish phonological substratum in Irish English", in Jerold A. Edmondson, Crawford Feagin and Peter Mühlhäusler, eds. *Development and Diversity: Language Variation Across Time and Space*. Dallas: Summer Institute of Linguistics, 147–72.

Ó hÚrdail, Roibeárd. 1997. "Confusion of dentality and alveolarity in dialects of Hiberno-English", in Jeffrey L. Kallen, ed. *Focus on Ireland*. Amsterdam, Philadelphia: Benjamins, 133–51.

Petyt, K.M. 1980. *The Study of Dialect An Introduction to Dialectology*. London: Andre Deutsch.

Philp, George. 2008. "Scotscreive", in *Lallans* 71, 46–49.

Purves, David. 1975. "The spelling of Scots", in *Lallans* 4, 26–27.

————. 1979. "A Scots orthography", in *Scottish Literary Journal* Supplement 9, 62–76.

————. 1997. *A Scots Grammar*. Edinburgh: The Saltire Society.

————. 2000. "Repone ti Report o the Scots Spellin Comatee", in *Lallans* 57, 50–53.

Pyles, Thomas and John Algeo. 1982. *The origins and development of the English language*, San Diego: Harcourt Brace Jovanovich.

Rennie, Susan. 1999. *Grammar Broonie: A Guide tae Scots Grammar*. Edinburgh: Scottish National Dictionary Association.

Robertson, R. *et al.* 1996. *The Kist/A' Chiste: Teachers Handbook (The Shottle)*. Edinburgh: Scottish Consultative Council on the Curriculum, Nelson Blackie.

Robinson, Mairi, ed. 1985. *The Concise Scots Dictionary*. Aberdeen: Aberdeen University Press. Republished in 1992 by W & R Chambers; in 1999 by Polygon (Edinburgh); in 2005 by Edinburgh University Press.

————. 1986. "The Concise Scots Dictionary" in Dietrich Strauss and Horst Drescher, eds. *Scottish language and Literature, Medieval and Renaissance: Fourth International Conference, 1984, Proceedings*. Frankfurt: Peter Lang, 19–34.

————. 1987. "CSD as a tool for linguistic research" in Caroline Macafee and Iseabail Macleod, eds. *The Nuttis Schell: Essays on the Scots Language presented to A. J. Aitken*. Aberdeen: Aberdeen University Press, 59–72.

Robinson, Philip. 1997. *Ulster-Scots. A Grammar of the Traditional Written and Spoken Language*. [s.l.]: The Ullans Press.

————. 2007. *Ulster-Scots. A Grammar of the Traditional Written and Spoken Language*. [s.l.]: The Ullans Press.

Rogers, Henry. 2005. *Writing Systems A Linguistic Approach*. Oxford: Blackwell.

Scots Language Society [David Purves]. 1985. "Spelling recommendations", in *Lallans* 24, 18–19.

————. 2017. *Concise Scots Dictionary*. Edinburgh: Edinburgh University Press.

Scragg, D. G. 1975. *A History of English Spelling.* Manchester: Manchester University Press.

SLD (Scottish Language Dictionaries) Ltd. 2002. *Standardisation of Scots. Some notes on spelling from Scottish Language Dictionaries (SLD).* A handout given at the 2002 Language and Politics Symposium, Queen's University, Belfast.

SND. *See* Grant, William *et al.*, eds. *above.*

SNDA et al. 1999. *Recommendations for writing, editing and transcribing Scots.* Edinburgh: SNDA.

Smith, G. Gregory. 1902. *Specimens of Middle Scots,* Edinburgh/London: Blackwood and Sons.

Smith, Sydney Goodsir, ed. 1952. *Robert Fergusson 1750–1774,* Edinburgh: Nelson.

Steiger, Otto. 1913. *Die Verwendung des Schottischen Dialekts in Walter Scotts Romanen.* Dissertation. Darmstatt.

Stevenson, Robert Louis. 1905. *The Works of R. L. Stevenson Vol. 8,* "Underwoods". London: Heinemann.

Stirling, A. 1994. "On a standardised spelling for Scots", in *Scottish Language* 13, 88–93.

Strauss, Dietrich and Horst Drescher, eds. 1986. *Scottish Language and Literature, Medieval and Renaissance: Fourth International Conference, 1984, Proceedings.* Frankfurt: Peter Lang.

Tait, John M. 2000. "A Tait Wanchancie", in *Lallans* 57, 67–73.

Todd, Loreto. 1989. *The Language of Irish Literature.* London: Macmillan.

Trudgill, Peter ed. 1984. *Language in the British Isles.* Cambridge: Cambridge University Press.

———. 1986. *Dialects in Contact,* Oxford: Blackwell.

———. 1999. "Norwich: endogenous and exogenous change", in Paul Foulkes and Gerhard Docherty, eds., *Urban Voices: Accent Studies in the British Isles.* London: Arnold.

Tulloch, Graham. 1980. *The Language of Walter Scott. A Study of his Scottish and Period Language.* London: Deutsch.

Venezky, Richard L. 1970. *The structure of English orthography.* The Hague: Mouton.

Wells, John. 1982. *Accents of English* vol. 2 *The British Isles.* Cambridge: Cambridge University Press.

Wettstein, P. 1942. *The Phonology of a Berwickshire Dialect.* Zürich: Bienne.

Williams, Nicholas, Michael Everson, and Alan M. Kent, eds. 2020. *The Charter Fragment and Pascon agan Arluth.* (Corpus Textuum Cornicorum; 1). Dundee: Evertype. ISBN 978-1-78201-182-8

Wilson, James. 1916. *Lowland Scotch as Spoken in the Lower Strathearn District of Perthshire.* Oxford: Oxford University Press.

———. 1923. *The Dialect of Robert Burns as Spoken in Central Ayrshire.* Oxford: Oxford University Press.

———. 1925. *Scottish Poems of Robert Burns in his Native Dialect.* Oxford: Oxford University Press.

———. 1926. *The Dialects of Central Scotland.* Oxford: Oxford University Press.

Zai, Rudolph. 1942. *The Phonology of the Morebattle Dialect.* Lucerne: Ræber.

12
SUMMARY TABLE
OF RECOMMENDED VOWEL
SPELLINGS

The first five columns in the table given here is based upon the tables given in Aitken 1977 and Aitken 2002, as given in §3.5 of "History of Scots to 1700" given on the DSL website.[283] A note to that table reads as follows:

> In the lists of graphemes, the semicolons divide spellings dominant in Early Scots from those which become common only in Middle Scots; the colon precedes word-final spellings. (A [triangular] colon after a phonetic symbol, however, indicates length.) Word-final position is indicated by a following # (for both sounds and spellings.)

---

283 "The vowel system of OSc" by Caroline Macafee, incorporating material by the late A. J. Aitken, https://web.archive.org/web/20210503032816/https://dsl.ac.uk/about-scots/history-of-scots/characteristics/ accessed 2021-10-30

Vowel number *Short vowels*	Early Scots (to 1450)	Middle Scots (to 1700)	Modern Scots	Principal Older Scots graphs	Suggested Modern graphs
1	iː →	ei →	əi / aˑe	iCe, yCe, y; yi, ay: y#	iCe, yCe
2	eː →	iː →	i	e, eCe, eC-; ei, ey, ea: e(e)#, ey#, ie#	ee, eCe, ei (*before* ch, r, st), ie (*before* f, l, v)
3	ɛː	*or*			ei, ea
4	aː →	eː →	e	a, aCe, aC-; ai, ay, e, ea: a#, ay#, ae#	aCe, (ai), ae#
5	ǫː →	ǫː →	o	oCe, oC-, o; oi, oy: o#, oo#	oCe, oa
6	uː →	u →	u	ou, ow; (ul): ow#	ou, oo, uCe
6a	ul			ul(l), (w)ol: ull#	
7	yː →	øː →	ø / i / e / ɛ / ɪ (*or*)	oCe, oC-, oi, oy, o(me), o(ne), (w)o, uCe, uC-, wCe, wC-; ui, uy, wi, wy, ou, ow, oo: o#, oe#, oo# ou#, ow#, u(e)#, w#	ui, eu (*before* ch, k), ae#
Diphthongs in -i 8	ai →	ɛi → (*or*)	ęː; ea / e	ai, ay, aCe, aC-, ae, ei, ey; e, ea	ai, (aCe), ay#
8a	ai# →	ǫi# →	əi#	ay#, ey#	ey#
9	ǫi →	ǫɪ →	oe	oi, oy	oi, oy#
10	ui →	ui →	əi	oi, oy; ui, uy, wi, wy, i, y, iy	iCe, yCe, (oi)
11	ei# → eː# →	iː# →	i#	ey#, e#, ee#, ie#	ee#
Diphthongs in -u 12	au →	ɑː → (*or*)	ɑ / ɔ	au, aw; (al): aw#, a# al, all, aul; aw, aw, aː: aw#, a#	au, aw(#), a#
12a	al				
13	ǫu →	ǫu →	ʌu	ou, ow; (ol): ow#	ow, owe#
13a	ǫl				
14a, 14b(i)	iu →	iu → (*or*)	iu / (j)u	eu, ew, uCe: ew#, ue#	ew, eu, u(e)
14b(ii)	ɛǫu →	iǫu →	(j)ʌu	eu, ew; ou, ow: ew#, ow#	ew
Short vowels 15	ɪ →	ɪ →	ɪ	i,y	i
16	ɛ →	ɛ →	ɛ	e	e
17	a →	a →	a	a	a
18	ǫ →	ǫ → (*or*)	o / ɔ	o	o
19	ų →	ų →	ʌ	u, o(m), o(n), w(o); ou	u

229

www.ingramcontent.com/pod-product-compliance
Lightning Source LLC
Chambersburg PA
CBHW020353100426
42812CB00001B/43